the social sciences

Bill Myers
Lin Shaw

Access to HE

Published in 2004 by:
Nelson Thornes Ltd
Delta Place
27 Bath Road
CHELTENHAM
GL53 7TH
United Kingdom

04 05 06 07 08 / 10 9 8 7 6 5 4 3 2 1

A catalogue record for this book is available from the British Library

ISBN 0 7487 8585 X

Illustrations by Northern Phototypesetting Co. Ltd, Bolton
Page make-up by Northern Phototypesetting Co. Ltd, Bolton

Printed and bound in Great Britain by Scotprint

Contents

Acknowledgements

For my first grandchild, Elena Rose.

The authors and publishers are grateful to the following for permission to reproduce copyright material in this book:

Crown copyright/MOD material is reproduced with the permission of the Controller of Her Majesty's Stationery Office © Crown copyright. All rights reserved. Core click-use licence no.C02W0002214

Every attempt has been made to contact copyright holders, and we apologise if any have been overlooked. Should copyright have been unwittingly infringed in this book, the owners should contact the publishers, who will make corrections at reprint

Chapter 1
Introduction to the social sciences

You will not be formally assessed on the contents of this first chapter – nevertheless it is essential reading. We start with a description of the scope of the social sciences and something of their history. In particular, it is important to understand how sociology and psychology differ from chemistry, biology and physics, the three major natural sciences.

For a short period after conception, there are no differences between identical twins. With this minor and temporary exception, all individuals now living, and all who have ever lived, are unique. We are different from each other for three reasons:

- We have different genetic inheritances.

- We are exposed to different environments.

- The interactions between inheritance and environment vary from one person to another.

Here, the word 'environment' is used in the broadest possible sense to mean any external influence that can alter an individual in any way.

Identical twins have different birth weights because, by an accident of position, one will have been better nourished in the womb than the other. Even before birth, environments vary.

In Japanese there is no single word for brother – *oniisan* means older brother and *otouto* is a younger brother. The distinction applies to identical twins – even to those born just minutes apart. In another way, in a more hierarchical society than ours, twins have different environments from birth.

Survival strategies

Most animals are capable of independent isolated existence from birth. Parents do not care for or protect their offspring and the species survives by sheer fertility and weight of numbers. A female cod lays millions of eggs at each spawning – if only a handful survive, the species prospers.

Some animals have evolved a different survival strategy. They have fewer offspring, but these are looked after until they can lead independent lives. As an extension to this idea, many animals spend their whole lives in cooperating family groups.

There are recorded instances of young children surviving alone following wars and natural disasters, but no human can have an environment that totally excludes social contact at all stages of life. The smallest human society is two people. Perhaps all of the world's population is now part of a single global village.

Natural versus social science

The natural and social sciences differ in several important respects.

Natural scientists study the physical environment; social scientists study the social environment. The widest definition of the social sciences is the study of human social contact and interaction.

- The characteristics that interest social scientists are often difficult or impossible to measure.

- The social sciences are not based on a single set of fundamental or universally applicable laws, theories and principles.

- Human behaviour is often irrational, or apparently irrational, rather than logical and predictable.

- Social science experiments and investigations usually involve small samples of a few hundred or a few thousand people. Conclusions drawn from small samples can be unreliable and unrepresentative of larger populations.

- Natural science works with numbers and with words that have precise and agreed meanings. Social science has to use words much more than numbers. This reliance on language often introduces uncertainty and differences of interpretation.

It is perhaps impossible to disentangle any major branch of the social sciences from a value judgement of some kind.

To give just one example, the natural and medical sciences have developed procedures that ensure safe termination of pregnancy. The 'right' science minimises the risks of blood loss, infection and permanent damage to the mother's reproductive system. The 'wrong' science, of the illegal back-street abortionist, is life threatening for the mother. Social scientists study the consequences of termination for the woman concerned and for society as a whole. Individuals and societies often have strongly held but often totally opposing views on the deliberate termination of pregnancy.

There is no 'wrong' or 'right' social scientific conclusion in this instance.

The natural sciences divide relatively neatly into three major disciplines – biology, chemistry and physics. There are blurred lines and overlaps, but little serious disagreement about the territory of any particular speciality.

Six social sciences

The social sciences are harder to define, but six subdivisions or disciplines are widely recognised.

A huge leap in our understanding of the physical environment began in the 17th century. This was based on advances in mathematics and the development of accurate measuring instruments and new technologies.

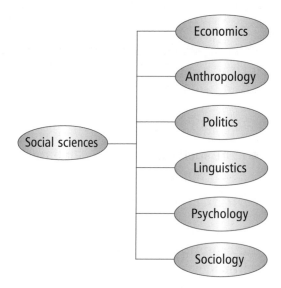

The birth of the industrial revolution is usually dated to 1712 and the invention of the first workable steam engine. Previously, we were totally dependent on the muscle of men and animals plus unreliable wind and water power. The industrial revolution began in the UK and over the next 150 years it spread across western Europe and North America.

Our greater understanding of the natural sciences led to the industrial revolution. The social sciences emerged as we tried to explain and predict its human consequences.

During the 19th century, the industrial revolution transformed society in large parts of the country. There was a huge population shift towards towns and cities, the power of landowners declined and a new class of industrial capitalists took centre stage.

For Access, the social science units concentrate mostly on applied sociology and psychology. It helps to outline briefly the focus of the other social sciences before we turn to the detail.

Economics

The central principle of economics is the concept of scarce resources. No individual, family or society has enough time, money or material to fulfil all of its needs and wishes. Economics is the study of the allocation of scarce resources or alternatively the examination of the behaviour resulting from this scarcity.

In the UK, the funding of the National Health Service is a superb example of how economics works in practice and the decisions faced by economists.

At the first level, the NHS competes with the demands of education, welfare, defence and all the other services that depend on money raised through taxation.

Within the NHS itself, there is continuous and inevitable argument about priorities. Should we spend money on preventative medicine, new research, children, the elderly, treating acute conditions, alleviating chronic disorders, and so on? The list is endless.

Different societies make different economic decisions. In the US, for example, healthcare is largely funded by individuals rather than by the state. In parts of Europe, higher tax rates are accepted in return for greater health spending.

No existing society, no matter how wealthy, has decided that the best possible healthcare for all of its citizens is an absolute priority. The cash demands of modern medicine are probably limitless.

Political science

Politics is the social science concerned with government and authority. Law and criminology can be seen as branches of political science. Economics and politics are obviously closely interrelated – different political ideologies produce different spending priorities.

Interestingly, in the UK, nearly all of our political leaders have had backgrounds in the social sciences or the humanities rather than in the natural sciences. The only trained scientist to have become prime minister in the UK was Margaret Thatcher, who studied chemistry. Before she entered politics, Mrs Thatcher also took a law degree.

Anthropology

Anthropology is the study of mankind and human groups, starting with the assumption that we are just another animal species. Physical anthropology is closely related to biology and the investigation of evolutionary change.

Beginning in the 15th century, large parts of the world were explored and then colonised mostly by the British, French, Spanish and Portuguese. For the first time, Europeans came into contact with totally unfamiliar cultures and societies. Comparative anthropologists study the variations in structure and organisation amongst different human groups.

The investigation of class differences within an apparently integrated society is another kind of anthropology.

Linguistics

The defining characteristic of our species – the thing which distinguishes us from all other living organisms – is our use of complex spoken and written language. Human social contact and interaction depends partly on language. Therefore, linguistics is a central social science.

Linguistics is best defined as the study of languages in relation to human behaviour and beliefs. The development of languages and language groups closely follows human history. The study of language differences and similarities gives many clues to the ways in which a society is structured and organised.

Sociology

It is impossible to be an effective health professional without some understanding of sociology and psychology. An individual's state of health and well-being, or lack of it, at any stage of life has resulted from tens of thousands of interactions between environment and inheritance.

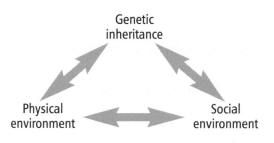

At a more practical level, any meeting between a health practitioner and a client or patient involves social interaction. This is nearly always much more than a simple objective exchange of information.

The term sociology was first used in the 1830s to describe the study of the new societies being produced by the industrial revolution.

The foundations of sociology were laid by four men who worked and published their research during the 19th century.

Karl Marx

Karl Marx was born in Germany in 1818. He studied law and philosophy at the universities of Bonn and Berlin. He was expelled from Germany in 1849 and spent the rest of his working life in England. He died in 1883 and is buried in Highgate Cemetery in North London.

Marx's political theories resulted in part from a study of working-class conditions in the newly industrialised cities of Europe – he was perhaps the first sociologist.

Marx thought that society inevitably involved conflict between classes with opposing interests. At its simplest, Marxist sociology says that the few groups and families who own most of a society's wealth will always try to exploit the majority – who have nothing to offer apart from their labour.

Marx predicted that rural feudal societies would evolve first into capitalist economies and that capitalism, at some stage, would be overthrown by a general and unstoppable move towards a more equal socialist structure. Marx believed the first truly socialist revolutions were likely to happen in England,

Germany or perhaps France. The Russian revolution of 1917, 34 years after his death, was the first attempt to instal a Marxist society.

The collapse of Russian-style communism in the 1990s is taken by many as the final proof that Marx's model was wrong and that Marxist society degenerates into conditions as bad or worse than pre-industrial feudalism.

The alternative political view is that Marx's model was correct in some major respects but wrong in detail. Modern democratic industrial societies have altered to include much that Marx may have admired.

Herbert Spencer

Herbert Spencer (1820–1903) was a British philosopher. He believed that societies evolved in the same way as living organisms or species. Spencer saw the family, political organisations, the church and the work environment as the main agents of change. He was especially interested in how control exerted by these four influences shaped the behaviour of children and hence the sociology of the next generation.

Towards the end of his career, Herbert Spencer's work was increasingly criticised. His theories were seen to justify the most extreme forms of capitalism, in particular the exploitation of the industrial workforce.

Émile Durkheim

Émile Durkheim (1858–1917) was born in France and trained as a philosopher. His work concentrated on the beliefs and shared experiences that hold societies together and, conversely, the factors that lead to social disruption, collapse and violence. He was the first sociologist to use the term 'collective conscience' and probably also the first to recognise the true complexity of and the interdependence needed to maintain large modern communities.

During his lifetime, Durkheim's theories were attacked by the established church. He thought that religion was a product of a society's shared values. The orthodox religious view held that the world worked the other way around – that religion is the civilising influence that produces common values and codes of behaviour.

Max Weber

Max Weber (1864–1920) was a German historian. He was the first sociologist to carry out and commission extended investigations and experiments to discover how large organisations really worked. His central concerns were the sources of power and authority, and the differences between logical and irrational behaviour in individuals and societies.

Weber recognised the true differences between the social and natural sciences. In particular he realised that, largely because of human irrationality, there could be no universal laws of social science to match those of chemistry and physics.

Clearly, advances in sociology did not end with the death of Max Weber in 1920, but his work, and that of Marx, Durkheim and Spencer, established the principles that underpin the applied sociology you will be taught as part of the Access course.

Psychology

Psychology is the newest of the social sciences and the one that provokes the greatest disagreement amongst its critics and supporters.

At one extreme, psychology has been described as a rag-bag of non-scientific assertions, unprovable by experiment and of dubious value in promoting human health and happiness. The defenders of psychology insist that its study goes to the heart of human existence and that it offers invaluable theories to explain human behaviour, in particular actions that seem to be self-destructive or irrational.

Psychology is the study of the human mind. This definition leads to difficult questions: What is the mind? Where is it located? How does it work? The word psychology derives from the Greek *psyché*. This translates into English as soul or something like 'the centre of a human being's life or existence'. The Greeks thought that the *psyché* was immortal and persisted as a vapour-like material after the death of the body.

The first recorded use of the word *psyché* is in the poetry of Homer, who died around 700 BCE. In the intervening 2,700 years, we have made considerable progress, but we still do not have a generally agreed definition of 'mind'.

If 'mind' is a physical object, it must be part of, or in some way associated with, the brain.

The brain is by far the most complicated structure ever encountered by mankind. Amongst many other things, the brain is a collection of specialist cells – neurones. It is thought that the physical basis of memory may be a series of permanent connections made between a network of neurones.

Psychology in healthcare

There are many overlaps between psychology, psychiatry and neurology. Some behaviour patterns that can be described as odd or unusual have proven biochemical origins. Psychiatry is the branch of medicine that deals with mental illness.

Returning to the realities of everyday medicine, very few practitioners dispute that psychology and psychologists make an invaluable contribution to healthcare. We do not know what 'mind' is, but we know for sure that there are intimate connections between state of mind and many physical diseases and disorders. Individuals vary enormously in their ability to cope with the stresses of modern life – some of this resistance or vulnerability is genetically inherited, but the rest must be due to environment.

Very few of us live totally blameless lives, in the medical sense. We are all tempted into lifestyles and behaviour patterns that threaten our health and longevity. Climbing one mountain, smoking one cigarette or spending one month without exercise may not be dangerous, but medicine has to cope increasingly with the effects of long-term self-destructive behaviour.

Psychology has a central role in preventative medicine. If we can begin to understand why people behave irrationally, then we stand a chance of altering this illogical behaviour.

The biopsychosocial model

From the outset, it is vital to recognise that healthcare does not involve conflict or forced choices between the social and natural sciences. Each makes an essential contribution. The modern NHS is firmly based on what is called the biopsychosocial model of health. Health and well-being, or the lack of it, is determined not just by the efficient workings of the body but also by psychology and the influences of society on its members.

Chapter 2
Health in a changing society

National unit specification
These are the topics you will be studying for this unit.

1   Defining health

2   Lifestyle, environment and class

3   Healthcare before the National Health Service

4   The National Health Service

5   Epidemiology

6   Healthcare legislation

7   Alternative medicine

8   Models of health

9   Health promotion and education

This chapter collects together material that may be taught as two units. These are usually called 'Health and society' and 'Changing patterns of health'.

1 Defining health

The word 'health' has descended into modern English from the Anglo-Saxon for wholeness or unity. Its meaning is also closely associated with the idea of being whole, holy or at peace. Throughout history, there have been strong connections between medicine, healthcare and religious belief.

There are many valid definitions of health. All have three things in common:

- Health is a positive concept. It is far more than just the absence of disease or disorder.

- Health involves emotional and psychological well-being, not just an efficient and properly functioning body. These two factors are always interrelated and often inseparable.

- Our health is partly determined by others. We, in turn, influence the health of the individuals we interact with.

The third idea defines the scope of this unit. Health is a concept that involves the structure and actions of societies. It cannot be properly studied or understood by considering individuals in isolation.

Definitions through the ages

Health is that state of moral, mental and physical well-being which enables a man to face any crisis in life with utmost facility and grace.

Pericles, Athenian politician 495–429 BCE

By health I mean the power to live a full adult living breathing life in close contact with what I love – I want to be all that I am capable of being.

Katherine Mansfield, New Zealand-born novelist 1888–1923

Health is a state of complete mental, physical and emotional well-being and not just the absence of disease.

World Health Organization Charter

'Health is for people'

The defining work on health and society is generally acknowledged to be *Health is for People* by Michael Wilson (1975). Michael Wilson practised medicine in Africa and in Birmingham. As well as being a qualified doctor he was also an Anglican priest.

Dr Wilson's writings give invaluable insights into the links between health and society – in particular into how patterns of disease and disorder alter with changes in social structure and material wealth.

We can summarise two of his most important ideas:

- Illness is a message. It can be personal and expressed in body language like pain or discomfort. It might also be a symptom of a failing in society – like poverty or stress – transmitted through the individual sufferer. An important function of healthcare is therefore to collect information about what is wrong with society.

- Treating disease and treating patients are very different things and they inevitably lead to different sets of priorities and resource allocation. Treatment of disease means attacking, inhibiting or destroying it in some way. Patient treatment involves fostering or nurturing the capacity to live a full life. The central purpose of a health system should be to care for patients. The treatment of disease is just one aspect of caring.

The model of health once implicit in the UK NHS was that health is obtained through the diagnosis, treatment and prevention of disease. Its unspoken goal is a perfect and flawless body. A better model of health is one that seeks harmony between individuals, families and wider society. Perfection is unobtainable and harmony has to be delivered by real people working together in real situations. It follows that models of health are not static but evolve as societies change.

In some respects, the NHS has failed because it has not produced a much healthier nation. The founders believed that once a backlog of untreated or neglected illness had been tackled, the NHS would then become smaller and cheaper to run. It has not turned out this way. As one pattern of disease has been defeated or dramatically contained, another has taken its place. The tools and structures of hospital medicine offer only partial solutions to the diseases and disorders triggered by materialism, stress and urbanisation.

Personal definitions of health

A physical examination, no matter how thorough, cannot prove the health of an individual – it can only show that on a particular day, there were no indications of disease or disorder. We all have our own definitions of health and these vary enormously from one person to another. A 20-year-old professional athlete with persistent injury problems might feel unhealthy. An 80-year-old man recovering rapidly from major surgery might describe his health as excellent.

Personal health definitions include:

- Feeling self-confident and physically attractive.

- Freedom from worry and anxiety and an ability to cope with stress.

- Enjoying the company of friends and family.

- Being able to handle the physical, emotional and intellectual demands of a job or profession.

- Being fit enough to enjoy physical leisure activities.

- Lack of dependence on alcohol, tobacco or drugs.

- Feeling that your health is 'good for your age'.

- Not suffering from anything more serious than colds, flu and mild stomach upsets.

- Not being reliant on regular prescription medication.

- Feeling optimistic most of the time, maintaining a sense of proportion and balance.

2 Lifestyle, environment and class

Anybody who is capable of some form of independent action can influence their own personal health. Infants, the very ill and sometimes the elderly rely on others, but even the fittest, wealthiest adults in the prime of life do not have total control over their health and well-being. To some extent, we are all influenced by the actions of others and by events beyond our control.

The diagram summarises some of the factors which can damage and/or promote personal health.

Factors influencing personal health

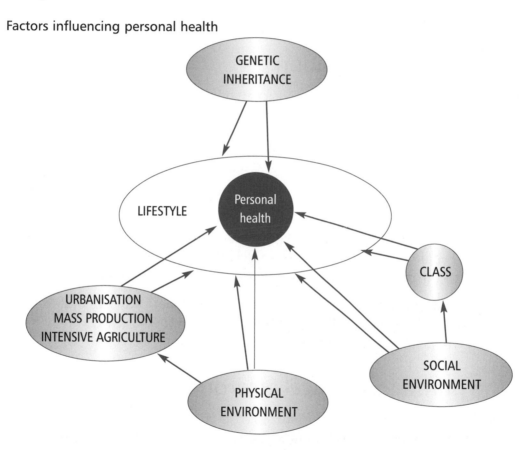

Some definitions

Genetic inheritance – nearly all of the more serious inherited disorders are as yet untreatable. For most people, genetic predisposition is a more important and relevant issue.

The broadest definition of physical environment includes any factor, apart from social interaction, that might influence health. Urbanisation, mass production and intensive agriculture have dramatically altered the physical environment.

Mankind is a social animal. We choose to live in groups for mutual comfort, protection and support. The **social environment** can be described as the total of all the human contacts and interactions we accumulate through our lifetime.

Attitudes towards health are formed largely by social interaction, but we cannot interact or feel a strong sense of belonging to a diverse community of many millions. **Class** is a convenient shorthand for the sub-groups within society that share common experiences, priorities and values. Put simply, class is a major determinant of health.

Lifestyle is another useful shorthand – it describes the sum of the personal decisions that affect our health and well-being. Lifestyle choices may be positive and health promoting, or they may be negative and reduce life expectancy. Very few people are blameless and most have lifestyles which are a mix of positive and negative behaviour. Irrationality is a major feature of human psychology.

Genetic predisposition

At the moment, most lifestyle advice can only be given in average or general terms. For example, we know that in the overall population a sustained diet high in saturated fats increases the risk of cardiovascular disease. However, we also know that some people can tolerate much more fatty diets than others without long-term harm. Differences in genetic inheritance can either provide resistance or increase vulnerability to many common diseases.

Predisposition is not a new idea. For a given level of exposure to sunlight, blue-eyed blond people are far more likely to develop skin cancer than Africans or Asians. People of northern European descent are genetically predisposed to skin cancer because they have less melanin in their body tissues.

Positive lifestyle decisions can reduce risk for the genetically vulnerable. If you have blue eyes, for instance, you should not use sunbeds; always apply a sunscreen when sunbathing and avoid midday exposure.

The primitive physical environment

The basic requirements for human survival are air, water, food, clothing and shelter. We can list the environmental threats to health that would have faced primitive pre-industrial communities.

- Extremes of climate and weather – in particular cold and drought.
- Natural disasters like floods, earthquakes and volcanic activity.
- Accidents and injuries – especially falls, drowning and poisoning.
- Diseases and disorders caused by other living organisms.

For most of human history, this fourth category has been much the most important.

The modern physical environment

Life in a 21st-century city bears very little resemblance to that of a small agricultural community of perhaps a thousand years ago. Some health risks have persisted, but the new environment has produced a different set of dangers and challenges.

In the developed world, very few die of food shortage or infectious disease, but this does not mean that health and well-being will automatically improve. We can list the modern environmental health risks:

- Food is relatively cheap and plentiful. High energy density manufactured products offer constant temptations to consume too many calories, too much fat and excess sugar.

- The connections between health, balanced diet, food hygiene, preparation and cooking are often poorly understood in large urban societies.

- Physical exercise is avoidable. Fewer jobs involve manual labour, public and private transport has replaced walking.

- Many adolescents and adults smoke.

- Relatively high levels of alcohol consumption are encouraged by advertising and cultural pressure.

- Addictive and dependency-forming drugs are available.

- Urban living is stressful, especially in competitive free-market economies. Many people react negatively to overcrowding, excessive noise and constant time pressure. There are related injury risks – most significantly crime, transport accidents and suicide.

- High urban land prices and planning restrictions mean that some of the housing stock in towns and cities are sub-standard and a risk to health.

- Pollution of air, water, land and food is a constant threat. Conservation and pollution-control legislation is often resisted and difficult to enforce. Allergic conditions may be a direct reaction to pollution in one form or another.

The return of infectious disease?

Medical science has contained infectious disease – it has not conquered or eliminated this most significant of all threats to human health. Urban living and urban lifestyles encourage the development of modified or new infectious disease, for instance:

- High population densities and international travel increase the mutation and transmission rates of influenza viruses. Influenza is potentially life threatening.

- Excessive and improper use of antibiotics has led directly to the emergence of resistant bacteria.

- New diseases evolve in response to changing lifestyles in large communities. HIV/AIDS is the best recent example.

Without intensive agriculture, most of the world's population would starve, but it can also produce problems. For example, we do not fully yet understand the links between BSE and Creutzfeldt-Jakob's disease in humans and, for similar reasons, UK public opinion is very much against the introduction of genetically modified foods.

Health inequalities

Most of what we have said so far applies more or less equally to all developed countries. For the rest of this unit, we will focus specifically on the UK.

If you stopped 10 strangers on a city street and asked them about the health history of the UK, perhaps eight or nine would be convinced of three things:

- The health of the nation has greatly improved over the last 100 years.

- The links between poverty and ill-health are no longer significant.

- The health gap between men and women has narrowed or closed completely.

These common perceptions are in many ways false.

Defining class

There are many ways of defining or measuring class. Some systems use the length and type of full-time education; some use the ownership of assets like houses, cars or consumer goods; and others use residential classifications based on post codes.

Since 1921, the 10-yearly census in the UK has collected information concerning the occupation of the heads of all households in the country. Most medical statistics still define class in this way. The method is not perfect but, interestingly, nearly all classification systems reach the same conclusions about the relationship between social status and health.

Occupations are allocated to one of six groups. The table gives examples.

Social class		Example occupations
I	Professional	Doctors, accountants, architects
II	Managerial and technical	Teachers, journalists, nurses
IIIN	Skilled non-manual	Clerks, office workers, shop assistants
IIIM	Skilled manual	Cooks, carpenters, electricians
IV	Partly skilled	Security guards, machine operators
V	Unskilled	Labourers, cleaners

Social class III is subdivided into manual and non-manual occupations.

The middle classes are taken to be groups I, II and IIIN; the working classes are groups IIIM, IV and V.

The general message

Healthcare is a major political issue. The UK National Health Service was founded in 1948 and its structure, efficiency and funding have not been far from the headlines ever since. To establish priorities and cash allocations, continuing surveys are conducted into health and health trends by government, the medical profession and other interested organisations. Since the early 1970s, virtually all health research has reached the same general conclusions.

- Death rates have fallen over the last century and there has been a corresponding increase in average life expectancy.

- Healthy life expectancy, however, has not been rising. The extra years of life are often characterised by disability or limiting long-standing illness.

- Significant gender differences in health still exist.

- The health gap between classes has widened rather than narrowed.

A full description of UK health trends is not needed for this unit, but it helps to have an overview of the most important issues and numbers. The statistics that follow are taken from a variety of government reports and green papers, census returns and statistical abstracts. We acknowledge Crown copyright.

Life expectancy

Life expectancy can be used to compare the health of large groups or to track health trends over time. A baby girl born in 2001 in the UK can expect to live for 80.7 years, and a baby boy for 75.7 years.

	Life expectancy at birth 2001	
	Women	Men
Japan	84.4	77.6
Norway	82.2	76.2
UK	80.7	75.7
US	79.8	74.4
Malawi	38.4	37.6

©Crown copyright

Average UK life expectancy has increased by about two years since 1980 and by something like 10 years since 1950. All classes can expect to live longer but the health of the fortunate has improved more rapidly than that of the disadvantaged. Professional men, those in social class I, live on average five years longer than unskilled male workers of social class V. Judged by life expectancy alone, the UK is relatively well placed. The table gives some international comparisons.

Healthy life expectancy

Health cannot be defined precisely because individual reaction to disease and disorder varies. Based on self-assessment, many middle-aged and elderly people describe their health as poor or limiting. Self-assessed poor health increases with age and especially with social disadvantage. Most research suggests that from about the age of 60, more than half of working-class and about a quarter of middle-class people think their health is poor.

These personal opinions are broadly confirmed by objective studies of factors like mobility, vision, hearing and dependency on prescription medicines.

Mortality rates

Mortality rates give a more accurate picture of changes in health patterns than life expectancy figures. Rates are quoted as the number of deaths per year per 1,000, or sometimes per 100,000, individuals. Lower overall death rates obviously correspond to greater life expectancy in large populations. The overall death rate in the UK in 1896 was 18 per 1,000; it was 10.2 per 1,000 in 2001.

Mortality and class

The following table could be seen as a snapshot of the central challenges to UK healthcare for the foreseeable future.

Mortality rates per 100,000, men aged 20 to 64

	1971	1991	20-year % reduction
Class I professionals	500	280	44
Class V unskilled manual workers	897	806	10

Death rates have fallen for all classes but the health of the richest and most fortunate has improved much more rapidly than that of the unskilled and poorly paid.

Similar trends are revealed by comparisons amongst all six classes and for all major causes of death such as heart disease, stroke, lung cancer, breast cancer and respiratory disease.

Mental illness, suicide and accident rates are also strongly related to class.

Mortality and age group

There are class-related mortality rate differences for all age groups from birth through to old age. An infant mortality is defined as the death of a child before his or her first birthday. In parts of Africa, the infant mortality rate exceeds 10% – that is 100 per 1,000. In 2001 in the UK, the mortality rate was 5.3 per 1,000 as a national average, but about seven per 1,000 for babies born into class V families and about four per 1,000 for professional couples.

Deaths from accident and injury are also strongly related to social class, in particular for young children.

Mortality and gender

Gender ratio is not fully understood. Simplistically, the sex ratios should be precisely 50:50 at conception, but this may not be a completely accurate prediction. At birth, boys outnumber girls by a few per cent, but by the late teens the sex ratio reaches one to one. From then on, women begin to outnumber men in all age brackets. The imbalance is most pronounced in the elderly.

UK population by selected age groups and gender 2001

Age range	Males ('000)	Females ('000)	Female (%)
0–4	1,786	1,700	48.8
20–24	1,765	1,781	50.2
75–79	818	1,149	58.4
80–84	483	831	63.2
85–89	227	526	69.9
90 and over	83	288	77.6

Source: Census 2001. © Crown copyright

It is entirely possible that men and women may have different genetically programmed lifespans – so that regardless of lifestyle, the average woman will outlive the average man.

Before the menopause, the female hormonal system protects the cardiovascular system. Testosterone and related male hormones encourage violence, aggression and risk taking.

Boys and younger men are more likely to die in accidents than the equivalent female age groups. This position only reverses amongst the elderly. Falls and domestic accidents are common causes and triggers of serious illness in older women.

Closing the gender gap

In the UK women still have a greater life expectancy than men, but the gender gap has closed by about two years since the 1970s. The causes are unclear but they probably relate to a narrowing of the gender gap in lifestyles. In particular:

● Increasingly, men seek medical advice and treatment when they first develop symptoms of the more serious diseases. Delay used to be a male habit.

● As a nation, we smoke less than we used to, but more men than women have given up. More teenage girls than boys smoke cigarettes. This is a reversal of the historical pattern.

Some gender differences have not altered. For all classes, women have more mental illness and men are more likely to abuse drugs and alcohol.

Diet and smoking

Currently, 73% of mothers in class I breastfeed for at least six weeks after the birth of their children. In class V this proportion is 22%. Class differences in diet have been found in all age groups. Fast, high-fat food is most popular in classes IV and V. There is a direct correlation between class and the consumption of fruit and vegetables. Up-market food retailers devote about 25% of their shelf space to fresh produce; at the other end of the social scale, this drops to around 5%.

It is difficult to track trends in smoking because in surveys and questionnaires many respondents under-report socially undesirable habits. Additionally, children younger than 16 are excluded from most routine government research.

Despite these problems of data collection, it is certain that the smoking habit has declined in the last 25 to 30 years. Historical figures are less reliable than recent surveys, but there are definite gender differences and a very strong correlation with social class.

Year	1975	2000*
% of women who smoke	40	25
% of men who smoke	50	29

* Social trends 2003. © Crown copyright

Smoking and class

		Year 2000 % who smoke	
		Male	Female
I	Professional	17	14
II	Managerial and technical	23	20
IIIN	Skilled non-manual	27	26
IIIM	Skilled manual	33	26
IV	Partly skilled	36	32
V	Unskilled	39	35
All aged 16 and over		29	25

Source: Social trends 2003. © Crown copyright

Exercise

The relationships between exercise, class and gender are complicated. Few class I or class II occupations involve regular physical work, but active leisure exercise is more prevalent at the top end of the social scale. Partly skilled and unskilled jobs usually include walking, lifting, carrying or heavy manual labour.

For men there is therefore no strong overall relationship between exercise and class, but for women those in classes IV and V are the least physically active.

Alcohol and health

Surveys of drinking habits are likely to be more accurate than research into smoking – moderate drinking is socially acceptable.

There is no safe level of cigarette consumption, but moderate drinking may not be damaging to health and some studies point to benefits. The medical evidence is contentious and confusing but there is no doubt that:

- Alcohol abuse is always dangerous – there are proven links between excess consumption and liver disease, stomach cancer, ulcers and some neurological disorders.

- The more you drink, the more you are liable to be involved in accidents, injuries and physical violence.

- As a generality, men's bodies are more tolerant of alcohol than women's. Pregnant women are advised not to drink at all.

- Regardless of initial consumption levels, some people are more likely to become alcohol dependent than others. Addictive personality is a reality, although it describes a complicated mix of psychological and sociological factors.

- Genetic predisposition is almost certainly involved in alcohol tolerance. The Japanese and many south-east Asians experience extreme discomfort at relatively low blood alcohol levels. Some evidence suggests that alcohol dependence runs in families. Genetic predisposition is probable but difficult to prove.

- Some kinds of drinks may be less damaging than others. There is no conclusive research, but dark spirits are perhaps the worst and red wine is possibly the least dangerous.

- For many reasons – medical and social – binge drinking is far more dangerous than regular, controlled alcohol consumption.

- There are interrelationships between alcohol abuse, smoking and poor diet.

- The mass production of alcoholic drinks is highly cost effective, but taxation makes drinking an expensive habit. In the UK, more than 70% of the retail price of beers, wines and spirits goes directly to the government as excise duty and VAT. Alcohol dependence can distort personal and family budgets which, in turn, increases health risks.

Alcohol, class and gender

The latest medical advice says that men should not drink more than 21 alcohol units and week and that women should not exceed 14 units a week. One glass of wine or a half pint of beer or lager contains roughly one alcohol unit. The table shows alcohol consumption by class and gender.

	Year 2000 Weekly consumption (alcohol units)	
Social class	Male	Female
I Professional	18	9
II Managerial and technical	18	8
IIIN Skilled non-manual	18	8
IIIM Skilled manual	16	7
IV Partly skilled	16	6
V Unskilled	17	4
All adults	17	7

Source: Social trends 2003. © Crown copyright

About 20% of men do not touch alcohol at all and the more you drink the less likely you are to tell a researcher the complete truth. It follows that the average reported UK male alcohol consumption of 17 units a week is probably an underestimate. It is difficult to escape the conclusion that men, on average, are drinking too much.

Working-class men are more likely to be alcohol dependent or to have alcohol-related health and social problems than middle-class men.

Women are different. The average alcohol consumption of seven units a week is safely below the recommended maximum intake of 14 units a week, but there is a strong class correlation. Professional women and the partners of professional men drink far more than the poorest and the most socially disadvantaged.

Housing

The assumption that the UK of the 21st century has become a classless society is totally disproved by any examination of the connections between health and social group. If you are well educated, fully employed, in a well-paid job and able to afford most of the consumer goods on offer, you and your family are much more likely to live a longer and healthier life than those who do not have, or cannot afford, these advantages.

About 14% of the current housing stock in the UK is officially defined as unfit or substandard. Owner-occupied suburban and rural houses and flats are almost all classed as adequate. Virtually all of the substandard dwellings in the UK are concentrated in the private rental sector and in older council estates. There is an obvious and direct relationship between class, income, housing quality and health.

3 Healthcare before the National Health Service

The National Health Service came into being on 5 July 1948. If you are younger than 60, you will have no personal memories of life before the NHS and may take its benefits and costs for granted.

Until the beginning of the industrial revolution, about 90% of the UK population lived in villages and other small agricultural communities. A voluntary system of charity developed, where the more fortunate supported the elderly, the sick and those that had fallen on hard times. The more fortunate nearly always meant the landowner and the church. No compulsion was involved, money rarely changed hands and the degree and quality of support varied a great deal from one place to another.

Most people were agricultural labourers or their families. Complete destitution – even starvation – threatened constantly.

Elizabethan upheavals

Elizabeth I was Queen of England from 1558 to 1603. By the early 1500s, a series of structural changes and crises were beginning to place intolerable burdens on the voluntary and charity-based system of health and social care.

For the previous 200 years or so, the English economy had become increasingly dependent on the wool trade. Hundreds of thousand of acres of high-quality land had been converted from tenanted smallholdings to sheep farming. The dispossessed tenants and their families grew into a sizeable and disruptive underclass roaming the country in search of work, somewhere to live and charity.

In the 1530s, Elizabeth's father – Henry VIII – had broken with the Catholic Church to form the Church of England. Part of this process involved the dissolution of the monasteries. Over the previous centuries the church had accumulated massive wealth and land. This was confiscated by the state. The monasteries and the church generally were no longer able to support the poor and the sick.

In the 1590s, the harvest failed catastrophically four or five times. Large parts of the country faced famine and starvation.

The Elizabethan poor laws

The UK welfare state is not a 20th-century invention. It dates from a law passed in 1572 introducing the first local poor-law tax. The tax was compulsory rather than voluntary and it recognised that alleviating suffering was the responsibility of the whole community.

Poor laws were not introduced entirely for the highest of motives. The unfortunate vastly outnumbered the wealthy and there was justified fear of violence, civil disruption and revolution.

The principles of infection were understood, as were the connections between poverty and disease. The poor could infect the rich just as easily as each other.

A relatively healthy and contented labour force was essential for food production and for military service.

During Elizabeth's reign, further laws were enacted in 1576, 1597 and 1601. The 1601 legislation consolidated all of the previous poor laws and, amongst other things, promoted the building of more workhouses, although these were first introduced in 1576.

Reform Act 1834

There were no substantial alterations to the poor laws between 1601 and 1834. During this period, the English population grew from 4.8 million to about 14.5 million, and the major shift from an agricultural to an industrial economy was well established.

The Reform Act 1834 made three major changes.

- Previously, parishes had been responsible for collecting and distributing the money raised by local taxation – they were amalgamated into a smaller number of larger and more efficient poor-law unions.

- In some places, poor-law administrators had become corrupt. New supervisory, report and control procedures were introduced.

- The workhouse became the main means for care and support of the poor. What we would nowadays describe as something like care in the community was discouraged.

Into the 20th century

The administration of the poor laws did not pass to central government and the Ministry of Health until 1918. During the second half of the 19th century, legislation was introduced in a series of attempts to improve the health and social conditions of the industrial working class. Rural poverty still existed, but much bigger problems were emerging in London, Birmingham and the northern industrial cities.

By today's standards, the workhouse system was harsh and even at the time it had many critics. The works of Charles Dickens are fiction, not sociological research, but they still reflect the real problems of poverty in the new industrial economy.

The National Insurance Act 1911 was the first major countrywide attempt to link general taxation directly with healthcare and social service provision.

Taxation

It is impossible to understand the connections between health and society without some knowledge of the history and principles of taxation. The main ideas are summarised briefly below.

By definition, a tax is compulsory and legally enforceable. Tax evasion is a criminal offence punishable by fines and/or imprisonment.

Broadly there are three kinds of tax:

- Tax on income.

- Tax on wealth, capital or property.

- Tax on the consumption of goods and services.

These categories often overlap. For instance, dividends on wealth accumulated as shares or on rent from land and property can be described as unearned income and may be taxed differently from wages and salaries. Sometimes, taxes are levied on the ownership of a particular kind of asset or a particular kind of behaviour – this is a form of consumption tax. In general, income taxes are called direct taxation; everything else is indirect taxation.

Taxes can be paid by individuals, often historically by couples regarded as a unit, and by businesses, companies and other organisations.

In the UK, taxes are levied by central government, by local government and by agencies acting on behalf of central government, for example Customs and Excise. Tax systems are supported by legislation which sets out how tax is collected and how much tax is to be paid – so revenue can be predicted quite accurately. Taxes are sometimes introduced for a particular purpose, but earmarking or ring-fencing is usually abandoned. Tax is collected from a variety of sources and goes into a central 'pot'. Government then decides the extent and priorities for public spending.

Most tax systems are progressive – meaning the more you earn, the more you pay. By accident or design, however, indirect taxes are often regressive – in proportion, the poor pay more than the rich. A TV licence costs the same for a family living on £15,000 a year as it does for one earning £150,000. In the UK, goods and services defined as essential are exempt from VAT, but this method of taxation is regressive in most other respects.

Redistribution and social engineering

All taxes are redistributive. They involve taking money from one group and giving it to another. Welfare or benefit, delivered as cash or as services, is a negative tax. Indirect taxes alter consumption patterns – we consume less of something if its price increases. Cigarettes are very heavily taxed in the UK for two reasons – to discourage smoking and to raise money for general public expenditure. Fruit and vegetables do not carry VAT but soft drinks, crisps and chocolate are taxed at 17.5%. Attempts to change behaviour through taxation are often called social engineering.

Politics, tax and health

Tax is a central political issue and therefore politics is the central issue in health-care and social services. The root cause of ill health is poverty, so taxation and redistribution can be seen as the foundation of preventative medicine.

Attitudes towards health define political difference. Those on the left generally favour higher taxes and greater redistribution.

The tax burden

As a broad generalisation, the total tax burden in the UK has gradually increased and the system has become more complicated. The official documents and pamphlets that describe all of the present UK tax regulations fill more than 7,000 sides of A4 paper.

During the 20th century, the tax burden in the UK varied between about 30% and 50% of total national income. At the moment, it is near the middle of this range, depending on whose calculations you care to trust.

The money raised by local government through council taxes only represents around a quarter of local expenditure. The balance comes from central government grants. Central government itself gets most of its money from four main sources:

- Personal income tax.
- Employee and employer National Insurance contributions.
- VAT.
- Excise duties (mostly taxes on alcohol, tobacco and motor fuel).

The big spenders

The total raised by taxation varies from one year to the next, as does the list of spending priorities. Major shifts usually follow a change in the governing party or are made in response to economic recession. The table summarises UK public expenditure for 2002.

Nearly 60% of all government spending is related directly to policies and strategies designed to promote health and well-being. If housing and environmental protection is added to this list, then the potential for redistribution increases to around two-thirds of all the tax collected in a typical year.

Social service payments like unemployment and housing benefit are obviously redistributive, but it should not be forgotten that the NHS is essentially a method for spreading the enormous costs of healthcare across the population and the economy as a whole.

The NHS is a logical consequence of the first Elizabethan poor law of 1572.

Spending department	% of total
Social services	28
Health	18
Education	13
Subtotal	59
Defence	6
Law and order	6
Debt interest	6
Housing and environment	5
Industry and agriculture	4
Transport	2
Everything else	12
Total	100

4 The National Health Service

By a wide margin, the NHS is the largest organisation in the UK. Judged by worker numbers, it is also one of the largest in the world. Only the Indian railway system and the Chinese army employ more.

About 1.3 million people work for the NHS in the UK and its present running costs are around £140 million a day.

The 1945 General Election

For most of the Second World War, the UK was run by an all-party coalition government. Winston Churchill, leader of the Conservatives, was prime minister from 1940 to 1945. The 1945 General Election, held two months after the end of the war in Europe, produced a landslide victory for the Labour party.

The 1945 election was one of the most important turning points in British history. It led directly to the foundation of the NHS in 1948.

The Beveridge Report

The Beveridge Report, named after its main author William Beveridge, has been called the blueprint for the Welfare State. Amongst other things, it recommended major reforms in social security and the creation of a National Health Service free to all at the point of use. The Report was published in 1942. The 1945 election ensured the implementation of most of its proposals.

Aneurin Bevan (1897–1960)

William Beveridge designed the NHS. His ideas were made real by Aneurin Bevan (known as Nye Bevan).

Bevan was born in 1897 in Tredegar, a South Wales coal-mining community. He first worked as a miner at the age of 13. He became an active trades unionist and won a scholarship to study in London in 1919.

His early background and later education made him a ferocious critic of capitalism. The defeat of the miners' union in the General Strike of 1926 convinced Bevan that his future lay in politics rather than trade unionism. He was elected Labour MP for Ebbw Vale in 1929.

Nye Bevan soon became noticed as a superb public speaker and a passionate opponent of the right-wing governments of the 1930s. In the Labour administration of 1945, Bevan was made Minister of Health with additional responsibility for housing.

Conditions in the late 1940s could hardly have been more difficult. The UK was more or less bankrupt: much of the housing stock and manufacturing capacity had been damaged or destroyed and there were shortages of coal, food and most essential raw materials. Demobilisation of the armed forces produced unemployment and social tensions – the divorce rate rocketed from a typical pre-war rate of around 2,000 a year to reach 38,000 in 1946 and 50,000 in 1947.

Against this unpromising background, Nye Bevan forced through the National Health Service Bill and this was made law in November 1946, although it was not implemented until July 1948.

The strongest resistance to the NHS came from the British Medical Association. Its chairman in 1946, Dr Guy Dain, advised BMA members not to cooperate or participate in health service reform. The consultants were Bevan's most active critics.

The Labour party won a narrow victory in 1950 but was defeated by the Conservatives in the third post-war election in 1951. The original budgets for the NHS proved to be gross underestimates and Bevan was blamed by many Labour supporters for the 1951 defeat and Churchill's return as prime minister.

Bevan's politics were widely thought to be too extreme for the average middle-of-the-road British voter. In a 1948 speech, he declared a 'burning hatred' of the Conservatives and described them as 'lower than vermin'. Through the 1950s, Nye Bevan was involved in a series of bitter internal Labour party disputes. He died in July 1960.

Politics and health

To this day, the Labour party, especially its left wing, sees the NHS as its finest achievement. Any attempts to dilute Bevan's and Beveridge's founding principles provoke the strongest opposition. The central concepts are that healthcare should be provided free of charge at the point of use and that provision should be based on medical need, regardless of income, wealth or social status.

During her time as prime minister, Margaret Thatcher frequently used expressions like 'the NHS is safe in Conservative hands'. Political generalisations are dangerous, but it is probably true to say that the NHS has become a permanent feature of British life.

Opinion research suggests that any political party that tried to dismantle the NHS would face electoral disaster. The NHS is differently structured in England, Wales, Scotland and Northern Ireland. Political devolution is an issue for the future. There are indications, for example, that the Scottish Parliament will favour higher health spending and greater levels of redistribution.

Hospitals before 1948

Before the NHS, the lowest-paid workers could consult a doctor without payment, but this service did not extend to their families. The slightly better off were obliged to pay, although many doctors reduced their fees or were prepared to treat first and wait for their money.

Most hospitals charged up front. The poorest could claim refunds, but this clearly did not help those who could not find the money in the first place. In London and some of the larger cities there were a few free hospitals supported by charity, but they were usually overwhelmed with patients and in constant danger of financial collapse.

In the larger towns, maternity care, the treatment of infectious diseases and care of the mentally ill were provided in municipal hospitals funded by the local authority. Some were excellent but others little more than warehouses. By modern standards, the care of the mentally ill, the disabled and the elderly infirm was harsh and inadequate.

The continuing challenges

The NHS was born on 5 July 1948. A full history of the organisation would fill thousands of pages; for this unit you only need an outline and an understanding of the challenges that the service has faced ever since its foundation. These can be summarised as follows:

- Shifting political priorities.
- Capital investment.
- Medical advance.
- Structure and organisation.
- Accountability and cost control.
- Staffing, education and training.
- Patient choice, expectations and attitudes.
- Demographic change.
- Public versus private healthcare.

Political priorities

It is impossible to divorce healthcare from politics. It is also true that long-term planning is essential if the NHS is to keep pace with changing health needs. Since 1940, there have been 11 UK prime ministers, 13 different administrations and more than 20 cabinet ministers who have had responsibility for the NHS.

The health planning cycle ought to be 10 years at least. UK political priorities have tended to alter every three or four years. Governments change policies between elections and major shifts have followed the periodic defeats of the Conservative and Labour parties. Planning becomes especially difficult in times of economic recession and high inflation.

Capital investment

The NHS capital budget is divided into two main categories – buildings and equipment. There was an acute shortage of hospital capacity in 1948. Few hospitals were built during the recession of the 1930s; many were damaged during the war. Post-war rehousing included slum clearance and the creation of many new towns to take the overspill from inner cities. New hospitals were built as a priority to serve relocated communities.

The running costs of the NHS cannot be avoided, but capital spending can be delayed or reduced. During the last 50 years, periods of cash shortage have alternated with major hospital building and replacement programmes – there has been no consistent policy.

Large general hospitals are expensive to build but are usually cost effective once in place. More of the capital budget now goes to smaller local healthcare facilities. Hospital-based medicine is no longer expected to meet all of our health needs.

Medical equipment costs have escalated beyond all original expectations. Surgery and diagnosis have improved dramatically. A fully equipped operating theatre costs millions of pounds, as do instruments like scanners and automated laboratory equipment.

Medical advance

Nye Bevan and one or two other post-war politicians recognised from the outset that the NHS would never have enough money. However, in 1948, it would have been impossible to predict the huge advances in medical science that have taken place. Three factors have combined to increase costs:

- The development and manufacture of new drugs and pharmaceuticals has saved millions of lives but at huge and increasing cost.

- The pattern of disease and disorder has changed. Long-term and chronic conditions are more expensive to treat or contain than acute illness.

- We have much higher expectations than 50 or even 20 years ago. Most of us no longer tolerate pain, discomfort or illness. The demand for healthcare is potentially limitless.

Medical cost inflation exceeds the average inflation rate for other goods and services. If NHS budgets are only increased in line with the general retail price index – as they often have been in the past – they cannot hope to meet the real growth in demand.

Structure and organisation

Every organisation is difficult to control and manage. Problems multiply as it gets bigger and more complex. Commercial companies are constantly reorganising and experimenting with new structures, but this happens in private. Most companies are accountable only to their shareholders provided their managements obey the law.

The NHS is different. It can do nothing in secret because it spends public money. We all have a vested interest in healthcare – so do our politicians and all sections of the media. Reorganisations are a continuing fact of life for the NHS and most have been an attempt to solve four kinds of problem:

- A centralised organisation promotes consistent national standards and it can be cost effective. However, health needs vary significantly from region to region and a centralised structure reacts slowly and impersonally to changing patient demands. Devolution and decentralisation are favoured by the present government.

- Healthcare is provided in hospitals, by GPs and by specialist local services. These three arms of the NHS can be integrated or compartmentalised. In recent years, there has been a major shift towards integration and away from hospital-based medicine.

- The NHS and the social services in the UK have traditionally operated as two separate organisations. The links between poverty and ill health are increasingly recognised and the distance between the two services has gradually reduced. Integration and cooperation between health and social services is critical for the elderly and the disabled.

- Every organisation needs managers and others who do not have front-line jobs or regular contact with customers. From time to time, the NHS has been heavily criticised for having too many administrators and not enough health practitioners. There is no single solution to this problem – more support staff are needed as medical science improves and the NHS is getting larger and more complex.

Accountability and cost control

Accountability has several dimensions. The NHS should be organised and run for the benefit of its customers, not for the convenience of the health professions. Accountability means that the service must respond to local and national public opinion. Departures from good practice should be punished or discouraged. Efficiency should be recognised and rewarded. Performance league tables have been introduced to inform patients and to incentivise the health professions.

The NHS is a nationalised industry and, unless you can afford private healthcare, it is a monopoly provider. During the 1980s, most of the UK's nationalised monopolies were broken up and privatised. The government of the day believed that public ownership reduced accountability, efficiency and cost control. The NHS internal market system was devised by the Conservatives and later abandoned by Labour.

Staffing, education and training

The NHS is a labour-intensive organisation. Wages, salaries, pensions and employer National Insurance contributions account for roughly half of its total running costs. In many organisations, machines can take the place of people – this is not usually possible in healthcare. The NHS will always need a very large workforce.

Starting with GCSE qualifications, it takes about eight years to train as a doctor and another 10 years of experience, at least, to become a specialist. Just as the NHS has never had enough money, it has always had to cope with shortages of skilled staff.

At many times during its history, the NHS has relied on recruiting foreign nationals to fill the gaps in the UK education and training system. The Commonwealth, Ireland and the Philippines currently provide many of our doctors, nurses and health professionals.

Attitudes towards pay, training and working conditions have varied with changes in government and government policies. This lack of consistency has generated many industrial disputes since 1948. At one time or another, nurses, GPs, hospital junior doctors and consultants have all been in open conflict with government.

Governments have often been accused of cynicism and short-termism in their handling of NHS industrial relations. Very few health professionals are prepared to endanger patients by going on strike or working to rule and there is no quick way of finding or training qualified staff.

Patient choice and expectations

The days when the average patient or client would treat doctors with deference and subservience are gone forever. We now expect to be treated with respect and courtesy and to be informed and consulted at every stage of treatment or therapy. Patients and clients have recognised their rights as the ultimate owners of the NHS.

Most of all, national expectations have risen. The average UK citizen expects high standards and prompt treatment. Politicians know that waiting lists, more than any other deficiency in the NHS, are likely to lead to problems on election day.

Managing expectation is a central political issue. Labour probably lost the 1951 election because it promised a better health service than it could deliver.

Demographic change

In material terms, the UK of the 21st century is utterly different from the country that emerged from the Second World War in 1945. The NHS has created some of this change; the rest it has had to respond to. The biggest demographic shift of the last 50 years has been a gradual ageing of the population.

The age statistics are not disputed, but their implications for the NHS are not clear or certain. Around 80% of the total cost of the health service is devoted to people in their first six years of life and in their last three. If healthy life expectancy can be increased, not just total life expectancy, then expenditure on the elderly will be postponed but not increased in total. The elderly use the NHS more than ever before, but so do most age groups. Some research suggests that the increase in consultation rates is directly related to improvements in diagnosis and treatment not to underlying real increases in illness. Much of this is contentious, but an ageing population has two implications that cannot be avoided or denied:

- Health promotion, education and preventative medicine will become more important. This is the best way of extending healthy life expectations.

- Increased social service spending will influence demands on the NHS. The longer the elderly can lead independent healthy lives, the better off we will all be. It follows that health and social service integration is the way ahead.

Public versus private medicine

You have to be very rich indeed to be able to afford to substitute all the services of the NHS with private healthcare. Regardless of wealth, complete substitution is impossible. An unconscious billionaire trapped alone in a car accident could not telephone for a private ambulance or arrange treatment in a private hospital.

Private medicine and private education have never been prohibited in the UK, but in both areas an uneasy truce has existed between the public and private sectors at least since 1945.

In 1946, Bevan said he would remove the consultants' opposition to the NHS 'by stuffing their mouths with gold'. Bevan accepted that the NHS could not be created if private provision was banned. The consultants were allowed to mix private and public practice with minimal restrictions.

Private medical insurance schemes have always existed but this sector has grown in response to real or perceived failings in the NHS. Private insurance is often given as an employee perk or benefit. For a period, premiums were tax deductible, but this incentive has now been removed.

More information

In this topic, we have tried to outline the history of the NHS and the changing issues it has had to face. As background or for assessments, you may need to study some current issues in greater detail. The NHS, the Department of Health, the Department for Work and Pensions and the Treasury run a number of user-friendly websites. The NHS is one of the most open and transparent organisations in the UK – information is freely available.

5 Epidemiology

An **epidemic** is an outbreak of disease that affects a large number of people, usually in one location and often over a relatively short period of time. Epidemiology is the study of epidemics. An epidemiologist is a specialist who is likely to be an expert statistician as well as a trained doctor.

An **endemic** disease or disorder is one which is always present in a particular group or location, or one which recurs consistently in a defined population or place. Malaria is endemic in some parts of Africa; tooth decay used to be endemic amongst British schoolchildren.

Epidemiology was originally concerned solely with infections, but its techniques have been widened to include the diseases and disorders that result from urban life in developed societies. There is an epidemic of cardiovascular disease in the UK where once there were epidemic infections like smallpox, cholera and measles.

Public health

The concept of public health is intimately linked with epidemiology. Public health is the branch of medicine that investigates patterns of disease, assesses the health needs of communities and establishes strategic plans to improve their health and well-being. The World Health Organization does this on a global scale; national governments and most regional and local authorities have public health departments.

The information base

Any census, survey or investigation that collects information from large groups of people is potentially useful in epidemiology. Routine data collection is backed up by analytical studies and experimentation to investigate or confirm the causes of disease. Individuals and health practitioners are legally obliged to disclose some kinds of information to the appropriate authorities. The following are examples of the UK medical information base.

Births, marriages and deaths have to be registered. Age at death and cause of death are included as part of registration. This relatively simple procedure is the foundation for medical statistics in the UK. It shows, amongst other things:

- Trends in major disease.
- Gender-related health differences.
- Fertility rates.
- Infant mortality.
- Regional and seasonal patterns.

There are procedures for recording and registering disabilities and illnesses that give entitlement to welfare payments and benefits.

The 10-yearly UK census is legally enforced. Members of households have to declare information that allows accurate planning for health and other services like education and transport. The census provides the demographic database for the UK. From it, we know not just total population size, but also detail such as age profile, regional population, family size, housing conditions, employment or profession, transport use and so on. Recent censuses have included specific health-related questions.

The first official census was taken in 1801 and there has been one every 10 years since, with the exception of 1941. The last census date was 29 April 2001; the next will take place in April 2011. We have 200 years' worth of demographic information in some categories. Clearly, the long-term trends which emerge from census analysis are exceedingly useful.

Notifiable diseases

Some diseases have to be reported to the authorities immediately on diagnosis, regardless of outcome. These are the notifiable diseases. The list has varied over time, and there are arrangements for temporary additions when the need arises.

Specialist databases

The census, birth and death registration, and disease notification provide core or basic information. These systems are supported by data collected to study specific problems and events. To give a few examples:

- A UK scheme has been in place since 1952 which monitors maternal deaths in pregnancy and childbirth.

- There are groups of medical researchers who cooperate in studying most of the more serious inherited conditions, like cystic fibrosis, haemophilia and Huntington's disease. Accurate family pedigrees are an essential prerequisite for this work.

- Some well-understood occupational diseases are notifiable. The best examples are the cancers and respiratory conditions caused by inhalation of coal dust, asbestos, metals and minerals. Other occupational diseases have emerged more recently or are less well researched. There are voluntary bodies and organisations collecting data in these areas.

- The study of sexually transmitted diseases presents major ethical problems. In the UK, notification of HIV/AIDS and other sexually transmitted disease is voluntary, not mandatory. Again, however, there are confidential systems in place which deliver accurate trend information. Diagnoses are nearly always reported but patients' identities are not disclosed.

Analysis

The full analysis of each UK census takes several years, employs thousands of people and costs many millions of pounds. Similarly, all information gathering is expensive and time consuming. Obviously, this is not a passive exercise and data is useless if it is just filed and forgotten.

Health information becomes more useful when two or more data sets are compared. This analysis often shows an association or correlation between two groups of numbers. Most medical research starts with statistical investigation. There are thousands of examples to choose from:

- Smokers suffer from many diseases and disorders that are rare in non-smokers. The same is true of heavy drinkers.

- There is a correlation between life expectancy and body weight.

- Meningitis is most common in the under 18s.

- Post-menopausal women have greater rates of bone fracture than men or younger women.

- Down's syndrome is associated with maternal age.

- Cross-cultural and cross-community studies can be revealing. Countries and classes whose diet includes a great deal of saturated animal fats have higher rates of cardiovascular disease than those who eat mostly unsaturated vegetable and fish oils.

- Many diseases and disorders are associated with dietary deficiency.

Experimentation

Statistical correlation or association does not prove that one thing causes another. Analysis is the starting point in medical advance, not the winning post.

In the early years of research into smoking and health there were theories that a particular personality type was more vulnerable to cancer and that these kinds of people were also, incidentally, more likely to smoke. These theories have been disproved by further statistical analysis – for example, with ex-smokers – and by animal experiments showing that tobacco smoke contains active carcinogens.

In complex situations, it is difficult to prove the direction of cause and effect. Does a high-sugar diet cause tooth decay? Or do bad teeth produce a craving for sweet foods? In this case, we know which is cause and which is effect because experiments have shown that sugars combined with oral bacteria produce acids that attack tooth enamel.

Analysis, combined with experimentation, cannot always give prompt and definitive answers. One of the largest debates in medical science concerns the relative contributions of genetic inheritance and environment or lifestyle to health.

The work of the epidemiologist

The history of the medical profession has been one of increasing specialisation. Despite the name we give to the job, a general practitioner is also a specialist. GPs act as the gatekeepers to the health service – their particular skills are first diagnosis, local community knowledge and differentiating between trivial, threatening or serious conditions.

In the same way, epidemiology subdivides into specialties. These consider:

- The causes of illness.
- The methods of transmission.
- The identification of risk or risk groups.
- Prevention.
- Cure.
- Control.

We need to look at each of these in turn.

Pathogens

'Path' or 'patho' means disease and 'gen' means a living thing, so a pathogen is an organism that causes disease.

The body of a healthy human is teeming with bacteria. Some of these play vital roles – in digestion and excretion, for instance. The immune system has evolved to destroy pathogens and to keep the population of beneficial organisms within acceptable limits.

Taking an historical view, the great majority of human deaths have been caused by pathogens or by malnutrition giving increased vulnerability to pathogens. Pathogens are viruses, bacteria, protoctista or fungi that produce toxins or disrupt the normal functions of the body.

All pathogens are parasites in one meaning of the word, but this term is usually reserved for larger or visible disease-causing organisms.

Symbiosis

No living thing exists in isolation. Symbiosis describes two or more species that live together to their mutual benefit. We have a symbiotic relationship with many kinds of bacteria. The dividing lines between a symbiotic relationship and that of host and parasite are difficult to define. Again in evolutionary terms, a parasite will not survive if it kills its host or has no method for transmitting itself to another host once the first one has died.

Evolution has produced infection. The polio virus, the bacteria that cause food poisoning and the parasitic protoctista that cause malaria would have become extinct if they could not move from one human host to another.

Dietary causes of disease

Malnutrition means any sustained departure from a balanced diet. Excess as well as deficiency causes disease and disorder.

Dietary deficiency diseases are rare in the UK, other than a shortage of iron which affects a significant proportion of women of childbearing age. Excess calorie intake and high consumption of saturated fats or added sugars are known to damage heath.

Pregnant women and younger children have extra need for protein, calcium, iodine and some vitamins. Spina bifida has been linked with low intakes of folic acid in pregnancy.

A previously well-nourished individual will not develop deficiency symptoms immediately if nutrients are withheld. Body fat is an energy store and most vitamins and minerals can also be stored in the liver and other tissues. In the poorest countries, food shortages tend to recur – sustained low protein and low vitamin A diets are common risks to health.

Alcohol, tobacco and drugs

There is no human nutritional need for alcohol but in the UK it provides around 6% of total calorie intake. The connections between smoking, alcohol abuse, drug addiction or dependency and ill health are very well established.

Substance abuse of all kinds is damaging to mental health as well as physical well-being.

Environmental causes of disease

In the precise meaning of the word, pathogens and diet are part of the environment because they are part of our physical surroundings. Environmental diseases are more often narrowly defined as those resulting from pollution in all its forms.

Many metals are toxic in very small quantities. Mercury, lead and cadmium are the most dangerous. These are cumulative poisons and as an animal at the top of the food chain, we are at the greatest risk. Public health legislation controls heavy-metal emissions.

Research showing that atmospheric lead pollution slowed brain development in children resulted in a ban of leaded petrol. This change cost the oil industry billions of pounds in new plant, equipment and processes.

Petrol and diesel engine exhaust will contain only carbon dioxide and water vapour if the engines are operating with perfect efficiency. However, even the most modern well-maintained vehicles give out carbon monoxide unburned fuel and very small particles of carbon. Over the last 20 years, much stricter legislation has been introduced to limit the health damage caused by ever increasing car ownership.

Coal burning and many industrial processes produce sulphur and nitrogen compounds that are direct causes of respiratory disease. Again, tighter legislation has been introduced as a public health measure.

Pesticides, fungicides and insecticides are complex chemical compounds designed to kill living organisms. They are not meant to damage non-target species like us, but most do.

Excessive or persistent noise is a health hazard. High frequencies are the most dangerous. Stress is an immediate consequence; hearing loss is inevitable if exposure is prolonged.

Radiation

We are constantly exposed to background radiation. This term describes the radiation reaching the earth's surface from space plus the natural radiation emitted by granite and some other rocks.

Background radiation is not damaging in most locations. Pubic health legislation controlling the nuclear industry is the most stringent of all. Leukaemia and many other cancers are direct consequences of excessive radiation. Medical X-ray machines and some industrial equipment work with radioactive materials.

Transmission and infection

Historically, epidemiologists spent most of their time trying to understand the mechanisms of infection. It is likely that the major infectious diseases evolved as a response to increasing human population and population density.

Infection most often involves direct contact or the transmission of pathogens via food, water, air, clothing or bodily secretions.

The Romans recognised the importance of clean water and efficient sewage removal. Victorian civil engineers made a major contribution to health by designing and installing the water and sewage systems that, to this day, make city life possible.

The detail of infection is not always obvious. We now know that apparently healthy people may transmit infections. Incubation periods differ and some individuals can be carriers of diseases like typhoid and dysentery.

The distinction between infections and contagious disease is largely a matter of degree. The skin and the immune system are our main defences.

Infestation, rather than infection, describes the parasites that reproduce in the intestines, on hair and on clothing.

Vectors

A vector is an intermediate involved in disease transmission. These can be biological or mechanical. Biological vectors are species that play host to pathogens as part of their life cycle.

A vector which is not biological has to be mechanical. Flies transmit disease to food via faeces, but the pathogens do not spend all of their life cycle in the fly. Water and food can also be described as mechanical vectors, as can air, water or food contaminated with toxic chemicals.

Social vectors

You cannot 'catch' heart disease, hypertension, obesity or diabetes, but these modern diseases still involve vectors.

Tobacco advertising is banned or tightly regulated because it is one of the main vectors for smoking-related diseases. Arguably, any social pressure or interaction that encourages an unhealthy lifestyle is a vector of disease and disorder. The least-healthy foods are the most heavily advertised. Some countries prohibit or limit 'unhealthy' advertising targeted at children.

Radical epidemiologists believe that society is, as a whole, unwell and that this is the root cause of most modern disease.

Investigating risk

In 1665, the great plague of London killed 70,000 people out of a total population of around 450,000. It did not wipe out the entire city – some recovered from the disease, others escaped infection altogether.

For thousands of years we have known that individual vulnerability to disease varies and that some diseases have regional and seasonal patterns. Infections often peak in spring and summer when pathogens and their vectors reproduce more rapidly. Before widespread immunisation, outbreaks of mumps and measles coincided with the beginning of school terms.

The identification of vulnerable and resistant groups has underpinned medical advance. In 1773, a Gloucestershire doctor, Edward Jenner, decided to investigate the popular belief that milkmaids were immune to smallpox. His discovery that a previous infection with cowpox prevented the related but much more serious disease founded the science of immunisation.

Prevention, control and cure

It is difficult or impossible to limit disease without a detailed understanding of its causes and means of transmission. Prevention and control may involve legislation and compulsion or education and health promotion. It is illegal to sell infected or contaminated food or water in the UK, but immunisation is voluntary and smoking is not prohibited.

We can illustrate prevention, control and cure by comparing two epidemics: cholera and coronary heart disease.

	Cholera	Coronary heart disease
High-risk groups	City dwellers in crowded conditions	Middle-aged and older men
Causes	Bacterium *Vibrio cholerae*	Unbalanced diet Smoking Lack of exercise
Transmission	Infected water, faeces, body fluids	Social vectors combined with self-destructive behaviour
Prevention	Capital investment in water and sewage system infrastructure Immunisation* Personal hygiene	Smoking cessation Dietary advice Exercise promotion Differential taxation** Anti-hypertension, cholesterol-reducing and other drugs
Control	Infrastructure maintenance Regular water-quality control	Regular health checks
Cure	Rehydration and antibiotic treatment	Heart surgery in extreme cases
Success rate	Virtually 100% in the UK	Some reduction in death rates now evident

*Cholera immunisation is not highly effective.
**For example, tobacco is very highly taxed in the UK, but fruit and vegetables are tax free.

Dr John Snow

Dr Snow was an anaesthetist but he is best remembered for his contribution to epidemiology and our understanding of cholera transmission. A major global cholera epidemic began in 1850 in the Far East, reaching Europe in 1853. Snow made maps of where cholera sufferers lived during an outbreak in Soho, which was then a crowded working-class part of London. He noticed that infection was concentrated in a small area close to a water pump. He removed and destroyed the pump handle, forcing the local residents to go elsewhere for water. Cholera subsided. Snow had proved that this particular pump was transmitting the disease.

Eternal vigilance

It is wrong to see epidemic infectious diseases as an historical curiosity or a thing of the past. We have driven the smallpox virus to extinction – the last recorded natural case was in October 1977 – but the complete elimination of other major infections is very unlikely. Many pathogens survive in animals and other living organisms and these pathogens are constantly evolving. The human immuno-deficiency virus (HIV), the cause of AIDS, was first described in 1981.

Eternal vigilance is required to maintain public health.

New for old

Overall mortality rates decreased significantly through the 20th century in the UK. This is the good news. The bad news is that we have swapped one set of killer diseases for another. The table gives the detail.

Mortality by major cause

Men in England and Wales				
		Rates per million of population		
Year	Infections	Respiratory disease	Cancers	Circulatory disease
1951	659	2,070	2,423	4,976
1961	186	1,633	2,584	4,887
1971	69	1,164	2,638	4,882
1981	34	811	2,489	4,331
1991	34	513	2,317	3,157
2001	47	423	1,866	1,983
2001 as % of 1951	7	20	77	40

Source: Office for National Statistics © Crown copyright

Mortality by major cause

Women in England and Wales				
		Rates per million of population		
Year	Infections	Respiratory disease	Cancers	Circulatory disease
1951	318	895	1,719	3,230
1961	76	556	1,670	2,676
1971	33	422	1,741	2,222
1981	19	384	1,794	1,865
1991	20	290	1,763	1,386
2001	34	285	1,483	893
2001 as % of 1951	11	32	86	28

Source: Office for National Statistics © Crown copyright

Disease classifications have altered several times since 1951, so these tables show broad long-term trends rather than precise comparisons.

Public health targets

The end products of epidemiology are targets for public health improvement and strategies to meet these targets. Public health policy is constantly reviewed and updated. In recent years, attention has focused on a relatively short list of issues.

- To reduce death rates for coronary heart disease and strokes.

- To reduce mortality caused by lung, cervical, breast and skin cancer.

- To improve mental heath and to reduce the suicide rate amongst the severely mentally ill.

- To reduce the incidence of HIV/AIDS.

- To reduce the number of teenage conceptions.

- To reduce deaths caused by accident amongst children and young people.

As an overriding priority, the present NHS plan aims to close the health gap between the poorest and the most advantaged in the UK.

6 Healthcare legislation

In this topic we outline how the law works in the UK. We then discuss some legislation and regulatory bodies in more detail.

Who makes laws?

The UK is unusual amongst modern democracies because it has no single written document defining and consolidating its legal framework. This contrasts strongly, for example, with the American system, where the US constitution defines precisely the relationship between its government and citizens.

Our law has evolved and developed over a period of more than a thousand years. It is a complicated mixture of Acts, precedents and customs.

The right to vote

The right to vote, and to be voted for, is the foundation of democracy and the legal system. There are some important dates in UK history:

- 1918: The vote was given to all men over the age of 21 and all women over 30. Previously, voting rights had been limited to male property owners.

- 1928: Sex discrimination was removed. All men and women over 21 became entitled to vote.

- 1969: The minimum voting age was reduced to 18.

Crown, Lords and Commons

Parliament is the House of Commons plus the House of Lords. The Parliament Act 1911 largely removed the power of the Lords to interfere with or block legislation proposed by the Commons – in particular, the Lords have no influence over tax or public expenditure. The present relationship between the two Houses remains complicated and difficult. Essentially, the Lords can delay legislation but not prevent it.

Recent law has altered the composition of the Lords, chiefly by limiting the number of hereditary members.

In the UK, the head of state is the monarch not the prime minister. Again as a generalisation, the monarch's present role in government is symbolic, ceremonial and advisory. No real or usable political power remains.

The legislature, the executive and the judiciary

The legislature is the House of Commons together with the House of Lords. The executive is the Prime Minister, the cabinet and other ministers. The judiciary is the courts and the judges.

A basic principle of government is that these three arms should be separated. This structure is designed to prevent the concentration or abuse of power. A government can do nothing without parliamentary approval; the judiciary interprets and enforces law. Through the jury system and via elections, the people have theoretical ultimate control over all three arms of government.

Many observers believe that the executive has tended to become too powerful in recent years. The UK party political system delivers a great deal of authority to the leader of the governing party.

Devolution and decentralisation

For historical reasons, the legislative and judicial systems of the four parts of the UK differ. These differences are widening with the devolution of power to the Scottish Parliament and the Welsh Assembly. Scottish and English law differ in many respects.

Health and social-care legislation is mostly devolved and decentralised, first to the four countries of the UK and then to local and regional governments.

European Union legislation has a significant influence on the UK especially regarding public health and environmental issues.

UK general elections

A UK-wide general election must be held at least once every five years. Within this period, the prime minister of the day can decide to call an earlier election at a time of his or her choosing. The average interval between general elections is now about three or four years.

The UK is currently divided into 659 parliamentary constituencies. Each elects a single MP on the 'first-past-the-post' system.

In theory, these 659 MPs then choose the government by a simple majority vote. However, few independent MPs are elected and general elections are reduced to contests between political parties. All MPs are free to vote against the wishes of their party, but these are rare events. A 'three-line whip' is an instruction for party MPs to support their group in a parliamentary vote – defying this instruction is more or less equivalent to resignation from the party. The last Liberal government lost office in 1922; ever since, UK politics has been dominated by Conservative and Labour.

How are laws made?

Most new law modifies, extends or repeals previous legislation. We can summarise the usual procedures:

- Parties continually develop policies through debate and discussion. Manifestos are published as part of general election campaigns. These outline the major legislation planned if the party wins the election.

- Governments often publish 'green papers'. These are consultative documents inviting public and specialist comment.

- A consultative document is usually followed by a white paper detailing the bill or proposed legislation.

- The first reading is largely a formality. The appropriate minister announces the bill to the Commons, after which it is printed and distributed.

- The second reading is a full debate, potentially involving all elected MPs.

- The committee stage is a detailed line-by-line examination of the bill by a standing committee or exceptionally by the whole House of Commons.

- The third reading is a final debate on the amended bill. It is then sent to the House of Lords and the cycle of readings and committees is repeated.

- Once both houses have agreed every dot, comma and line of the bill, it then receives the Royal Assent and the bill becomes an Act of Parliament.

In emergencies, parliament can make new law very rapidly, but most legislation takes months and sometimes years. A bill can be defeated by a vote of the House or by a committee at any stage.

An Act of Parliament may end up looking very different from the original manifesto or green-paper proposal. Governments usually have to make concessions and amendments to be sure of full party support. Health legislation is always politically contentious. Delay, dilution and spending restriction have been the rule, not the exception, since the formation of the NHS.

Ministers and ministries

The government divides its work into specialist departments or ministries. The politicians in charge of the larger departments are members of the cabinet. The cabinet is chosen by the Prime Minister – no election is involved. The cabinet decides policy by a secret vote. A cabinet decision is binding on all of its members, even those who have voted against a particular proposal. From time to time, ministers resign from the cabinet because they cannot support some piece of suggested legislation under any circumstances.

The history of the Health Service is littered with ministerial resignations. In 1951, Nye Bevan resigned from the Labour cabinet rather than support the diversion of funds away from the NHS and into military expenditure.

Departments and ministries are continually reorganised and not many ministers keep the same job for more than one parliament.

At the moment, the Department of Health is responsible for social care and the NHS. Health-related legislation can also originate from the Department for the Environment, Food and Rural Affairs and the Department for Work and Pensions.

Public offices and bodies

Many functions of government departments are delegated to public bodies and there are other similar organisations whose responsibilities cut across departmental boundaries. Some of these have direct influence on healthcare and healthcare legislation. The table gives a short summary.

Public body	Function
Audit Commissions	To audit and examine expenditure by the NHS and local authorities to ensure value for money. There is a separate audit commission for Scotland
British Pharmacopoeia Commission	Sets standards and quality specifications for all human and veterinary medicines used in the UK
Environment Agency	To prevent and control pollution and to manage water resources
Food Standards Agency	A new body set up in 2000 to oversee all aspects of food consumption as they relate to health. Also responsible for local authority food inspection and enforcement of the hygiene regulations. There are separate FSAs for the four countries of the UK
Health & Safety Commission and Executive	Oversees and enforces the provisions of the Health & Safety at Work Acts. Largely concerned with ensuring safe working environments
Health Protection Agency	Established in 2003 to integrate emergency procedures in cases of infection, chemical pollution and radiation hazards
Human Fertilisation and Embryology Authority	Oversees an Act passed in 1990 which controls the creation and use of human embryos outside the body
Human Genetics Commission	Advises on the ethical implications of human genetic research in healthcare
Mental Health Commission	To protect the rights of people detained or restricted under the Mental Health Acts. To receive complaints and enforce codes of practice
National Radiological Board	To oversee the Radiological Protection Act 1970. Mostly concerned with the health risks posed by X-rays and, more recently, mobile telephone systems
Office for National Statistics	The body that collects and processes most of the information used by government. This includes the registration of births, deaths and marriages and many other health-related databases
Parliamentary and Health Service Ombudsman	Receives and considers complaints concerning maladministration in the NHS
Live Transplant Authority	Organ transplants between unrelated living individuals may not take place without this Authority's consent

Acts of Parliament – principle versus detail

To close this topic, we outline the principles of two important pieces of health legislation:

- The Access to Health Records Act 1990

- The Mental Health Act 1983.

Most of what follows is reproduced from the text of the Acts involved or their summaries, published by HMSO. We acknowledge Crown copyright.

Access to health records

This is a relatively short and simple piece of legislation. Its main aim is to allow individuals the right to see their health records. The Act also provides a system for correcting inaccuracies.

A health record is defined as information relating to an individual's physical or mental health from which that individual can be identified.

A health record holder is a GP, somebody working for a GP or the appropriate health body – most usually a hospital. Individual health professionals are also included.

Applications for access to a health record can be made by the patient concerned, a person authorised in writing by the patient, a parent or guardian of a patient under 16, somebody authorised by a court to manage the patient's affairs, or the personal representative of a person who has died.

Once an application is made, the record holder must supply the record or a copy of the record. The Act includes provisions to minimise cost and delay.

Access may be denied if, in the holder's opinion, the information would cause serious harm to the patient's health or to the health of another individual.

If the record includes terms which are not intelligible without explanation, the holder must provide an explanation along with the record.

An applicant may insist that anything that is incorrect, misleading or incomplete is put right. A corrected version of the record must then be supplied.

Mental health

Most healthcare is based on consent. However, for the protection of some individuals and the community, mental health law has to include the option of compulsory treatment and detention. Safeguards and controls to prevent abuse and misdiagnosis must, therefore, be as effective as possible.

Mental illness can be hard to diagnose and define. A patient presenting physical symptoms might have an underlying mental illness.

The Mental Health Act 1983 is a piece of narrowly focused legislation designed to protect the most severely mentally ill from harming themselves or others.

The majority of the mentally ill give voluntary consent for treatment or hospital admission – in these cases, the Act does not apply.

The full texts of Acts of Parliament are always divided into sections. The expression 'to be sectioned' has come to mean compulsory admission for treatment under one of the sections of the 1983 Act.

Admission, treatment and consent

An application for compulsory admission has to be made by a social worker or by the person's nearest relative. Two doctors then have to agree that admission is in the best interests of the person concerned. Most forms of treatment are then legal without patient consent. Only one doctor's recommendation is needed for emergency admission.

The police have powers to enter premises and take people thought to be severely mentally ill to a place of safety for a maximum of 72 hours. A place of safety may be a hospital, nursing home or, exceptionally, a police station.

Treatment without consent cannot continue for more than three months unless a second independent psychiatrist agrees that this is in the patient's interests. There are extra safeguards concerning electro-convulsive therapy, neurosurgery, hormonal treatment and some other hazardous procedures.

Discharge and aftercare

A patient may apply for discharge at any time or a doctor can discharge a detained person if that doctor decides the patient is no longer a danger to themselves or to the community. The closest relative can apply for discharge, but this can be refused on medical grounds. A Mental Health Review Tribunal can also discharge a patient. Many patients continue treatment on a voluntary basis once a section order has expired.

In most cases, recovered patients are then free to lead their lives without legal restriction, but there are exceptions:

- A supervision register is administered by local authorities. It creates a duty of care for ex-patients at risk of suicide or self-neglect.

- Those previously detained can also be discharged into the care of a guardian. A guardian may be a local authority or a responsible individual. The guardian has rights to decide where ex-patients live and they are expected to make sure that they attend for regular treatment and keep to prescribed drug therapies.

- Supervised discharge is the third option - this is guardianship with extra restrictions. Refusal to comply with the conditions of a supervised discharge usually results in compulsory readmission.

Financial provisions

The 1983 Act includes wide and comprehensive powers to control all of the financial affairs of people who are thought to be permanently or temporarily incapable through mental illness. The bodies involved are the Court of Protection and the Public Trustees.

7 Alternative medicine

Western, scientific or orthodox medicine are all taken to mean the body of knowledge that began to accumulate in Europe during the 19th century. Modern surgery first became possible with the discovery of chloroform as an anaesthetic in 1831, for example. The role of pathogens could only be guessed at before the invention of efficient microscopes.

Orthodox medicine uses all of the sciences and a great deal of advanced technology. It tends also to focus on specific diseases and disorders rather than the whole person. The term 'hospital medicine' is a common shorthand for all this.

The failings of orthodox medicine

A UK survey conducted by Mayor and Sharpe (1997) gave some startling results. About a quarter of those consulting a GP and nearly half of those visiting outpatients departments presented with a collection of vague ill-defined symptoms. Without firm diagnosis, orthodox medicine usually fails.

Many studies since have supported these findings, and there are other issues. The extent and speed of recovery from illness or surgery varies considerably, even amongst patients whose age and physical condition are virtually identical. We also know that general health during pregnancy, childbirth and the post-natal period differs hugely from one woman to the next. Orthodox medicine cannot easily explain the extent of this variation.

Anecdotal and informal evidence further suggests a growing resistance to hospital medicine amongst some groups – not necessarily the poorest and the least educated. This phenomenon is difficult to pin down. However, it includes a dislike, distaste or lack of trust in major interventions like surgery and complex or continuous medication.

Increasingly, we are turning to unorthodox medicines and therapies. At any one time, it is thought that about one-third of the adults in the UK are using some kind of unorthodox treatment. Spending more money on scientific medicine seems to accentuate the trend. France has one of the best and most expensive state health services in the world, but about 60% of French people are regular users of unorthodox medicine.

Unorthodox medicine

Unorthodox medicine is also called alternative, complementary or holistic treatment. There are dozens of techniques, but common features are:

- They are mostly long established and the products of non-European or pre-scientific cultures. China, India and Japan feature most often. Consequently they do not rely on advanced science and technology.

- The scientific base for much unorthodox medicine is unknown, unproven or, as far as we know, non-existent.

- Unorthodox therapies are usually holistic – they treat the whole person and their environment rather than narrowly diagnosed symptoms of disease and disorder.

The dangers

To call an American a 'snake-oil salesman' is an insult. It describes any kind of fraudster, cheat or liar. The original snake-oil salesmen were unorthodox 'doctors' who travelled the US in the late 19th and early 20th centuries selling snake oil at vastly inflated prices. Snake oil was supposed to cure most diseases and disorders.

It was sold as a special extract produced from rare or exotic reptiles, but was usually some kind of vegetable oil bought for a few cents a gallon. Financial exploitation is one of the dangers of unorthodox medicine, but there are others.

Practitioners might not be trained, registered or accountable for their actions. Codes of conduct may not exist or they might not be enforced.

Unorthodox treatments can be harmful or mask the symptoms of more serious disease. Some patients reject conventional medicine, with a proven track record, in favour of alternatives that are less effective or not effective at all.

Protective legislation

Legislation protects the public against the worst excesses of disreputable or dangerous treatments. Impersonating a registered medical practitioner is a crime, as is any infringement of the rules relating to prescription-only medicines. Financial exploitation is a different issue. Manufacturers and retailers must not make false claims for their products but they are free to charge whatever their customers are prepared to pay.

Good doctors are good scientists

There is a body of evidence pointing towards the benefits of many unorthodox treatments. A good scientist cannot ignore this evidence – we may not know how they work, but that does not mean that they do not work.

Increasingly, GPs and other practitioners give complementary treatment alongside conventional medicine – acupuncture, osteopathy and homeopathy are the most popular. Younger GPs use more unorthodox medicine than older ones. Some branches of complementary medicine have introduced formalised training, professional registration and codes of practice.

Below is a brief description of some of the more important and widely used complementary therapies. This is not a complete or exhaustive list.

Acupuncture

Acupuncture is part of traditional Chinese medicine. It has been practised for more than 2,000 years. The technique assumes that there is a network of meridian lines around the body and that these transmit energy, thus ensuring good health. The meridian lines can become blocked but also relieved by inserting needles into the skin at predetermined points. The ear is thought to include a particularly important collection of meridian lines.

Scientific or western acupuncture is a variant of the traditional methods. It is taught as a formal postgraduate course, leading to examination and registration. Acupuncture is a proven substitute for chemical anaesthesia in minor surgery. Its efficiency in the treatment of some disorders is recognised by the NHS.

Aromatherapy

The Romans used aromatherapy. It probably originated in what is now Iran or Iraq. Plant oils and extracts are applied to the skin, accompanied by massage and sometimes relaxation techniques. Different oils are used to treat a range of conditions.

There is a plausible scientific basis for aromatherapy, but little formal research exists. Plant oils are complex mixtures of organic compounds, some of which are biologically active. There is also a strong but ill-understood connection between smell and memory. It is possible that pleasant aromas evoke agreeable memories, thus improving well-being. Relaxation and massage are known to decrease stress and anxiety.

Aromatherapy is not formally regulated in the UK, but there is a register of trained practitioners.

Chiropractic therapy

This is a relatively new procedure, first developed in Canada in about 1905. Joint manipulation and massage are used to treat muscular and skeletal pain and disorder. X-rays are commonly part of preliminary diagnosis.

There are undergraduate and postgraduate degree courses in chiropracty and a British association of qualified professionals. It is widely used in sports medicine.

Herbalism

Herbalism is the ancestor of pharmacy and the drug industry. Plant products are used to relieve pain and to treat symptoms. Some of the most effective modern pharmaceuticals are man-made variants of naturally occurring plant materials. The scientific base for herbalism is self-evident but, once again, not widely researched. Herbal medicines are usually dilute mixtures of several active ingredients, whereas modern drugs are mostly a single compound delivered in a more concentrated form.

Herbalism has been established in the UK since the Middle Ages, but it is not regulated. There is a National Association of Clinical Herbalists.

Homeopathy

Homeopathy was known to Hippocrates, the Greek physician of the 4th century BCE. It became widespread across Europe and North America in the 19th century. In the UK, several hundred conventionally qualified doctors are also registered homeopaths and the profession is regulated and controlled through formal education and codes of practice.

Patients are given greatly diluted solutions of natural products that in concentrated form would produce the symptoms of the disorder being treated. The mechanism for homeopathy is unknown – it may be similar in principle to immunisation, although homeopathy does not involve pathogens or the treatment of infectious disease.

Hypnotherapy

Hypnosis is an ancient art. It was first employed medically in the UK by surgeons in the 19th century. The main aims of hypnotherapy are relaxation, pain relief and to bring about changes of attitude towards disease and disorder. It is used by a small minority of doctors and dentists, more so by psychiatrists.

Hypnotherapy is not regulated in the UK.

Osteopathy

This was the first branch of complementary medicine to be controlled by law in this country. Legislation now protects patients from untrained therapists. Education, training and registration are now compulsory.

Osteopathy and chiropracty use similar techniques of massage and manipulation to treat musculoskeletal disorder.

Reflexology

Reflexology originated in the Far East more than 4,000 years ago. After herbalism, it is the oldest-known complementary medicine. Compression and massage of the hands and feet give pain relief and effects similar to local anaesthesia in other parts of the body, notably the ear, nose and throat.

There are codes of practice and several national associations.

T'ai chi

This is a Chinese therapy that was originally part of the Confucian and Buddhist religions. T'ai chi involves a series of postures and movements that promote health and well-being. Relaxation is an essential part of treatment.

Yoga

Yoga was introduced from India into the UK by the Victorians. It is probably the most familiar unorthodox therapy and combines physical exercise, breathing control and meditation. Yoga is known to be effective in treating anxiety and stress.

Why do complementary therapies work?

There are few healthcare professionals who see complementary medicine as an insult or an affront to conventional methods. The key word is 'complementary' rather than 'alternative' – the orthodox and unorthodox should work together.

Social science, rather than natural science, perhaps explains the success of complementary medicine. Holistic treatments recognise the intimate connections between mind and body, even if they do not understand the detail of cause and effect.

The patient/client-practitioner relationship also explains a great deal. We all respond well to personal attention delivered in a calm, peaceful, non-threatening environment. The immune mechanisms and the body's ability generally to heal itself are not fully understood, but we do know that these systems are weakened by stress.

What has been called the 'dentist's chair effect' may be significant. The procedures and equipment of hospital medicine produce patient reactions that range from mild anxiety through to abject terror. Complementary medicine can help prepare patients for conventional treatment and help aid recovery.

8 Models of health

The expression 'model of health' needs explanation: it describes the set of theories, attitudes and assumptions that lead to beliefs concerning how health and illness are caused.

Different societies, classes, groups and individuals have different health models. The models used by health professionals sometimes bear little resemblance to those of their clients and patients. A model need not be documented or even consciously recognised – it is often just a series of assumptions accumulated through experience and social contact.

No single model fully describes a particular person or group, but we can distinguish between some alternatives. The figure explains.

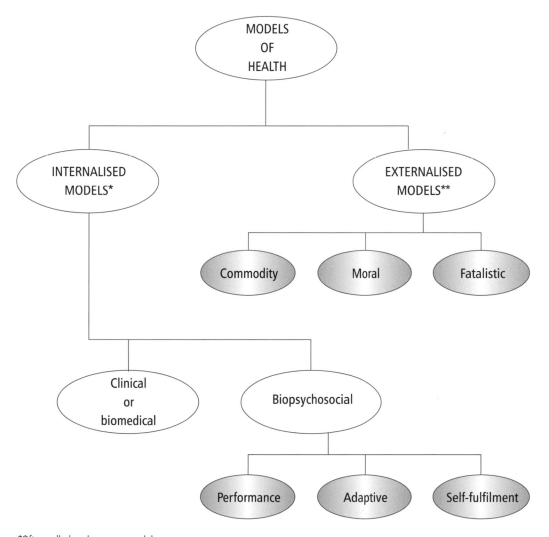

*Often called endogenous models.
**Often called exogenous models.

Externalised models of health

Under this heading we group together the beliefs that health is something external or imposed on the individual.

One externalised model of health says that it is a commodity that can be produced and traded. By implication, this means that the rich can afford better health than the poor and perhaps also that this state of affairs is normal, defensible or inevitable.

The primary motive of the NHS is to ensure that health is not a commodity to be bought and sold. The successes of the last 50 years have been very significant, but in this chapter and elsewhere we discuss the continuing connection between poverty, disease, disorder and ill health.

The moral model of health

There is a widespread but usually unspoken belief that good health is connected with being a good or moral person – that it is some kind of reward for upright or praiseworthy behaviour. Morality is associated with moderation, thrift, hard work, sexual fidelity, cleanliness and decency. If good people become ill, this may be seen as unjust, but bad people 'deserve what is coming to them'.

Some groups take the guilt and punishment concept to cruel and ludicrous extremes. One school of reincarnation believes that disability is a punishment for bad or immoral behaviour in a previous life.

There are clear connections between good lifestyle and good health, but morality is a different issue. A psychopathic serial killer could have a perfect diet and be an accomplished non-drinking, non-smoking athlete.

Fate and luck

Fatalism is the most common externalised model of health. It assumes that health is just a matter of luck or fate, over which we have no individual control. Superstition is nourished and encouraged by fatalistic health models – some objects and some behaviour patterns are thought to be lucky or unlucky.

In 21st-century Britain, black magic and witchcraft are not common, but fatalism still is. Illogical or self-destructive lifestyles can be excused if our destiny is preordained or just the result of some cosmic lottery. The language of conception and contraception is a good example: 'I fell pregnant' implies an accident or chance event.

Internalised health models

Internalised or endogenous models of health all include beliefs that, to some extent, we can determine or influence our own health. These models further subdivide into two groups.

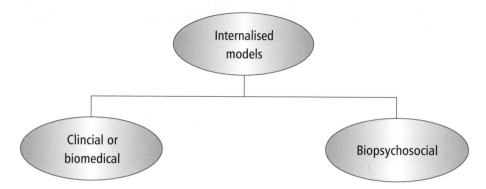

Clinical or biomedical models see people as organisms that can be understood just by reference to measurement and the natural sciences. Biopsychosocial models describe beliefs that emerge from a mixture of the natural and social sciences. They recognise that society and social contact play a role in our understanding of what causes disease and illness.

The biomedical model of health

The biomedical or clinical model once dominated the health profession and health education.

Health is said to be the absence of disease and disorder. By implication it is not therefore a positive concept. The body is thought of as a mechanism that can be repaired when it goes wrong; every disease and disorder has physical symptoms that lead to a firm diagnosis. As medical science advances, the clinical model seems to become more appropriate. A heart, liver or kidney transplant is just the replacement of an important working part, for instance.

The pure clinical model defines health as a series of numbers that lie within an acceptable or normal range – things like height, weight, blood pressure and the results that come back from the pathology laboratory.

Health, according to the clinical model, is a personal responsibility. It may follow that those in poor health are irresponsible or in some way inferior.

The performance model

Many people define health as the ability to function according to their own or to society's expectations. Health is related to duty and to performance in a particular role. This model was the rule in working-class communities before the NHS – it is still widespread. A woman needed to be healthy enough to care for the home and her children; a man would not define himself as unwell provided he could earn enough to support his family.

The performance model can easily lead to denial of symptoms and an acceptance of steadily deteriorating health. It may also produce healthcare rationing based on a narrow judgement of an individual's economic worth. Healthcare professionals sometimes use the performance model to decide priorities for scarce resources. A surgeon is perhaps more likely to recommend a liver transplant for a 40-year-old dentist with three dependent children than the same procedure for a 75-year-old living on a state pension.

The welfare state and the NHS have in some respects turned the performance model on its head. Rather than feeling they have a duty towards society, many now believe that society has a duty towards them. This kind of thinking makes the following connections: 'I pay for the NHS through taxation, therefore I have a right to expect "enough health" to be able to continue working and to carry on paying taxes.' This is another way of saying that good health benefits society as a whole – not just individuals personally.

The adaptive model

The adaptive model sees health as a continuing process, not as a fixed state or condition. From birth to death we continually have to adapt to changing circumstances. All of the important milestones in life present new challenges and opportunities. Good health is the ability to make the best of the positives and to cope easily with the negatives.

The idea of a strong or delicate constitution flows directly from the adaptive model. At its simplest, it equates good health with physical strength and a cheerful, optimistic disposition. This model instinctively recognises that both mind and body are involved in health. A scientist would reach similar conclusions, but the explanation might be given in terms of a well-developed immune system and a stable, secure personality.

Often, physical weakness is seen as the cause of illness, not its consequence.

The self-fulfilment model of health

The self-fulfilment model is broad and multidimensional. It is therefore difficult to describe. It is also the most optimistic and productive of the alternatives that we have considered. An individual is self-fulfilled if he or she has the energy, enthusiasm and fitness to do all that they want to do. Peace of mind is an essential element, as is rewarding social interaction. The model makes little distinction between physical and emotional or psychological health.

Self-fulfilment includes the ability to control immoderate or excessive consumption, being liked by others, having an affectionate nature, feeling physically and sexually attractive, having a sense of purpose and self-worth, along with being creative, alert, inquisitive and self-confident. Most of all it includes being healthy enough to achieve the goals, targets and ambitions we all set for ourselves.

Models of health and health education

By historical accident, the NHS was founded and designed to deliver curative medicine in the decade when the balance between cure and prevention first tipped in favour of prevention as the better alternative.

Health education and promotion is the ground floor of preventative medicine but it will not work if it does not recognise that many common models of health are based on false assumptions.

The current 10-year plan for the NHS is written around the biopsychosocial model of health. The clinical model has been overtaken and is now seen as false or misplaced.

9 Health promotion and education

The first international conference on health promotion and education met in Ottawa, Canada in November 1986. The definition of health promotion that emerged is written in elaborate English, but it would be difficult to improve on:

> Health promotion is the process of enabling people to increase control over, and to improve, their health. To reach a state of complete physical, mental and social well-being, an individual or group must be able to identify and realise aspirations, to satisfy needs and to change or cope with the environment. Health is, therefore, seen as a resource for everyday life, not the objective of living. Health is a positive concept emphasising social and personal resources as well as physical capacities. Therefore health promotion is not just the responsibility of the health sector, but goes beyond healthy lifestyles to well-being.

The historical context

All societies include health education and promotion as an important and often a central part of their culture. Health information is passed from one generation to the next through custom, ritual, religion and law.

For thousands of years, communities have made the links between health, personal hygiene, wholesome food, clean water and preventing the transmission of infectious diseases.

The UK public health movement began in the 1840s when it was politically accepted that high population density, poverty, bad housing and poor infrastructure combined to cause misery, disease and reduced life expectancy.

Promotion versus education

Amongst health professionals, the biomedical model of health grew increasingly dominant with the advances in medical science made across the four or five generations between about 1850 and 1970. Health education in the narrow sense was based on several assumptions:

- Medical science had pinpointed the causes of most diseases and disorders.

- Hospital-based medicine could cure most things. Medical educators could also formulate sound medical advice that would prevent or delay the development of many health-threatening conditions.

- If this advice was presented to the general public, then in their own best interests, people would alter their lifestyles and behaviour to increase their health and well-being.

- Politicians were another target audience for the health educators. Again, it was assumed that they would allocate priorities and spend public money based on proven medical principles.

By the 1970s, it was clear that pure or narrowly defined health education was not working, or at least not working very well. A simple presentation of the facts did not change behaviour, or it did so painfully slowly.

The emergence of health promotion

The shortcomings of health education were evident throughout Europe, North America and the developed world. The emergence of health promotion as a bigger and broader idea than simple health education is usually attributed to Marc Lalonde, the Chief Canadian Medical Officer of Health in 1974. In that year, he published research (1974) which formalised the equal importance of individuals and societies in determining health and well-being. Lalonde was amongst the first to recognise that health education might be failing because most of us do not behave logically, even when we are given proven inescapable medical truth or fact. Social scientists express this same idea in different language – they say that the simple biomedical model of health is not widely or universally accepted.

In 1978, the World Health Organization shifted its emphasis from education to promotion following a conference at Alma Ata in the USSR. However, as we have indicated, the major turning point came with the 1986 Ottawa conference and the publication of what is now called the Ottawa Charter for Health Promotion. The principles of the charter are important enough to list in detail.

The Ottawa Charter 1986

- The fundamental conditions and resources for health are peace, shelter, education, food, income, a stable ecosystem, sustainable resources and social justice. Health improvement requires a secure foundation in each of these.

- Health is a major resource for social, economic and personal development, and a major determinant in quality of life.

- Political, economic, social, cultural, environmental, behavioural and biological factors can all favour or damage health. Health promotion has to include or consider all of these elements.

  Health promotion focuses on achieving equality in health. Action should aim to reduce difference in current health status, ensure equal opportunities and allow equal access to health resources. Health resources are defined as a supportive environment, information, life skills and the ability to make informed choices.

- Health promotion policies should apply equally to men and women.

- Health cannot be secured or improved by the health sector acting alone. Health promotion requires coordination and cooperation amongst governments, voluntary organisations, industry and the media. Health professionals should act as agents and intermediaries to bring together these different groups in the interests of health.

Ottawa as an ideal

Nearly all of the world's developed countries and many developing nations signed the Ottawa Charter. A signature is one thing, appropriate policy change and action is another. The original aim of the Ottawa Charter was to achieve health for all by the year 2000. Clearly this has not happened. The Ottawa ideal is only readily achievable in relatively rich countries which can agree on a level of taxation sufficient to fund an extensive health sector. The main message of Ottawa is health promotion through political change – many nations are unwilling or unable to enforce the policies required to ensure 'health for all', at least in the short term.

The changes in the UK NHS which began in 1997 closely follow the Ottawa Charter.

The Yale communication model

The failures of health education can be seen as failures of communication.

Yale University is generally acknowledged as one of the most prestigious centres of learning in the US and in the world. The Yale model of communication was developed there in the 1970s. It is especially relevant to promotion, education and communication in health.

The model says that communication has five stages.

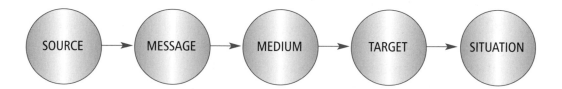

The source

For communication to be effective, its source must be credible or believable. It must also have expertise and be trustworthy. It cannot be assumed that all advice delivered by health professionals is passively accepted as the truth, the whole truth and nothing but the truth.

There are, for instance, class and gender issues. As an example, doctors tend to be middle-class men, and working-class women suffer more than most groups from the newer urban diseases and disorders.

Credibility and expertise are different ideas. Different groups in society see credibility in very different ways. For example, a bald middle-aged GP wearing a cardigan has expertise but may lack credibility amongst teenagers experimenting with drugs.

Expert professionals often give conflicting advice, or a single source can alter its recommendation from one year to the next.

Trust is the most important issue of all. The government is the ultimate source of official health education and promotion. If you do not trust a particular politician, or any politician at all, why should you change your lifestyle on their say so?

After tobacco, an unbalanced diet is probably the single greatest cause of ill health in the UK today. However, we do not buy food and drink at GPs' surgeries – we have to rely on profit-orientated manufacturers and retailers. Amongst the most heavily advertised of all products on UK television are alcohol, high-sugar soft drinks, snack foods and fast food restaurants. There is conflict between food advertising and health promotion in a free society.

The message

The more important and the more urgent the message, the simpler it has to be. Road signs and hazard warnings are good examples – some dispense with words altogether. Red and yellow mean danger, and a skull and crossbones mean death in most languages. Health messages are rarely simple matters of life or death – most reduce to something like, 'If you carry on doing this, something bad will probably happen to you'.

A message may be two-sided (presenting the case for and against) or one-sided (delivering simple or overwhelming support for a single viewpoint or piece of advice). In all circumstances, the message must be clear and appropriate. If possible, it should also be vivid and memorable.

Two-sided presentations become more and more effective as the level of expertise in the target audience increases. A research paper giving the results of an investigation into the links between exercise and heart disease would be two-sided if presented to a conference of heart surgeons but one-sided if it had to be converted into a 30-second TV advert.

Clarity, brevity and appropriate language are always important. This also means that most health messages have to omit detail and focus on generalisations – simplification and 'dumbing down' are almost unavoidable.

Shock and horror

Horrific and shocking messages can be counter-productive, particularly those that include disturbing visual images. Those most likely to benefit from the message are usually the groups who try hardest to ignore it.

Horror has a limited shelf life and its impact can reduce with repeated exposure. Campaigns to reduce drink driving in the UK have only succeeded because they have been maintained over many decades.

There are also issues of taste, decency and language, although standards and expectations are fluid. Condoms were never mentioned on daytime TV and radio before the safe-sex campaigns designed to limit the spread of HIV/AIDS. You cannot reduce the rate of teenage pregnancies by targeting only those young people above the age of consent, but frank words and honest pictures are certain to offend the parents of some 14-year-olds.

The medium

There are two ways of delivering a message – either through direct human contact and social interaction or through a remote or mass medium like TV, cinema, radio, newspapers or magazines.

A message transmitted by human contact can be one to one, confidential and tailor made for the individual concerned. TV and radio cannot deliver personal messages, but the most effective health promotion campaigns use techniques that mimic conversation and informal social contact.

For most of us, our first health promoters are our parents – our mothers more often than our fathers. In developing countries, health promotion is often targeted at women with families and/or the senior women of the community.

The target audience

The medium and the target audience cannot be considered in isolation from one another. Most health promotion is, or ought to be, targeted at particular groups or subsets of the general population. Mass media advertising is expensive and the industry has developed techniques to identify and reach many different audiences. The main variables are:

- Class – the *Sun*, *The Times* and *The Financial Times* have different readerships; Radio 4 and Radio 1 have different listeners. Sunday newspapers, some magazines and most books are better media for more complex health messages than tabloid daily papers.

- Region – all advertisers, which includes all health promoters, can buy air time or advertising space region by region. Class inequalities in health translate into regional variations. A health message aimed at Glasgow or Sunderland might not be effective in Surrey.

- Gender – men and women have different health needs because their patterns of health and illness vary. Many TV programmes have a pronounced gender bias, as do most magazines.

- Age – very few health promotion messages apply equally to all age groups. Dietary advice does not vary much according to age, but there is obviously little point in directly targeting healthy-eating campaigns at people like young children or the many men that do not buy food. Educating children to eat properly is usually a two-stage process – parents first and children second with perhaps a different message.

- Targeting requires market research because common sense can be misleading. Most of the motorists convicted for drink driving are middle-aged men, not the younger or older age groups. Similarly, health-threatening sexual behaviour is not confined to the under twenty-fives and the gender gap in sexual attitudes has narrowed very significantly in the last 20 years.

Time slot, attention span and permanence

These factors influence the message and the medium. The watershed protects children from exposure to adult material on TV – or is supposed to. Our definition of adult material has altered, but clearly a message broadcast on Sunday afternoon has to have a different approach to that taken after 11 o'clock on a Saturday evening.

Attention span is critical. Some advisory booklets are meant as reference documents to be kept and consulted over months or years. A roadside poster is visible to a driver for just a few seconds. TV and radio deliver fleeting messages that are easily missed, whereas print media give a life of days or weeks, and potentially a permanent record.

Sympathy and knowledge

Commercial mass media advertising has much to teach health promoters and educators, but the parallels are not exact or precise. Most TV and newspaper adverts are aimed at people who are likely or able to buy the product or service concerned. The audience is sympathetic to the message. Health promotion has bigger problems – it is by definition preaching to the unconverted. Those most likely to benefit from the message are also those most resistant to its content.

Knowledge is another issue. It can be argued that health education is the first stage of health promotion. The facts have to be presented but, in a free society, individuals can only be encouraged or persuaded to take appropriate action – force or coercion is not an option.

Situation and context

The fifth element or stage in the Yale communication model is situation or context. Where will you be and who will you be with when you receive a health promotion message?

Sex education and the promotion of safe sex behaviour clearly illustrate the importance of context. A booklet that explains the facts of life to primary school children would obviously be nothing like a 30-second safe sex cinema advertisement shown on a Friday evening.

Opinion formers

Health promotion is about changing attitudes and opinions. In most situations, this is a two-stage process at least, rather than a straightforward sequence of source, message, medium, target and context.

Commercial advertisers have always recognised the central importance of role models and endorsement. Manufacturers and retailers of football boots, soft drinks and beauty products pay large fees for celebrity endorsement because these well-known people are opinion formers. An opinion former has a unique combination of expertise, credibility and trust. Health promotion is no different – there are opinion formers and a much larger group of opinion receivers.

If good health is more about prevention than cure in modern society, and if health promotion is the foundation of preventative medicine, then health professionals must have opinion forming and role model status.

Matching the models

Previously we considered the various models of health that are commonly held by different individuals and groups.

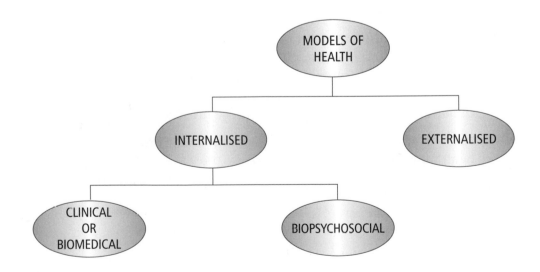

Health education in the narrow sense of simply presenting information only works or works well amongst groups who believe that the clinical or biomedical model applies to them in their present situation. Even in the best-educated societies and communities only a minority hold these views and beliefs. Biopsychosocial models see health or illness as being caused by a variety of factors, only some of which are under the individual's control. Because most of us do not subscribe to the simple biomedical model of health, education has to be combined with health promotion.

Health promotion, attitudes and behaviour

Health promotion aims to change attitudes and then to change behaviour. Not all changes in attitude produce alterations in behaviour. Attitudes take many years to form and behaviour patterns can become deeply entrenched. Health promotion campaigns usually extend for years or decades – they are never a quick fix, and reversals are common.

Change in behaviour depends on:

- What people think the consequences of change will be.

- How important they think the results of a behavioural shift will be.

- The opinions of partners, children, extended family and close friends.

- How much notice the individual concerned takes of these opinions.

- How strongly the individual is motivated, in particular their wish to conform to what might be described as normal sensible behaviour.

Nurses as health promoters

Among many other things, the Ottawa Charter foresaw the need for changes in education, attitude and organisation in the health sector. Nurses have an indispensable and growing role in health promotion.

In hospital situations, the number of contact hours and the number of social interactions that patients have with nurses vastly exceed the contact they have with doctors. In primary healthcare there is a similar pattern.

A specific objective of the new NHS plan is to remove demarcation lines and increase flexibility amongst doctors, nurses and other health professionals. Nurse prescription of some medicines illustrates this trend.

The diffusion of healthcare away from large general hospitals and into the community will inevitably give nurses a bigger and wider role.

The UK of the 21st century no longer accepts relationships based purely on power, hierarchy, paternalism and authority. The role of the nurse will alter more than that of most other health professionals.

Chapter 3
Social structures and personal identity

National unit specification
These are the topics you will be studying for this unit.

1   Identity and socialisation

2   Culture

3   Identity and family

4   Identity and class

5   Social difference in education

6   Identity and gender

1 Identity and socialisation

Personal identity is the way we see ourselves. In a practical sense, it could be defined as all the labels and descriptions we use to distinguish ourselves from others. We ascribe identities using a hierarchy of levels and layers. Some are unique to the individual concerned; some indicate our membership or sense of belonging to smaller groups like family; others denote affiliation to much larger communities:

> My name is Fiona Jane McAllister. I am a Scot, living in London, and a mother of two children.

Personality and personal identity are different ideas. Personality involves characteristics like extroversion, shyness, aggression and timidity.

Most job application forms begin with the same five questions. You are asked to give:

- Surname or family name.

- Forenames or given names.

- Address.

- Date of birth (day, month, year).

- Place of birth.

You share some of these descriptions with others, but taken together they are enough to distinguish your personal identity from that of the other six billion people in the world, and all those that have gone before.

In the beginning, we have no control over our identity – gender is determined by chance, babies do not choose when and where to be born, and our parents decide our names.

Self-worth

Identity develops with age and accumulated experience. This is called socialisation.

Theories of socialisation were first used to explain how infants and young people acquire identity, but it is a general idea not limited to childhood. Immigrants to a new country go through an adaptation or socialisation process; so do adults faced with life changes or altered social environments.

As part of our personal identity, we reach conclusions about our self-worth. An understanding of identity and socialisation is important for caring professionals:

- Every client or patient has the right to respect for their identity and beliefs.

- Fragile or confused identity is the root cause of many – some would argue most – behavioural and psychological problems. Reversing the argument, those with high self-esteem tend to recover more rapidly from disease and physical injury.

- Good-quality health and social care is impossible if the client is seen just as a collection of tissue, organs and symptoms. Care and therapy has to involve the whole person, including their identity and self-worth.

There are three commonly accepted theories of socialisation. They differ most in the importance given to socialisation in early childhood.

Sigmund Freud

Sigmund Freud (1856–1939) spent nearly all of his working life in Vienna. He developed psychoanalysis, one of the most important techniques in practical psychology. Freud believed that everyday actions and behaviour are caused by motives that are far more complex than common sense suggests. He also thought these motives were often unconscious or unrecognised.

Freud's theory of socialisation concentrates on emotions rather than logical thought processes. He believed the first two years of life were critical and laid the foundations of adult personality. The relationship between mother and infant could result in a secure balanced individual or it could establish anxieties that become permanent features of later life.

Freud's theories explain much about phobias, anxieties and neuroses that persist into adulthood, but they are criticised because they take little account of secondary socialisation – the processes that continue through life as people adjust to new circumstances. Freud's approach can be seen as essentially pessimistic.

George Mead

George Mead (1863–1931), an American sociologist, suggested a second theory of socialisation. Mead believed that identity develops through play in childhood. By reversing roles with others, children begin to realise the influence that their behaviour has on those around them. Freud saw socialisation as almost entirely resulting from mother–infant interactions. Mead took a wider view.

The recognition of self comes first. This is followed by behaviour learned through interaction with a small group of 'significant others' – typically parents, brothers, sisters and close friends. At a third stage, a child develops a more general view of 'others' and what constitutes acceptable behaviour.

Researchers have extended Mead's work, proposing that play or acting continues throughout life. Adults present different self-images in different social situations. Importantly, this flexibility is seen as normal behaviour and a sign, amongst other things, of consideration for others.

Mead's theory is called symbolic interactionism.

The functionalist theory

The third theory of socialisation has emerged from observation and experiment rather than from the work of any one sociologist. It is the role learning or the functionalist theory.

Children learn how to behave by social interaction, first with their parents and then with larger and more varied groups as they develop a wider circle of social contacts. The functionalist theory emphasises social control, reward and punishment.

Primary socialisation is usually complete by the age of four or five and this lays down guidelines for secondary socialisation at school, work and in other groups.

Identity – an overview

In the rest of this unit we consider in detail the impacts on personal identity of family, class, education and gender, but we begin with a general overview.

At birth, our identity is determined by chance and by others. As we grow and develop we can choose to be identified with particular groups. This is an active process not a passive one. Although our identification choices usually become more numerous, they are never limitless. Some parts of our identity are always shaped by others or by forces beyond our control. Agency is the term used to describe the degree of control we can exert over who we are.

Identity is a two-way process – it is how others see us just as much as how we see ourselves.

Identity confusion creates stress and conflicts that can damage health. To give three examples:

- Continual striving to achieve an identity that is beyond reach for whatever reason, justified or unjustified, is an established cause of stress-related illness. Prejudice and bigotry in all of its forms are good examples. It was only in the 20th century that all of the professions in the UK became open to women. Similarly, a teenager from a high-achieving academic family is under enormous pressure to do well at school, so that he or she can also be identified as an academic.

- The rejection in later life of an identity firmly ascribed during childhood is often problematic. The British-born children or grandchildren of immigrants may wish to reject their family identity and adopt another. Similar patterns of rejected identity are common among the children of working-class parents who have become upwardly mobile and adopted middle-class lifestyles.

- A multiplicity of identities is part of a natural and healthy human condition. Most of us at some stage accommodate the triple identities of child, partner and parent, but sometimes identity conflicts become unmanageable. Many Access students have to come to terms with being a parent, an employee, a partner and a student – it is often impossible to meet all of your own and others' expectations all of the time.

The determinants of identity

The diagram summarises the main impacts and influences that determine identity.

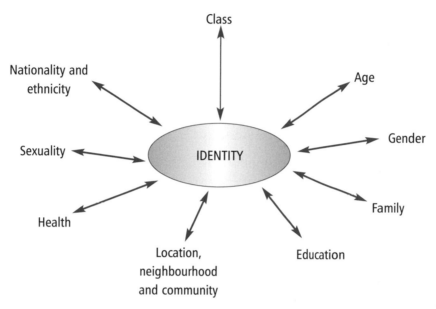

This diagram is a simplification – it would be impossible to chart all of the interactions that shape identity. Class, education and health are closely interlinked, for example, and it would be easy to subdivide and divide again all of the influences we have shown as single elements.

2 Culture

An interesting and productive definition of culture is based on a model taken from biology. Culture is all those aspects, activities and characteristics that can be transmitted from one generation to the next by social contact and interaction. Just as every group has a gene pool, all societies have a culture pool or a specific and characteristic culture.

Many words come with an associated bundle of value judgements. These associations are a particular problem in the social sciences. As commonly used, the word culture has overtones of social refinement, something to be admired, the preserve of the wealthy, the well educated, and so on.

Sociology should begin with the assumption that culture is value free. Opera, ballet, the plays of Shakespeare, Beethoven's symphonies and *The Times* crossword are culture, but so are the inside pages of the *Sun*, the FA Cup final, *Eastenders*, line dancing and punk music.

Disapproval, disdain, repression and censorship almost inevitably flow from cultural difference. A truly objective sociologist would argue that there is no right culture and no wrong culture – just different cultures.

Cultures change and evolve in the same way as species. Some researchers have extended the biological analogy and use terms like 'cultural cross-fertilisation' and 'cultural mutation'.

Theories of culture

Sociologists try to understand how cultures work. Theories of culture and theories of socialisation are different sides of the same coin. Karl Marx was among the first to study the culture of the newly industrialised societies – his theory has class conflict as its central theme.

Marx saw that all societies were unequal and that wealth, power and status were concentrated in a few hands. Industrialisation produced even greater inequalities and society diverged into a small capitalist class and a very much larger working class. To protect their interests, Marx thought that the economically powerful socialised the working class into passive acceptance of inequality and their lower social status.

The capitalist class had control of religion, education and the media. These were used as cultural instruments. In the last resort, force was used to control and repress resistance – the capitalist class also 'owned' the police and the military.

As a development of Marxism, later researchers suggested that 'divide and rule' was a more subtle cultural force. The capitalist class makes concessions to the majority of the working class but marginalises minority groups such as foreigners and those who do not follow the state religion. In this way, the status of the so-called respectable working class is relatively increased.

Alternative cultural theories do not see class conflict as inevitable. Consensus sociologists have suggested a more flexible model where economic factors, religion, education, family and political institutions each contribute to culture. Culture is reinforced and stabilised by socialisation and people learn to conform to a set of cultural standards. The consensus theorists define culture as a combination of roles, status, shared values and acceptable behaviour patterns.

A third school of cultural theories says that culture is a product of constant social interactions. This is another consensus model, but it emphasises the fluidity of culture and its ability to alter rapidly and dramatically.

Mass culture

Later we consider the interrelationships between class, culture and identity in some detail. Here it is appropriate briefly to consider the importance of mass or popular culture in the shaping of personal identity.

Major cultural shifts are occurring throughout the developed world, but we need to be most concerned with the growth of mass culture in the UK.

Before about 1750 and the beginnings of the industrial revolution, culture – as narrowly defined – was entirely produced and consumed by small elites. One view held that the working classes had no culture or no culture worth respect or investigation. The reasons for this cultural divide were obvious – participation in cultured society demanded a minimum level of income, leisure time and literacy that was beyond the means of almost all of the population.

Those from ordinary backgrounds who showed exceptional talent were often marked out for special attention, patronised and absorbed into the high-culture elites.

If anything, the early and middle stages of the industrial revolution accentuated the cultural separation amongst the classes. The beginnings of mass culture in the UK probably date to the early part of the 20th century and a series of legal reforms which improved factory working conditions, expanded the electorate and introduced elementary or basic education for all.

The Britain of the first half of the 20th century would be alien and unrecognisable to most people today. Without doubt, there was a popular culture based on universal literacy, greater prosperity and increased leisure time, but this was still widely regarded as inferior to high culture.

The cultural changes that have transformed the UK since the 1950s are sometimes encapsulated in expressions like 'the death of class' or the 'rejection of deference'. The degree of unquestioning respect that was once given to political leaders, the church, the royal family and professionals like lawyers, doctors and teachers now strike most of us as faintly absurd.

The mass market

Consumption patterns, product preferences and leisure activities are now very significant determinants of personal identity. People no longer define their identity simply in terms of family, class and occupation. Most of all, identity has diverged according to age and stage of life. Very few mass-market products and services are advertised to or targeted at a broad age range of potential consumers.

The central importance of mass culture is self-evident, but sociologists see dangers as well as advantages in the growing association between consumption and identity. Many labels are used to categorise opposing views, but these boil down to a debate between optimists and pessimists.

The optimists

The optimists believe that:

- Mass culture has not destroyed a superior, more traditional way of life, because the golden age theories are an illusion. Working-class existence was never close-knit, warm, cohesive and self-supporting. The reality was harsh, brutal and characterised by poverty, illness, exhaustion and despair.

- Mass culture offers a vast array of goods and services plus information that enables consumers to choose wisely amongst these options. Freedom of information limits exploitation.

- Consumers are free to decide their own cultural mix and are no longer forced to conform to narrow cultural stereotypes. Diversity is encouraged and the artificial walls between high culture and popular culture have been demolished.

The pessimists

The pessimists think that:

- Working-class culture was authentic, vibrant and provided emotional security for its members.

- The majority have exchanged their dignity and political independence for an indulgent, spoon-fed and placid lifestyle. The mass market inevitably leads to 'dumbing down' and a loss of interest in participative democracy or politics in general.

- The choice of goods and services is dictated by large companies, not by the buying decisions of individual consumers. Product differentiation is a sham and this leads to overcharging and exploitation.

- Mass culture is no more than standardisation in disguise or by deception. This has global as well as local, regional and national consequences. The greatest fear of the pessimists is that valuable local cultures will be overwhelmed and destroyed because this suits a few very large and powerful multinational interests.

3 Identity and family

It would be ridiculous to deny the fundamental importance of the family in shaping identity, and no respected sociologist ever has. Instead, social scientists have turned their attention to other aspects of family life:

- The role of the family in raising and socialising children.

- The family as the basic building block of larger groups and societies.

- The possible consequences of dysfunctional families and the definition of dysfunction.

- Family structure and how this differs between cultures and how it changes over time.

- The relationships, especially those of power, between men and women.

The typical family?

Television is a powerful cultural influence, but many of the images of family structure that it delivers are unrepresentative or atypical. TV advertising suggests that all or most UK families have four members – a '30-something' married couple with a son and a daughter. The advertising agency picture of the average or nuclear family is no longer true – it probably never has been.

Most people in the UK used to spend the majority of their life within a few miles of their birthplace. Cohabitation was virtually impossible because of cultural pressures. Conception outside marriage nearly always resulted in social disgrace or irresistible pressure for the parties to marry. Your husband or wife would very likely have been born within walking distance of your parent's house and you would start married life surrounded by both extended families. Poverty, the lack of welfare provision and the need to care for the sick and the elderly meant that many households contained several generations of the same family. Families had many children although infant mortality was high. Serial marriage following the death of a woman in childbirth was common, single-person households were exceptional.

This rural household and family structure relocated to towns and cities during the first half of the industrial revolution.

Modern families

Like most of the sociological changes that have reshaped the UK, the variety we now see in family structures can be traced back to the 1950s, increasing prosperity and relaxing cultural constraints.

The total number of households in the UK is increasing a lot more rapidly than the population overall.

Completed family size is smaller than ever before. Families of four or more children were the rule in the 19th century.

On average, women are delaying marriage and the birth of their first child. Young adults are more often living as singles and then cohabiting before marriage and/or producing children.

Divorce and separation produce two households where once there was one. Not all divorced people remarry or enter into new long-term relationships; those that do often spend years living alone.

Life expectancy is increasing and there are growing numbers of the elderly, usually widows, living singly. Welfare provision and social support extends the time during which independent living is feasible.

There are growing numbers of same-sex households. Many communities are now tolerant or supportive of openly homosexual relationships. Relatively few gay or lesbian households include dependent children or young adults.

Matrifocal households with mother, grandmother and dependent children living as the family unit are a common feature of Afro-American and Afro-Caribbean communities in the US and the UK.

The kibbutz movement

The nuclear family as we presently understand it in the UK is not a universal feature of all societies. The matrifocal structure is a positive and sensible defence against poverty and isolation. Some societies have experimented with structures that eliminate the nuclear family altogether.

The kibbutz movement was founded in 1909 by a group of Russian emigrants to what is now Israel. A kibbutzim is a collective that shares property, work, defence and the care of its children. The children are raised by the community as a whole, not as a part of a nuclear family. About 100,000 Israelis live in kibbutzim and the movement has largely stood the test of time.

Far less successful experiments in communal child-rearing were tried and abandoned in the USSR in the 1930s.

Some traditional societies in central America, West Africa, New Guinea and the Pacific islands are structured to exclude the nuclear family.

The sex rules

All cultures have rules that limit sexual freedom. These have major implications for family and household structure. The sex rules operate at three levels – through religion, via the legal framework and by informal but often very powerful cultural pressures. The traditional Christian approach is simple – sex outside marriage is forbidden and remarriage is only possible following the death of one partner. Blood relatives closer than first cousins are not allowed to marry; there is a minimum age of sexual consent. 'Thou shalt not commit adultery' is the seventh commandment and only murder is a worse crime than rape.

The traditional Christian rules, or relaxed variations of them, are by no means common to all societies, even to those in the developed West.

Most of the legally permitted departures from the 'one sexual partner for life' model result from the unequal distribution of power and wealth, in particular from male power and wealth.

Islam and some other religions allow polygyny – one husband taking several wives. However, in these societies, only the richest men are able to support the large households involved. The traditional Mormon religion allows multiple marriage, usually one man marrying sisters or groups of female relatives.

The marriage of close relatives is an effective way of preserving royal, aristocratic or tribal power. The Egyptian pharaohs sometimes married their brothers or sisters.

The sanctions used to prevent or discourage pre-marital and extra-marital sex vary enormously across cultures and within cultures.

In the UK, under-age sex is still regarded as a serious crime; adultery is not a criminal act. Most cultures have an institutionalised or informal difference in their approach to adultery – women are often punished more heavily than men. For example, a British politician who was discovered to be supporting a wife, a mistress and two families would perhaps be forced into resignation; in France, Italy and much of South America, this set-up is seen by some as normal and acceptable.

In the UK before the 1950s, cohabitation was exceptional. It is now the norm and is seen as a natural stage in the progression from living with parents to formal marriage as recognised by the state and/or the church.

It should not be forgotten that any social structure that prevents or limits contact between children in their formative years and both of their parents is a departure from the allegedly ideal nuclear family. For example:

- One or both parents may have jobs involving long working hours or extended travel.

- Illness, imprisonment or homelessness disrupts the nuclear family.

- Some parents, most often men, have social lives which greatly reduce contact with their children.

- We often delegate some parental responsibilities to outsiders, like childminders, nannies and the staff of boarding schools.

A good thing?

There was once a widespread unspoken belief that, except in the most extreme circumstances, the family was 'a good thing'. Behind this view there are untested assumptions: at best, the conviction that caring for children is innate and that no sane adult would harm a child; at worst, children were seen as the property of their biological parents, to do with as they wished.

The legal framework in the UK recognises the dysfunctional family at several levels. Child neglect and cruelty are punishable by imprisonment. The state has the right to remove children from parents – temporarily or permanently. Corporal punishment at school is forbidden and severely limited in the home. Local authority social service departments are responsible for identifying and monitoring children at risk.

Socialisation theories differ, but they all recognise the crucial importance of primary socialisation (i.e. the first five years or so of social contact and interaction that takes place in the family). Behaviour patterns are learned. Very young children cannot distinguish good from bad or, put more correctly, they cannot know whether the norms of their family are different from those of wider society.

Secondary socialisation begins at school and continues throughout life. The differences between dysfunctional family norms and the ideals of a stable, functional society can be compared.

Dysfunctional family norms	Functional society norms
Materially destructive, lack of respect for personal property	Respect for property; theft and vandalism are illegal
Verbally aggressive – shouting, 'bad language', limited vocabulary	Verbal skills highly valued, orderly conversation rewarded Some words unacceptable
Irregular sleep patterns Chaotic or non-existent daily routine	Punctuality and good attendance required at school and work
Poor diet, no or few formal meals	Good diet essential Meals are social events
Physical aggression and bullying	All physical aggression illegal and unacceptable
No books, little regard for literacy. TV dominant or only cultural instrument	High literacy vital for success Cultural discrimination and taste highly praised
Unemployed or casual work No work ethic	Welfare only justified for 'deserving' families. Work equals status
Little history of, or regard for education	Education equated with success. Well-educated much more highly regarded than ill-educated
Alcohol abuse Drug and solvent abuse	Social drinking acceptable Intolerance of drug-dependency and 'drug culture'
Financially disorganised Persistent debt; no concept of saving or investment	Thrift and financial planning admired regardless of income

Two political views

In most societies – the UK included – reactions to change in family structure split very broadly along political lines.

Many on the traditional right, typified by parts of the Conservative party in the UK and the Republicans in the US, see the changes of the last 20 or 30 years as almost entirely negative. They put the rising divorce rate and the increasing number of children born outside marriage at the centre of the 'problem'. Their greatest fear is crime fuelled by drug dependency. Right-wing solutions include harsher prison sentences, more policing and a less generous welfare system.

The left wing, socialist or liberal view, sees the social exclusion of relatively small groups as the root cause of the 'problem'. It believes that the American experience is proof that a stricter, less tolerant culture does not work.

The left argues that the diversity of modern family life is a liberating influence and insists that it produces the greatest good for the greatest number. It does not regard mass culture as second rate or as inferior to high culture.

Patriarchy

A patriarchal society is one dominated by men, in which women accept, or are forced into, subservient roles. The feminist movement is a broad general term used to describe attempts to increase or extend the rights of women.

Patriarchy, and attempts to justify it, have an anthropological base. Men are bigger, stronger and (as a generalisation) more violent than women. In societies dominated by force, and ultimately by military power, men have a biological advantage over women. For most of human history this advantage was seen as natural and to the benefit of both sexes. A whole range of biological or anthropological gender differences were assumed – most significantly that men were better at organisation and government and that men were cleverer than women.

The birth of modern feminism is agreed by most sociologists to have followed from the publication of four books:

- *Le Deuxième Sexe*, Simone de Beauvoir, English translation 1953.
- *The Feminine Mystique*, Betty Friedan, 1963.
- *Sexual Politics*, Kate Millett, 1969.
- *The Female Eunuch*, Germaine Greer, 1970.

In essence, these works turned feminism from a personal movement into a political one. There are many historical precedents – notably the UK suffragette movement that in 1928 secured votes for women over the age of 21.

Some sociologists believe that feminism has been the major cause of structural family change in the UK since the 1950s:

- Reliable female contraception and abortion law reform means that women are no longer forced into having large families.

- The law prescribes equal treatment for women in employment and in access to financial services like loans and mortgages.

- As a society, we no longer believe that every marriage should be preserved at all costs.

- Physical aggression within marriage is now recognised as a serious crime. Many more women than previously are totally intolerant of any kind of male violence.

- It is now possible, both culturally and economically, for women to raise families alone or without the help of a permanent partner.

4 Identity and class

Animals that live in cooperative groups develop a hierarchy or class system. Expressions like 'leader of the pack', 'pecking order' and 'queen bee' are instantly recognisable.

Class arouses fierce emotion. From time to time the word itself becomes politically incorrect and expressions like social stratum or socioeconomic group are preferred.

Class is a major area of study and a central concern of sociologists – it can be an effective shorthand for the differences in norms, status and value systems among human groups.

Income and wealth

There are two kinds of money, or economic power:

- Income is what you are paid in return for your labour. The more valuable or the rarer your skills, the more you will be paid. In a feudal society, most people were paid just enough to ensure survival. If income only meets the basic human needs of food, clothing and shelter, there is no surplus.

- If income exceeds expenditure, as an individual or as a group, then you have to do something with the surplus. This surplus is a second kind of economic power – defined in general terms as wealth or capital.

Capital can accumulate. It often, but not always, produces an income. Land and houses can be rented, shares give a dividend, capital invested in your own business can make a profit.

You can borrow money from others. If this money is used wisely, the income it produces will exceed the interest rate on the borrowing – and your capital will grow. Interest is the rent you pay for the temporary use of somebody else's accumulated wealth.

The surplus of income over expenditure can be used to buy or manufacture physical objects or assets – land, animals, houses, jewellery, gold, silver, works of art, and so on. These are 'stores of value'. If well chosen, these become worth more over time. Selling appreciated assets also produces capital growth.

In a feudal society, capital accumulates almost entirely into the hands of landowners, their families and close associates.

Marx and Weber

Marx believed that the industrial revolution would make no difference to, or would even accentuate, the unequal distribution of capital. The essence of Marxism is class conflict leading to revolution – the overthrow of the capitalist class by force.

Capital is still concentrated in relatively few groups and families, but the sharp distinction between 'haves' and 'have nots' has softened and blurred. Middle classes have emerged – those who have managed to accumulate capital and pass it on to their children.

The majority of sociologists do not now define class as simple differences of wealth and income. Modern theories revolve around the idea of cultural capital. Economic and cultural capital are related but not identical.

Put at its simplest, you will not and cannot buy a book until you have paid for dinner. The book will be useless unless your social group could excuse you from work for long enough for you to learn to read.

Max Weber defined class in a wider sense than Karl Marx. Members of the same class have similar life chances and broadly similar skills. Weber recognised that assets or capital can be intellectual as well as physical. Surgeons are paid more than shop assistants because they have accumulated more intellectual capital during many years of education and experience.

Weber saw class struggle as competition between those who lend money and those that have to borrow. In his view, Marx's conclusions about conflict between industrial owners and industrial workers was just a special case of this general theory.

We describe or assign class to ourselves and others using a range of signs, symbols and indicators. Most of us reach conclusions rapidly and tend not to think through their implications. The table on the next page gives some examples.

Class versus income

It becomes clear that outward signals are used as codes for things like wealth, income, health, education and taste – things that cannot be directly observed or measured. More importantly, class is a relative idea: 'People like me are members of the same class. People that are different from me belong to another class.' It is probably impossible to ascribe difference without some assumption of rank or status.

Some groups have very significant cultural capital but little economic capital – that is, no wealth and low incomes. Others have considerable economic power but no 'culture' as usually described. Our society now includes many workers that have opted out of the race to accumulate wealth. Typically these are concentrated in the public sector and in vocational occupations.

The Registrar General's classification

In topic 2 of Chapter 2, we described the Registrar General's subdivision of UK households into six social classes. This system is far from perfect:

- Pensioners and the unemployed are grouped according to their last occupation. Everyone living at the same address is assumed to be of the same class as the person describing himself or herself as the head of the household.

- Social class C or III is subdivided into non-manual jobs, assumed to be middle-class C1 or IIIn, and manual jobs, regarded as working-class C2 or IIIm. Supermarket checkout assistants are officially middle class; central-heating engineers and electricians are working class, even though they are highly skilled.

- Occupation, class and status are not directly related. Bus drivers might be magistrates, councillors or lay-preachers in their spare time.

- The census classification does not separately identify the wealthiest families of all. Depending on definition, somewhere between 20,000 and 40,000 people own between 5% and 10% of the country's total wealth. This group is tiny but potentially very powerful.

Dozens of different social classifications have been designed for specific purposes. Most of these are used to predict consumer behaviour and how many people are likely to buy particular goods or services.

Class indicators

Indicator	Subjective conclusion
Body image and physical appearance	We see departures from the typical appearance as indicators of lower social class
Dress	Whatever style is adopted, clean and tidy suggests higher status than dishevelled and scruffy. Style in itself is no longer a major class indicator – for example, jeans and trainers
Accent	In England, this used to be the defining class indicator. Some regional accents were high status – Edinburgh Scottish and Southern Irish, for example. Others were seen as inferior – East London, Belfast, and West Midlands, for instance
Vocabulary	Limited vocabulary, poor communication and verbal aggression are indicators of lower status. Attitudes to 'bad language' are fluid and unpredictable
Wealth indicators	Most people still see a direct relationship between class and the ownership of capital. Exceptions are thought to be due to chance – lottery winners and very rich footballers, for example
Income and consumption signals	The most widely used indication of class in the UK now groups together people with similar tastes and consumption patterns

Class mobility

The English fascination with class is perhaps more accurately described as an abiding interest in class mobility. Most politicians in most democracies promise equality of opportunity in return for votes. Nobody is condemned to stay in the class into which they were born. Conversely, there are no guarantees that high status can be preserved.

Intergenerational social mobility, combined with the feminist movement, has been a major determinant of class change in UK society since the 1950s. The more able, more fortunate or more industrious sons and daughters of working-class families promote themselves into the middle class and all that entails in terms of income, values, taste and lifestyle.

Education, provided at no cost by the state for the children of poorer families, has been the cornerstone of equality of opportunity in UK society. The bitter arguments between the supporters and the critics of higher education tuition fees and the replacement of student grants with student loans are perfect illustrations of cultural capital debate. The supporters of a fee and loan system believe that individuals should pay for cultural capital. The critics are convinced that the state should pay, because eventually the state benefits. The state, of course, has no money apart from that raised by taxation.

Marriages across class barriers were statistically insignificant in the 19th century and very rare before the 1950s. A woman was thought to acquire the social class of her husband – for richer or poorer.

Luck is an important influence in social mobility. Many of the wealthiest families in the UK have been in the right place at the right time or have benefited from chance decisions. You can alter your social class by winning the National Lottery or by mortgaging the family's land holdings in a business venture that goes disastrously wrong.

A classless society

There is little evidence to support the fashionable assumption that the UK is now a classless society. Sociological investigation reaches three broad conclusions:

- Since the 1950s, the UK class structure has become more fragmented and complex. Mass-market consumerism is now a major factor in class identity. The pace of change has accelerated since the 1980s.

- Class structure is increasingly based on merit and achievement.

- However, a considerable residue of privilege is still an important indicator of class.

The 1997 House of Commons

In the UK general election of May 1997, 659 MPs were elected to parliament. The final result by party was:

The backgrounds of MPs and parliamentary candidates are well documented. A fascinating snapshot of class in the UK emerges if we compare the education and occupations of the 418 Labour and 165 Conservative MPs elected:

	Number of MPs
Labour	418
Conservative	165
Liberal Democrat	46
Others	30
	659

- The median age of the Labour MPs was 48; the Conservatives were slightly older at 50.

- 10 Labour MPs and one Conservative were under 30.

- The Conservative group was predominantly male. Neither party approached gender equality:

	Labour		Conservative	
	No.	%	No.	%
Men	317	76	152	92
Women	101	24	13	8
	418	100	165	100

- Educational background shows stark differences between Labour MPs, Conservative MPs and the UK overall:

Educational background	Conservative MPs (%)	Labour MPs (%)	UK average (%)
State schools	34	84	93
Public schools	66	16	7
Total	100	100	100
University graduates	81	66	11
Non-university graduates	19	34	89
Total	100	100	100

Source: D. Butler and D. Kavanagh (1997), *The British General Election of 1997*

- The table shows MPs' stated occupations at the date of their election (1 May 1997):

Occupation	Labour MPs (number)	Conservative MPs (number)
Barristers and solicitors	29	29
Doctors and dentists	3	2
Architects and engineers	3	2
Scientists	7	1

Occupation	Labour MPs (number)	Conservative MPs (number)
Accountants	2	3
Central and local government officers	30	5
Armed forces	–	9
	74	**51**
University lecturers	22	1
College lecturers	35	–
School teachers	57	9
	114	**10**
Company directors	7	17
Company executives	9	36
Other business people	21	12
	37	**65**
White-collar workers	69	3
Political organisers	40	15
Journalists	29	15
	138	**33**
Farmers	1	5
Miners	12	1
Skilled workers	40	–
Semi-skilled workers	2	–
	55	**6**
Total	**418**	**165**

Source: D. Butler and D. Kavanagh (1997), *The British General Election of 1997*

- The Registrar General's classification system shows major differences between the two largest groups of MPs:

Occupation	Labour		Conservative	
	No.	%	No.	%
Professionals	74	18	51	31
Educators	114	27	10	6
Business and commerce	37	9	65	39
White collar	69	16.5	3	2
Politics and journalism	69	16.5	30	18
Skilled and semi-skilled	55	13	6	4
	418	100	165	100

- Miners and landowners were once seen as typical representatives of the traditional class divide. These groups are no longer significant in the House of Commons.

- The role of education and educational interest in class mobility is well demonstrated – more than a quarter of Labour MPs have been teachers or lecturers. In contrast, nearly 40% of Conservatives have business backgrounds.

Social exclusion

Social mobility has introduced tensions and anxieties that did not exist 100 years ago.

Sociologists, politicians, educators, the health professions and the forces of law and order are increasingly concerned with social exclusion – the creation of small groups who feel they have nothing to gain by 'cooperating with the system'. Poverty is a social stigma – the reverse of social esteem. The excluded have no common identity with the more fortunate and often no common cause amongst themselves.

The causes of social exclusion are varied and interrelated:

- Unemployment, leading to low income and/or a culture of dependency.

- Poor housing, poor diet, chaotic family life.

- Large families, unstable relationships.

- Criminality and related drug abuse.

Many sociologists have concluded that a disregard for education in primary socialisation is the root cause of social exclusion.

5 Social difference in education

The word 'education' comes from the Latin *educare*, whose broad meaning is to lead or to bring up children. Education has three purposes:

- To preserve and transmit knowledge or cultural capital.

- To teach practical skills and attitudes.

- To extend knowledge and create new cultural capital through original research and investigation.

A society that does not educate its children cannot survive. An education system of some sort must always have existed. In cultures without written language, this would have been informal and by example. In the past, skills were often passed from father to son – many surnames describe occupations: Smith, Archer, Cooper, Fletcher, Cartwright, Miller, Baker and so on.

The Greeks and Romans educated the children of their elites. The Romans in particular had a state-funded system that taught boys between the age of six and 16.

Much of our present science and mathematics is based on Arab learning and education. The word 'alchemy' and hence 'chemistry' derives from Arabic, as does our number system, using the ten digits from zero to nine.

The table below gives a brief history of the development of formal education in the UK.

1167	Oxford – the first British university founded
1207	Cambridge University formed
1780	First Sunday schools
1801	First non-conformist voluntary schools
1808	First Church of England voluntary schools
1828	Thomas Arnold begins public-school reform
1833	Factory Act makes two hours per day of schooling compulsory for nine to 11-year-olds. Funded by government
1868	Regulatory Public Schools Act
1870	First Education Act. Locally elected school boards established
1880	Second Education Act. Schooling for all children aged five to 10 becomes compulsory
1902	Board schools come under the control of local education authorities. Beginnings of secondary-school system
1918	Education Act raises school leaving age to 14
1944	Butler Education Act provides free and compulsory education to age 15. Free school meals and milk for all. Tripartite system – selection between grammar, technical and secondary modern schools, decided at age 11
1951	GCEs introduced
1963	Robbins Committee recommends major expansion in the university sector
1964	Government encourages introduction of comprehensive schools
1965	Polytechnics established
1969	Open University founded
1973	School leaving age raised to 16
1976	All state schools required to become comprehensive
1979/80	1976 Act repealed. LEAs required to publish first 'league tables', but no longer obliged to provide free meals and milk
1987	GCSEs replace GCEs and CSEs
1988	National Curriculum introduced with testing in major subjects. Schools allowed to opt out of LEA control
1994	National Curriculum revised. National Curriculum and Assessment Authority established
1997	Expansion of nursery-school provision. Setting up of Education Action Zones, phasing out funding of grant-maintained schools. Means-tested grants for university students replaced with a loan system. Tuition fees introduced
1998	Compulsory literacy and numeracy hours in primary schools

The school system

Primary and secondary education in the UK is a national service but it is locally administered. Policy decided by parliament is implemented by Local Education Authorities (LEAs). A slightly different system operates in Scotland and Northern Ireland. State education is politically controlled and the results of general and local elections can alter policy.

State schools have boards of governors selected from parents, the local community, the LEAs and teachers. These governing bodies have financial responsibility and, amongst other things, interview and select senior teaching staff. The head teacher manages the day-to-day running of the school.

Some state schools are allowed greater independence and special funding. These grant-maintained schools are politically contentious and are being phased out by the present government.

Under UK law it is a criminal offence not to educate a child, but state schooling is not compulsory. Some parents choose to teach their children at home. About 7% of British children attend private fee-paying schools. For historical reasons, these private institutions are called public schools.

Most of the funding for state schools is provided by central government grants to LEAs. Schools are free to raise extra money through parent teacher associations and approved sponsorship schemes with business and commercial organisations.

Compulsory education begins at five, although many schools now accept four-year-olds. Nursery education is not compulsory. Secondary education begins at 11, or 12 in Scotland. Public schools commonly recruit at 13.

The state system allows some schools to be run in partnership with religious denominations. A majority of UK voluntary-aided schools are associated with the Catholic Church or the Church of England. There are a relatively small number of Jewish schools, and recently several Muslim schools have been approved for state funding.

An LEA is obliged to offer a choice of single-sex or mixed secondary education.

Nearly all state secondary schools are comprehensive – children are admitted regardless of ability. A few LEAs maintain grammar schools with selective entrance.

The state provides special schools for children with disabilities or earning difficulties that prevent them from benefiting from mainstream education.

Compulsory schooling ends at 16. The majority of young people now continue full-time education at least until 18.

State schools are regularly inspected by the Office for Standards in Education, Ofsted. Inspection reports are published and OFsted has the power to close schools in some circumstances.

Corporal punishment was made illegal in state schools in 1986 and in public schools in 1998.

The public schools

It is impossible to understand the links between class and education in the UK without knowing something about the public schools.

Private education is expensive. The highest-status schools charge about £20,000 a year for boarding pupils. To educate two children from the age of 13 to 18 requires an investment of about £200,000.

Entry is selective. The selection methods used are private decisions made by the school. Single-sex education is the norm; coeducation is the exception.

Some public schools have centuries of history. Eton College was founded by Henry VI in 1440.

Some of the older institutions have accumulated significant wealth. Additionally, fee structures are pitched to fund a high level of resource and support.

Public schools are free to pay higher salaries in order to attract staff. Typically, the staff:student ratio in public schools is 1:10. This compares with about 1:30 in the state sector. Teaching hours, especially for boarders, can spread into evenings and weekends. Homework is supervised and unavoidable.

Few features of UK society polarise opinion more sharply than attitudes towards private education. The table summarises the usual arguments.

Supporters of private education	Critics of private education
In a democracy, every citizen has the right to spend their money as they wish	Buying privilege is wrong Education should depend on ability, not money
The public schools are centres of excellence that make a major contribution to UK society	The public schools teach a socially disruptive set of class values. These damage UK society
Public schools establish lifelong networks of civilised, like-minded adults	Public schools produce badly socialised adults. Closed social networks perpetuate elitism
If banned, the public schools would relocate overseas. UK society would be the loser	Legislating against the public schools is by far the best way of improving the state sector

Generally, public schools are registered as charities and therefore pay less tax than mainstream commercial organisations.

6 Identity and gender

Gender is concerned with the different social roles of men and women – how these are established, how they change over time and how they vary from one society to another.

Sexuality or sexual identity is different from gender. There are two genders but many patterns of sexual orientation and behaviour.

Patriarchy, the rule of men, is or was justified in terms of proven or alleged biological difference.

Male	Female
Physically bigger and stronger	Physically smaller and weaker
Hormonally aggressive, especially towards other men	Hormonally placid, unless in defence of children
Leaders and decision makers	Followers and decision accepters
Material and resource providers	Materially dependent
Large geographical territory	Confined to private and domestic spaces
Logical and rational	Emotional and irrational
Minimal role in childcare	Carers for children, sick and the elderly
Dress and physical appearance a low priority	Deeply concerned with clothing, ornamentation and body image
Responds mostly to visual signals	More complex responses
Programmed to be sexually aggressive and to seek out many sexual partners	Programmed to be sexually passive and to prefer one or few sexual partners

Gender identity is established during primary socialisation. An infant learns, and is taught, a gender identity from the first months of life and this is nearly always firmly established by the age of four or five. Appropriate behaviour is rewarded and inappropriate behaviour discouraged or even overtly punished.

The reinforcement of gender continues beyond the family, first at school, then at work and wherever there is social contact and interaction.

Gender and education

Education in the UK has moved through a number of phases, each with a different set of commonly accepted gender roles.

The earliest English public schools were all-male institutions and many still are. Thomas Arnold, the great reformer of the public-school system, said its objective should be to turn out Christian men of gentlemanly conduct, emphasising values of self-discipline, public service and team spirit. There was no mention of women.

The UK state system has never openly discriminated in favour of one gender, but this often happened by default. Historically, some teachers favoured boys, leading to lower self-esteem amongst girls. Subjects were generally thought of as male or female with little middle ground.

Male school subjects	Female school subjects
Woodwork, metalwork, technology	Domestic science, art, music
Maths, physics, chemistry	Biology
Latin, Greek	Modern languages
Greater emphasis on team sports	Greater emphasis on individual
– soccer, rugby, cricket	sports – athletics, tennis, swimming

These are coarse generalisations. For example, it is difficult to assign genders to subjects like geography and history.

The division of secondary education into grammar, technical and secondary modern schools was meant to be gender neutral. In fact, it reinforced many class and gender roles.

One of the reasons for the withdrawal of the eleven–plus exam was its tendency to discriminate against girls. Gender differences in compulsory education ensured their continuation into the college and university system. In some university courses during the 1960s and 1970s, men outnumbered women by 20 to one – typically in engineering and physics. The university student population was predominately male.

More recently, there has been a fascinating shift in gender expectation and performance in secondary schools. The biggest underperformers are now teenage boys, in particular amongst lower-status groups. An anti-school culture is causing deep concern in some areas. The factors involved include male unemployment, lack of appropriate role models and the rise of 'girl power', leading to male insecurity and loss of self-esteem.

Gender and employment

Gender stereotyping in employment has followed the same broad pattern as that for education. Gender discrimination at work is now illegal, but the traditional pattern of male jobs and female jobs persists.

Women are now equally educated, and in theory have equal opportunities in the job market. There is still a significant gender gap in average salaries but this is partly explained by two factors:

- Women still predominate in lower-paid occupations – on a job-for-job basis, pay rates are equalising rapidly.

- A time lag is at work. If it takes 30 years to achieve a senior position, the current gender mix, in the best-paid and highest-status jobs, will reflect the society of the 1970s. For example, investigations at entry level into medical and law schools show a gender balance close to equality. Recently, slightly more girls than boys have been admitted to degree courses in the UK. (See the table below).

Male occupations	Female occupations
Armed forces, police and fire services	Childcare professionals
University lecturer	Infant-school teacher
Doctor	Nurse
Plumber	Florist
Finance director	Human resources/personnel director
Barrister	Barrister's secretary
Chef	Cook
Orchestral conductor	Harp player

Gender and the mass market

By definition, mass-market goods and services are provided by large corporations, not by small businesses and individuals. The narrowing of the gender gap, preferably its complete demolition, is in the interests of big companies.

To take a theoretical illustration: if a product that was previously only bought by men can be redesigned and readvertised so that it appeals equally to men and women, the sales of that product will double. Provided costs are controlled, a doubling of sales produces something like a tripling or quadrupling of profit. The temptation is irresistible. None of these changes have happened overnight, but very clear long-term trends are observable and measurable in all parts of UK society. It is interesting to note that the gender gap in the marketing and advertising professions has virtually disappeared.

There are thousands of examples of gender gap reduction marketing. To give one example, the UK spends billions of pounds a year on alcoholic drink. This market is being feminised.

- Sales of dark spirits like whisky and dark rum are declining. Sales of lighter spirits such as vodka, gin and white rum are stable. The big growth market is wine and, to a lesser extent, light beers.

- The alcohol market share of pubs and clubs has fallen dramatically. We now drink more at home and in mixed company.

- Alcoholic drink as part of a meal, at home or away from home, is becoming the rule rather than the exception.

In conclusion, at the beginning of the 21st century in the UK, three facts are undeniable:

- The gender gap is narrower than it used to be.

- However, the gender gap still exists and it still explains vitally important differences in the expectations and behaviour of men and women.

- Gender signals and gender roles are increasingly subtle and more and more the subject of debate.

Concerning gender difference, there are many shades of opinion. The table summarises the two extremes.

On the one hand	On the other hand
Men and women are different but equal	Men and women are different, equality is a meaningless concept
Gender differences are largely cultural and therefore changeable	Men will inevitably try to dominate women – given the opportunity.
The closure of the gender gap is social progress and irreversible	The closure of the gender gap is just a symptom of prosperity. This may change – it is not irreversible
Society will inevitably move to narrow gender differences. No special action is required	Constant vigilance, legislation and perhaps positive discrimination is the only way of maintaining equality
Men and women are genetically programmed to cooperate	Gender conflict is biologically determined and cannot be avoided
'New man' is real. 'Macho man' will become extinct	'New man' is a temporary phenomenon. Inside every 'new man' is a 'macho man' longing to escape

Chapter 4
An introduction to ethics

National unit specification
These are the topics you will be studying for this unit.

1 Why study ethics at all?

2 What is ethics?

3 Moral development

4 Ethical theories

5 Thiroux's five principles of ethics

6 Ethical codes

7 Legal issues and client rights

Ethics is a practical subject and most of your teaching and learning will be based around class discussion and case studies taken from real life. This chapter presents the theory and essential background; it does not include an extensive list of group exercises or examples – these will be provided by your subject lecturers.

1 Why study ethics at all?

Ethics is the study of moral behaviour and morality can be described as a branch of philosophy.

Some people have trouble coming to grips with this unit – in particular those with a practical or down-to-earth approach to life. Many ask questions such as:

> I know how to behave properly, so isn't this unit a bit of a waste of time? Why do we need to be taught what is simple common sense?
>
> How can the writings of long-dead philosophers ever be relevant to my daily life as a health professional?
>
> Why is the language and vocabulary of ethics so unnecessarily complicated? What is the point of arguing over the slightly different meanings of two very similar words?

These questions have to be answered before we can begin.

Moral absolutes

A common-sense view of what is right or wrong is relative, not absolute. There are no moral certainties that apply in all situations, at all times and for all groups or societies. This idea can seem odd at first, largely because most of us lead relatively sheltered lives. We tend to think that our particular group or cultural values are universal.

'Thou shalt not kill' seems like a moral absolute, but virtually all societies make exceptions. Warfare is often justified as the lesser of two evils; so, on a smaller scale, is killing in self-defence. Capital punishment, suicide, euthanasia and abortion are prohibited in some societies but allowed by others.

Moral dilemmas

In Greek, a *lemma* is an assumption or statement used as the starting point for an argument and then a conclusion. The word 'lemma' is rare in English, but dilemma – meaning 'two lemmas' – is common. A moral dilemma can be precisely defined as a choice that has to be made between two morally defensible actions. There is no right decision and nearly always no convenient or good decision. There are no common-sense solutions to moral dilemmas.

Medical ethics

Moral dilemmas present in every walk of life but they are major and continuing issues for health professionals. Often, decisions cannot be avoided, cannot be delayed and may have to be made using incomplete information. Doing nothing or 'letting nature take its course' is a decision in itself, because an alternative is always available.

Dilemmas may involve conflict between the ethical stances taken by different branches of the same profession. For instance, there are no guarantees that a GP, a surgeon, a nurse and a medical researcher will reach the same conclusions concerning a particular client or treatment.

As medical science advances, ethical issues become more complex and more frequent. The greater our ability to intervene, the harder it is to decide if intervention is morally justified.

Decisions concerning resource allocation in healthcare are moral dilemmas not financial calculations with a single correct mathematical solution. These dilemmas are certain to multiply if the last barrier to medical advance is funding alone.

Teaching and learning ethics

Teaching and learning for the ethics unit is based around case studies, scenarios and class discussions. These often become heated and prolonged – which proves several points:

- Everybody has an ethical code, but even those with very similar backgrounds find agreement difficult.

- Ethics is real and relevant – it is not an abstract or theoretical concept of little use to practical people.

You might be asked to invent a scenario or one may be given to the class by your lecturer. In any event, you will be spoilt for choice.

The most common ethical case study used to be that of a Jehovah's Witness refusing a lifesaving blood transfusion. This religious group believes that transfusions are expressly forbidden by the Bible and the dilemma has occurred many times in real life. The study can be widened. What should be done if the patient becomes unconscious? Do the ethical considerations change if parents refuse a transfusion for a child?

A typical Access class can immediately come up with half a dozen scenarios that pose even more difficult dilemmas. A greater understanding of human genetics raises ethical issues that did not exist 20 years ago. We can now extend existence to the point where quality of life sometimes has to be weighed against sheer longevity – how do we decide when enough is enough?

Changing patterns of disease and disorder in the Western world create yet another new set of ethical dilemmas. Should priority be given to patients and clients with responsible, healthy lifestyles, or should we see self-destructive behaviour as a disorder and its sufferers as victims? Should we care for people who do not care for themselves?

Philosophy, morality and ethics

As a mature student, you will not be meeting subjects like literacy, mathematics, chemistry, biology and sociology for the first time. From school, you will have some idea of their scope, relevance and application. Philosophy, morality and ethics are different – these disciplines are not school subjects and, by definition, they will be unfamiliar.

Loosely translated, again from the Greek, a philosopher is a lover of wisdom or knowledge. A critical thinker or researcher in any field or discipline could be called a philosopher. Philosophy is concerned with concepts like value systems, goodness, evil, truth, justice and freedom. Morality and ethics are branches of philosophy. Many modern moral dilemmas are old issues in new clothes. The words and thoughts of men and women who lived many years ago are therefore still relevant and useful.

Much of the maths you are taught as part of the Access course is based on the original work of Greeks like Euclid and Pythagoras who lived more than 2,000 years ago. To most students, this is not startling or surprising. In a similar way, Aristotle (384–322 BCE), was one of the greatest philosophers. He said and wrote a great deal that still applies directly to 21st-century medical ethics.

Language and vocabulary

Because there are no moral absolutes, it follows that words must be used carefully and precisely in ethical debates and discussions. A particular therapy or treatment might be described as 'good', 'right', 'correct', 'beneficial', 'advantageous', 'appropriate' or perhaps 'the best available option'. These words may mean different things to different people – and different things to the same person in different circumstances.

Assumptions are culturally determined and therefore should be avoided wherever possible. You should not assume that a colleague, patient or client means exactly what you mean when they use the words you use.

2 What is ethics?

Previously, we have defined ethics as the study of moral behaviour. The *Concise Oxford Dictionary* (Eighth edition) says **ethics** is '**the science of morals in human conduct**'. These definitions are virtually identical but both are unhelpful unless we can pin down the differences between ethics and morals.

Ethics derives from the Greek word *ethos* and morals from the Latin word *mores*. Confusingly, both translate to mean custom or convention. In conversation, we sometimes use the words interchangeably; to say 'she is an ethical person' means much the same as saying 'she is a moral person'. In everyday language, most of us associate morality with sexual conduct – 'he was living off her immoral earnings'. Ethical behaviour and its negative is also commonly used to describe actions which may be legal but might also be seen as wrong – especially if financial exploitation is involved. Somebody might say: 'An interest rate of 32% p.a. is certainly legal but it is also unethical.'

Ethics and morals – some definitions

We define morals and morality as values, rules and codes of conduct that are accepted by individuals, groups and societies. Morals and morality emerge from shared beliefs. These may be religious in the first instance, or practical with no reference to a God or a creator. It is worth restating the point that morals and morality are culturally determined and therefore vary from one society to another and from one time to another.

An ethic, in the singular, is one of these values, rules or codes of conduct. For example, a politician could say, 'An overgenerous welfare system destroys the work ethic.'

Ethics, in the plural, is the science whose object of study is morals and morality. The table gives some examples and comparisons to underline the point.

Objects of study	The science
Mass and energy	Physics
The plant kingdom	Botany
The heart	Cardiology
Values, rules and codes of conduct	Ethics

Metaethics

Metaethics, sometimes called moral philosophy, is the study of the relationships between theories that lead to systems of morality and morals. 'Meta' used as a prefix in this way just means at a second or higher level. Apart from this passing reference, metaethics is not mentioned again in this unit.

Ethics as an applied science

We shall be looking at ethics at the first level – as a practical applied science, not as a body of theory unrelated to everyday life and experience. We can list the characteristics of applied sciences:

- They are active processes, not passive ones. Theory is applied to achieve a predetermined goal or objective, and to benefit people.

- They are group or communal activities, not private or personal concerns. Individual bias, opinion and attitude must be eliminated whenever possible. Subjectivity and false assumptions are often difficult to identify.

- The central purpose of applied science is to find solutions to intractable problems.

- Applied sciences have to be taught. They are not self-evident and they cannot be deduced by intuition, instinct or 'gut feeling'.

- Sciences are applied to bring about advance, progress and reform.

- There is nothing fixed or static about applied science. New discoveries, observations and developments mean that new methods are needed to solve new problems.

We can now put together a second definition of ethics – this time using words that will probably appeal to practical people.

Ethics is a system or series of steps that help us decide which actions are good and right.

The opposite of good is bad, and the opposite of right is wrong – but this does not mean that good and right are the same thing – and clearly also, bad and wrong are different concepts. You cannot be an efficient and caring health professional unless you give some more thought to what these four words really mean.

Good versus bad and right versus wrong

Compare the following incidents.

An ambulance and a fire engine are responding to an emergency call. Three young children are trapped in a top-floor bedroom of a burning three-storey house. Both vehicles at times exceed 70 mph in a built-up area and pass through several red traffic lights.

On the following day, over exactly the same route, two young men decide to see who has the faster car. Both vehicles at times exceed 70 mph in a built-up area and pass through several red traffic lights.

No traffic or pedestrian accidents occur, none of the drivers are drunk, all of the vehicles are roadworthy, taxed and insured and all of the drivers have valid licences.

In the UK, it is always illegal to jump a red light or to exceed 30 mph in a built-up area – no exceptions are allowed. All of the drivers have certainly broken the law – their actions are wrong. However, the vast majority would see the first action as good and the second as bad.

Four boxes

With just a few minutes' thought it is easy to construct any number of four-grid box examples to compare good, bad, right and wrong. These can be straightforward and obvious or deeply contentious and thought-provoking.

	GOOD	BAD
RIGHT	Working hard to feed your children	Charging £10 for a loaf during a bread shortage
WRONG	Destitute parents stealing food to feed their children	Setting fire to a bread factory

Once you start asking questions like 'What if …?', the real scope of ethics emerges. In the example, what if:

- The hardworking parents had little quality time to spend with their well-fed children?

- The destitute parents had no money because they were compulsive gamblers?

- The market price of a loaf had risen to £25 in an acute food shortage?

- The bread factory was selling contaminated or poisoned bread?

These questions may not be troublesome, but in which of the boxes would you put abortion, euthanasia, withdrawal of life support from those in a persistent vegetative state, explicit sexual images, foxhunting, under-age contraception or the sale of genetically modified food?

Ethics in real life cannot be reduced to four boxes. How many different combinations of good, bad, right or wrong are possible once you begin to ask 'What if …'?

Right and wrong – black and white

An action can be right or wrong. It cannot be both and it must be one or the other. These definitions seem to offer a way out of, or a way around, ethical dilemmas. All you need to do is to consult a rule book and uncertainty evaporates. In essence an individual who always obeys every rule is letting somebody else – the rule giver or law maker – make his or her ethical decisions. We can be certain only if we accept the rules unquestioningly and in all circumstances.

Without an extensive system of laws, enforcement and punishment, no civilised society could exist. Laws are essential precisely because they leave no room for doubt as to individual rights and obligations. Most rule or law systems have an appeal procedure. This amounts to saying, 'We cannot decide what is right or wrong, so let us ask the rule giver – he or she will tell us what we can and cannot do.'

The problems with right and wrong

The first problem with rules and laws is that they are difficult to frame or to write in a way that is completely unambiguous. Millions of people accept that the Ten Commandments are divine law as revealed by God to Moses. An early English translation gave the commandment 'Thou shalt not kill'. Later translations say 'You shall not murder'. These are different laws. Which is right? Which is wrong?

Historically, laws were made by the powerful and enforced by the powerful for the benefit of the powerful. A good working definition of democracy is the process that leads to a set of rules that limit the actions of the most wealthy, fortunate and aggressive groups in society.

Our definitions of right and wrong change constantly. In the UK, capital punishment is now wrong and – as legally defined – abortion, attempted suicide, homosexuality and selling tobacco to adults are right. There are no universal laws. In the US, some states allow capital punishment whilst others do not.

In the UK, an individual may do anything that is not specifically prohibited by law. This means that laws are of little use in the most difficult situations – they are a starting point but they offer nothing approaching a conclusion or solution to ethical or moral dilemmas.

Good and bad – judgement, responsibility and risk

A fundamentalist is someone who accepts an externally imposed set of rules without question. This acceptance may be the result of years of agonising personal thought and deliberation, but this does not mean that the actions that result are both right and good. Immediately we are in very deep and dangerous water. Terrorism is often justified in terms of fundamentalism. The universally admired and respected devout Catholic nurse who will not under any circumstances become involved in the termination of a pregnancy, is also a fundamentalist.

Choosing between good and bad is much more difficult than deciding what is right or wrong. Certainty is not available, because judgement, responsibility and the risk of an incorrect choice are always present. There is no simple appeal procedure. You are faced with a decision, and the decision must be made.

Yet again, the real meaning of words is a central issue. There is no simple appeal procedure, but there is, and has to be, an appeal process. In deciding between good and bad, appeals have to be made to evidence, available facts and the experiences of others who may have been faced with similar decisions in the past. An ethical code, in contrast to a set of laws, is a collection of rules that have been developed by the interaction between evidence and experience.

3 Moral development

Jean Piaget (1896–1980) was a Swiss psychologist. During a remarkably long and productive career, his work centred on the study of how children learn. Many of his theories and ideas can be transferred directly to all learning. The processes used by adults in adjusting to new situations and circumstances closely resemble the stages of childhood development.

Moral maturity

Piaget (1948) distinguished between mature and immature morality. The table summarises his major conclusions.

Immature morality	Mature morality
Rules and laws come from those in positions of absolute authority	Rules and laws develop and change. They derive from the need for human interaction and cooperation
Motive and intention are irrelevant	Motive and intention are vital in the judgement of behaviour
The rules must not be broken or disobeyed	Disregard for authority and the rules need not be bad
Punishment for rule-breakers is retribution – an eye for an eye	Punishment should aim to reform and educate so that rule-breakers can begin, or begin again, to make a contribution to society
The rules and laws are absolute	Rules and laws are relative and subjective
If in doubt, the rule-giver will decide what is right or wrong	There is no hard, firm or precise distinction between good and bad
You can tell how wrong an action is by the punishment it brings	You can tell how bad an action is by the amount of harm it does to others
Reciprocity is no reason to obey the rules	Reciprocity is often a justification for good behaviour – do unto others as you would be done by
Misfortune or accident following wrong actions is natural punishment or retribution The two events are connected	Good things happen to bad people and bad things happen to good people Any connection between fate and morality is coincidental and determined by chance alone

Age and moral maturity

Piaget's views on mature and immature morality came after extensive observation and experiment involving children from birth through to adolescence. However, his findings make no direct link between age and moral maturity. Extending Piaget, we can reach three conclusions that are directly relevant to ethics:

- Adults, in other words the physically and mentally mature, may be morally immature.

- Groups of adults, societies and organisations may be morally immature.

- Adults faced with new circumstances and situations are likely to be morally immature. This sounds like negative or destructive criticism, but it is not. Using different words, we can make a constructive statement. When coming to terms with new or unfamiliar situations, most people are untrained and inexperienced – therefore education and exposure to new ways of thinking are essential.

History, in particular political and legislative history, has moral maturity and immaturity as a continuing theme. England under William the Conqueror, for example, was a morally immature society. Laws were absolute and derived ultimately from the teachings of the church and the military power of the king. On a smaller scale, families and communities were patriarchal. Rules were made or interpreted by a few adult men. Nearly 1,000 years ago, all of this was thought to be normal, natural, right and God given.

Political debate is never-ending and this makes the point that morality and moral maturity are matters of judgement. It also implies that some law is bad law and that laws may have a limited shelf life. During the 20th century, social codes relaxed and legislation followed suit. Some people see this as increasing moral maturity, others as a dangerous collapse in standards. 'I don't know what the world is coming to – it wouldn't have happened in my day' is the stereotypical response of older people to the attitudes of the young.

No socially active group can insulate itself from shifts in behaviour and beliefs. More than most professions, nursing, midwifery and healthcare are in the front line of these moral arguments and debates.

Moral maturity and language

The use of inappropriate language can be seen as a lack of courtesy, imagination or thought, but in more general terms it is a sign of moral immaturity.

Sexist and racist language is only tolerated in groups or societies where sexism and racism are accepted or not actively discouraged. It may not always be obvious that some words will be offensive or transmit the wrong meaning to many patients or clients. The best advice is to use words cautiously and never without thought. Language reflects morality – unmarried couples no longer 'live in sin', 'bastards' are now 'love children'. Never assume that your morality – the source of much of your vocabulary – is the same as that of the patient or client in your care.

Theories of moral development

Piaget's work is widely accepted as a good definition of what moral development is – the growth from moral immaturity to maturity. Other researchers have looked at how moral development happens. The different explanations are called theories of moral development.

Maccoby (1980) defined moral development as a child's acquisition of rules that govern behaviour in the social world. Three contributing factors were identified.

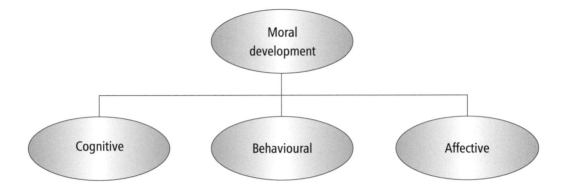

To cogitate is to think. Children come to know and understand that actions have consequences. This is the cognitive element in moral development.

Behavioural development describes the acknowledgement of rules imposed by others – of parents in the first place and then those of school and wider social groups.

As used by Maccoby, the words 'affective development' mean the emergence of feelings like guilt, shame and pride.

Taken together, these factors lead to a sense of right and wrong, good and bad, and cause and effect. There is a difference between knowledge and action. A child or an adult may know that something is wrong or bad, but proceed anyway. The reverse is also true. Many of us do not do things that we know we should do. Guilt and shame are the results of conflict between moral knowledge and immoral action.

Individuals vary enormously in their ability to feel guilt, shame and pride. Some would not dream of stealing a paper clip; others can find moral justification for armed robbery.

Learning theories and morality

Nearly all psychologists believe that morality can be taught and learned – this is the view we have taken in our description of what ethics is and how it should be applied. However, some faiths take a different stance – they do not see a newborn child as a clean sheet of paper or a blank canvas.

The concept of original sin is fundamental to some religions. It is thought that we are born bad – that is our natural condition. In contrast, secular humanists and some political theorists suggest we are born with a sense of morality and this can be built on to produce a society which is eventually perfectible.

In a practical sense, none of these theories concerning our innate or original condition invalidate the need to teach morality.

Morality can be taught and learned just like any other discipline or skill. It follows that the theories of learning that are known to apply for subjects and skills like mathematics and driving a car must also apply to morality. There are four generally accepted learning theories.

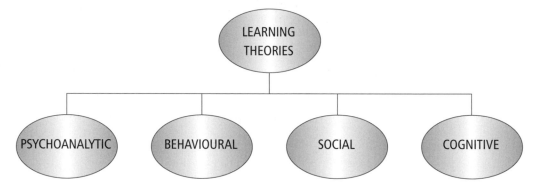

The psychoanalytic learning theory

Sigmund Freud pioneered psychoanalysis in the early part of the 20th century. His theories came from attempts to treat adults suffering from anxiety, depression and a number of phobic conditions. Freud believed that adult personality was largely fixed and determined by very early life experience, most often by the relationship between mother and infant. Freud suggested the existence of the super-ego – a part of the mind that contains conscience and the ego-ideal. The ego-ideal, according to Freud, is a set of standards by which behaviour can be judged.

The super-ego is formed by observation and identification with parental values.

The existence of the super-ego cannot be proved and Freud's approach does not explain why and how morality can change from childhood through to maturity.

The major contribution of Freudian psychoanalysis is the recognition that motives and drives can be deeply rooted and not consciously recognised.

Behavioural learning theory

Behavioural theory coincides with what most people would describe as self-evident common sense. Children are taught how to behave by reward and punishment. The greater the departure from normal behaviour, the bigger the reward or the harsher the punishment. Behaviourists think that morality is a conditioned response that becomes ingrained and persists into adult life. Anxiety in anticipation of a wrong or bad act deters us from actually committing the act.

The behaviourist school includes many shades of opinion. These differ mostly in their assumptions concerning the replacement of existing conditioned responses with new ones. At one end of the scale, this substitution is thought to be rare and difficult; at the other end, behaviourist learning is said to continue throughout life.

At first glance, behaviourism seems to give a complete explanation of how morality is learned – making every other theory redundant. With a bit more thought, however, it becomes clear that behaviourism cannot answer many central moral and ethical questions:

- Why do some people actively rebel or refuse to conform to accepted standards of behaviour?

- How can 'good' parents produce 'bad' children, and vice versa?

- Why do most of us behave well, even when we are certain that some bad or wrong actions will never be detected or punished?

- Why is our legal system of crime and punishment not perfect? Why do some people persistently reoffend?

Social learning theory

Behaviour which is admired or seen to be relevant or useful is likely to be copied. The more powerful the role model, the stronger the influence on the observer. Social learning and behavioural learning can reinforce moral behaviour, or they can set up conflict and confusion. Parents are usually the first role models for children, but actions may not match instructions – 'I try not to smoke in front of the children'. There is a thin dividing line between role model and authority figure. Children, and society generally, may reject the traditional authority of parents, the Church, the police and teachers only to transfer their imitation and social learning to different role models.

Celebrity culture is a perfect illustration of social learning. An individual with exceptional skills in one field is often taken to have authority in unrelated areas. We no longer universally admire politicians and archbishops, perhaps because they seem irrelevant to everyday life. So we look up to musicians, singers, actors and sports celebrities. Does violence on the football field encourage aggression off the field? Does the behaviour of a few popular musicians promote drug taking and sexual irresponsibility?

Celebrity endorsement in advertising assumes that social learning has a powerful influence. Censorship in all of its forms is partly justified as an attempt to prevent social learning.

Cognitive learning theory

This theory says that human beings learn by thinking problems through and by applying logic and reason. It stresses the process of intelligent adaptation to the social environment rather than reward, punishment, unconscious motivations, desire or imitation. As with behaviourism, this theory can seem like common sense dressed up in difficult language – but, again, cognition is not a full or complete description of how morality is learned.

If cognition explained morality, then the most intelligent members of a society would be the most moral. By sheer brain power, they could work out what was right and good, and also that it was illogical to be bad.

Common experience and the lessons of history prove that morality involves much more than intelligence, reason and logic. Some of the most evil actions imaginable have been planned, designed and authorised by very intelligent men and women. Most religions make connections between simplicity, innocence or naivety and the highest moral standards.

Moral development in nursing

It should now be clear that studying the applied science of ethics is as much a part of preparing to enter the health professions as studying the applications of say chemistry, biology, sociology and psychology. Each science has its own specialist vocabulary and language – none is more difficult than the others and none is intrinsically more or less valuable.

In the next topics we discuss the theories of ethics and then the five ethical principles that have been shown to be effective working guides to ethical behaviour in all professions. We are moving on from philosophy and towards a practical approach that will become part of your daily working routine.

4 Ethical theories

Ethical theories are the starting point of a framework that offers solutions to ethical dilemmas.

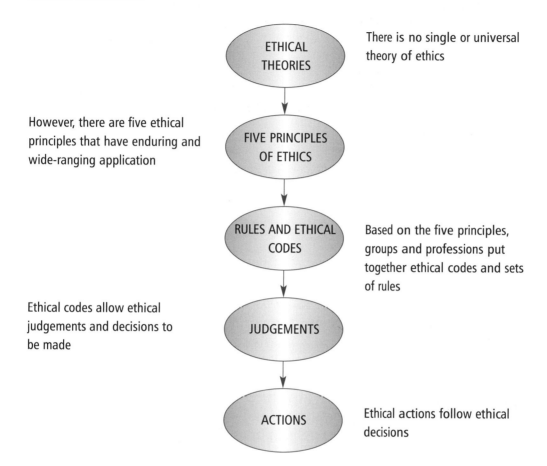

There is no single or universal theory of ethics

ETHICAL THEORIES

However, there are five ethical principles that have enduring and wide-ranging application

FIVE PRINCIPLES OF ETHICS

RULES AND ETHICAL CODES

Based on the five principles, groups and professions put together ethical codes and sets of rules

Ethical codes allow ethical judgements and decisions to be made

JUDGEMENTS

ACTIONS

Ethical actions follow ethical decisions

Two major theories

Religious faith determines morality and ethical behaviour for very many people. Medical ethics has its roots in the belief that to care for the sick and the vulnerable was a duty owed to God or the Creator – and that not to do so was an offence or a sin against God. Jews, Christians and Muslims share the belief that ethical codes are revealed in the Old Testament, the New Testament or the Qur'an and interpreted by religious leaders.

The refusal to accept that morality is determined by, and depends solely on, religious belief is not a new idea. The separation of faith and ethics features in the writings of Greek philosophers, but the two most widely accepted theories of ethics were proposed in the 1780s. The names can be confusing, but the table explains.

The ethics of duty	The ethics of consequences
also called	also called
Deontological ethics	Teleological ethics
Kantian ethics	Utilitarianism
The ethics of obligation	Consequentialism
formalised by	formalised by
Immanuel Kant	Jeremy Bentham
1724–1804	1748–1832
Prussian/German	English
first published in	first published in
Critique of pure reason	*Introduction to the principles of morals*
in 1781	in 1789

Immanuel Kant, 1724–1804

Kant could be described as the most important man that most people have never heard of. He was born in Königsberg – then in east Prussia – now renamed Kaliningrad and part of the Russian Federation. His parents were poor and deeply religious. Kant never married and spent virtually all his life in his home town, first studying and then lecturing at the University of Königsberg. His intellect was prodigious and wide ranging – he was especially influenced by David Hume, an English philosopher, and by the most famous mathematicians of the day, Newton and Leibniz.

Kant's major contribution was finally to dispel medieval ways of thinking based on assertion and superstition. He believed the problems of science and morality could be solved by reason, logic, observation and experiment.

Jeremy Bentham, 1748–1832

Bentham and Kant could hardly have been more different. Jeremy Bentham was the son of a wealthy English family. A private income allowed him to spend most of his life studying and writing. He was educated at Westminster School and Queen's College Oxford, after which he became a barrister. In today's terms, Bentham would be described as an eccentric left-wing intellectual – he questioned all of the accepted establishment norms, in particular the legal system. He was an early campaigner for prison reform. Bentham's work was much admired in France and the US. He founded University College London, providing money on condition that the College admitted Methodist, Catholic and Jewish students.

The ethics of duty

Kant believed that people act morally only when they act out of a sense of duty to do good, regardless of their own inclinations. Motives and intentions decide if an act is ethical, not its result or consequences.

Deontology focuses on rights, duties and justice.

Under the Kantian theory, an act cannot be ethical if its motivation or purpose is personal gain or benefit. Kant also believed that there must always be a personal conviction that an action is right. This means that 'I was only obeying orders' cannot be an excuse for unethical behaviour. In a competition between externally opposed moral authority and personal conviction, the internal view of the individual must always win out and determine the action.

It also follows from Kant that people must be treated with respect, they must not be manipulated and must not be exploited or used as a means to an end.

There need be no conflict between Kantian ethics and religious belief if that belief is the source of an individual's personal conviction. 'Do unto others as you would be done by' is a good summary of Kant's ethical theory, but it presupposes that all of the parties involved will reach the same conclusions based on the same interpretation of duty.

Act deontology and rule deontology

Kant's theory does not list or prescribe a set of moral actions, it only gives ways of deciding if an action is ethical or unethical. In its pure form, deontology is of little practical use in resolving ethical dilemmas – any course of action could be justified by personal conviction, and this could vary from one individual and one situation to the next.

This interpretation of Kant is called 'act deontology'. It rapidly degenerates into situational ethics where every action, or perhaps no action, can be ethically justified. A different way of applying the theory is, however, an invaluable practical tool – this is 'rule deontology'.

Personal conviction as the decider or determinant is replaced by a group conviction leading to a mutually acceptable definition of duty. The group arrives at its concept of duty by discussion based on experience. The duties so defined usually extend beyond the minimum dictated by law – they incorporate the right and the good. Duty is formalised into a written ethical code, or code of conduct. No exceptions are sought by the professionals concerned, and none are given.

The ethics of consequences

Under this system, an action is judged by its outcome or consequences. The Greek word *teleos* means an end or a result, so this can also be called the 'teleological theory of ethics'. A third description is 'utilitarian ethics' – utility being another word for usefulness. An action is good if it is useful.

This theory feels more modern and liberal than Kantian ethics, but it dates back at least as far as Aristotle, who believed that the pursuit of happiness was a natural human condition. At the individual level, the ethics of consequences is a relatively simple matter of avoiding pain and acting in a way that brings pleasure and satisfaction – this idea is called hedonism.

Even at the personal level, the theory produces immediate problems – how do we judge actions that are pleasurable in the short term but damaging in the long run? An even greater difficulty is how to predict what consequences might result from a particular action. At what level of risk does a good action become a bad one? Motor racing and mountain climbing result in pleasure and satisfaction, but sometimes in death or crippling injury.

Utilitarianism is most closely associated with the work of Jeremy Bentham. For groups and societies he defined an ethical decision as one that produces the greatest good for the greatest number. If there is no good to be had, then the ethical choice is the one that produces the least harm.

Bentham's theories grew as a reaction to religious restriction and the reluctance of the governments of the day to repeal laws that had become antiquated and useless. He defined a bad law as that which had outlived its utility.

The ethics of consequences underpins a great deal of modern life. Preventative medicine aims to provide the greatest good for the greatest number, as does our legal system and democracy generally. Taxation and the resulting public expenditure on the NHS, education and welfare are justified by utilitarian ethics.

The greatest good for the greatest number is an ideal not a foolproof formula for ethical decision making. There are drawbacks and uncertainties:

- Good, happiness and satisfaction are difficult to define and usually impossible to measure. What produces most happiness – opera, cricket, clean streets or trees in the park? Who decides?

- Resources are always limited. In other words, there is never enough good or happiness to go around. Somebody has to decide priorities and compromises – who should do this? How should the rationing system work? This is a perpetual dilemma in healthcare at all levels. Who gets the liver transplant? What do you do on the ward if you have eight patients but only five clean pillows?

- Should the greatest good for the greatest number be imposed or voluntary? Parents are free to refuse immunisations for their children, but they will be sent to prison – eventually – if they do not pay their income taxes.

Act utilitarianism

Act utilitarianism is an individual weighing up the consequences of a proposed action, for themselves and for others. We all do this everyday, often without recognising the process. Arguably, act-based Kantian ethics is of little practical use, but its equivalent, working from a consideration of consequences, has value. It helps divert attention away from personal bias and focuses on concern for others.

General utilitarianism is an extension of considering the consequences of a one-off act or situation. It asks the question, 'What would happen if everybody did what I am planning to do?' Actions that seem ethical in isolation may then be revealed as unethical for society at large and therefore as unethical under all circumstances.

One person exceeding the speed limit because he or she is late for work may not have bad consequences, but if everybody did the same, there would be more fatal road accidents. Therefore, exceeding the speed limit is always unethical.

Rule utilitarianism

This application of the theory comes closest to what most people would regard as a common sense view of right and wrong and good and bad.

Some actions produce consequences that always or nearly always result in harm, unhappiness or damage, irrespective of context. The ethics of consequences seems to lead to an absolute definition of wrong and bad. Therefore, there must be rules and laws to prohibit this behaviour.

With a few illustrations, we can show again that there are no moral absolutes and that no single theory of ethics has all the answers:

Societies grade crimes and the punishments they impose on rule-breakers. Immoral or unethical behaviour is judged quantitatively and qualitatively. Stealing an apple is not as bad as stealing a car; genocide is far worse than manslaughter.

The worst crimes?

Almost without exception, and throughout history, the worst crimes have generally been agreed to be murder, rape, treason and violence towards children. Blasphemy and sedition can be seen as treason against the accepted state religion or belief. Rule-based utilitarian ethics does not give totally defensible solutions, even in the most extreme contexts.

- Life is not sacrosanct. Taking life might be considered justified in the context of abortion, euthanasia, self-defence, capital punishment, protection of the home or the homeland, a crime of passion or the unwillingness to act to preserve the life of a grossly deformed or incapacitated infant.

- Until relatively recently in the UK, marriage was taken to imply sexual consent, but rape within marriage is now a crime as bad, in theory, as rape by a stranger. Would you distinguish between the alleged rape of a nun and of a prostitute if you were a member of a jury?

- Treason is a crime defined by the established order or the military victor. When does a terrorist become a freedom fighter? What would you do if your home or country was invaded by a foreign army?

- Spare the rod and spoil the child was the traditional moral justification for corporal punishment at home, school and for young people at work. Would the world be a better place if parents, policemen and teachers were still allowed to inflict considerable pain on thoughtless or ill-disciplined teenagers? What is good and what is bad, judged purely by consequences?

Where do we go from here?

We started by defining ethics as an essential applied science, without which we could not resolve ethical dilemmas. The two major ethical theories seem to make matters worse because they do not lead directly to a set of rules. Kant and Bentham only seem to confuse the issue. If duty or consequences are a matter of debate, how can we ever distinguish between right and wrong or good and bad?

These questions have been asked many times before and there is a way ahead. A set of consistent principles that apply in all circumstances does not exist, but the relatively recent work of Jacques Thiroux (1980) is widely thought to be the closest we are likely to get. Thiroux's five principles of ethics are discussed next.

5 Thiroux's five principles of ethics

As always, we must use words carefully. The *Concise Oxford English Dictionary* (Eighth edition) says a **principle** is '**a fundamental truth or law used as the basis of reasoning or action**'. Thiroux's own definition is very similar. He describes the five principles as near absolutes or enduring ethical values.

Labels and descriptions

You can choose between straightforward names for the five principles or more complicated alternatives.

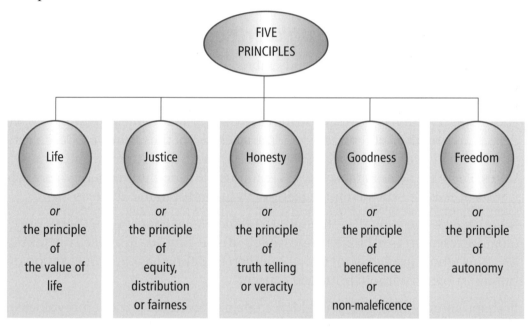

Life	Justice	Honesty	Goodness	Freedom
or	*or*	*or*	*or*	*or*
the principle of the value of life	the principle of equity, distribution or fairness	the principle of truth telling or veracity	the principle of beneficence or non-maleficence	the principle of autonomy

The principle of the value of life

Respect and reverence for life is the first ethical principle and it is central to ethical theory and morality. Thiroux believes, however, that respect for life also implies the acceptance of death and that reverence does not mean the preservation of life at all costs.

The concept of futility is long established in healthcare. At some stage, for some conditions, the continued striving to maintain life becomes futile or pointless. The ethics of consequences applies because the results of further treatment may be judged to cause more harm than good; or there may be no good decisions left.

The interpretation of the first principle has altered in the UK within the lifetime of most adults. Many religions hold that respect for life should be absolute, but in a secular society – one not controlled by religious belief – more tolerant attitudes become ethical and acceptable. Recognising the futility of continued treatment is not the ethical equivalent of actively choosing to end or shorten life. At the moment, in the UK, euthanasia is an illegal act, although it is permitted in some circumstances in other countries. Under UK law, a mentally competent adult may decline treatment at any time, even if the result of this refusal is certain to cause his or her death. Ethical codes have been devised to help define the point of futility. These also recognise consent and withdrawal of consent.

The biological and legal definitions of life, death and what is living do not always coincide, and the separation between the two widens as medicine advances. Once a child is born, there is no concept in UK law of a second-class life – a profoundly physically and intellectually disabled infant has the same rights as the most fit, powerful and wealthy adult.

Abortion and embryological research

Case studies involving abortion and embryological research are widely used in teaching ethics. Societies that we would all regard as civilised take dramatically different ethical stances on the abortion issue. In Russia, much of eastern Europe and Japan, abortion is routinely permitted for social and financial reasons and, by default, as a method of contraception. The teachings of the Church produce a very different set of values in much of southern Europe, South America and some US states. There are no moral absolutes. It is impossible to define precisely when a collection of cells becomes a human being with full indisputable rights to life.

If you accept the view that the right to life begins at conception, then embryological research is ethically impossible – discarding fertilised cells is taking life. This whole branch of medicine can then be defined as experimentation on human subjects without informed consent.

Perhaps Jeremy Bentham would have taken a positive view of embryological research. He might have seen some of the existing legal restrictions as bad or outdated law and argued that this new work produces the greatest good for the greatest number.

The principle of goodness

Through history and across societies, moral people have been defined as those that do good and resist evil. Goodness has been described as the ability to resist temptation or to inhibit behaviour that is bad even though it may be pleasurable or profitable. Bad people, by contrast, do not control impulses or desires, and they pursue their immediate satisfaction. Beneficence is an action that results in good consequences; maleficence results in bad consequences. Non-maleficence is the avoidance of actions with bad consequences.

Good and bad as concepts can be contained within a religious framework. The seven deadly sins of pride, covetousness, lust, anger, gluttony, envy and sloth are taken by many Christians as yielding to temptation and therefore as acts that offend God.

As with all morality, a strict code or set of laws seems to offer certainty – if it is unquestioned – but distinguishing bad from good need not be straightforward, obvious or derived from religious belief.

Non-maleficence

We can all be placed in situations where there are no good decisions left – when we have to choose between the lesser of two evils. These ethical dilemmas are an everyday, almost routine, fact of life in healthcare. It may not be possible to do good, but at the very least, a health professional must do no harm, or must act to reduce harm. This idea, called non-maleficence, is a universal ethical principle embodied in all ethical codes.

In many real-life situations, non-maleficence involves judgement and hence risk. Invasive major surgery could never be described as good, but it may be the only action available to reduce further harm. Much less dramatic choices are made every hour of every day in all hospitals. Most medical procedures produce discomfort; some, like anaesthesia and X-ray investigations carry a small but definite risk of harmful or even lethal consequences.

Parentalism

Non-maleficence is universally regarded as the first or minimum duty of parenthood. Parentalism flows directly from the ethical principle of goodness, but it also assumes an imbalance of knowledge and power: 'I'll smack my children if they play with matches – this is for their own good. I'm a better judge of good than they are.'

Parentalism is seen as good, but in most societies only within limits that are difficult to define. Indulging your children and giving in to all of their demands produces bad consequences, but so does locking them in cupboards for hours on end if they steal food.

Paternalism

Like parentalism, paternalism results from an imbalance of power and knowledge. It has several different definitions.

Taken literally, paternalism means rule by the father, and therefore the dominance of men over women and children. Nearly all traditional societies are or were paternalistic – men making decisions because of their greater physical power and aggression.

The concept of paternalism extends to medicine and medical ethics, but it need not involve male dominance. A 35-year-old female surgeon treating a 60-year-old man would be acting paternalistically if her thoughts and actions were based on ideas like 'doctor knows best' or if she used words like 'Don't worry about the detail – the operation is very complicated'.

In this instance, the principle of goodness is being wrongly applied. In a contest between paternalism and informed consent, informed consent must be the winner.

It may be impossible to avoid paternalism in the treatment of mentally ill or mentally incapacitated patients or clients. Legislation and the appropriate ethical codes acknowledge these difficulties.

In a third sense, paternalism is an issue in medical ethics because the upper reaches of the profession are still predominantly male. A male senior consultant should not automatically assume that he 'knows better than' a junior female nurse. The biopsychosocial model of healthcare suggests that nurses and others with frequent patient contact can make invaluable contributions to ethical decisions.

The principle of justice

Because there is never enough good to go around, what there is must be distributed justly or fairly. The principle of justice has practical relevance throughout the health sector. Like the principle of the value of life, related ethical decisions are becoming more difficult as the costs of healthcare escalate.

The NHS was founded on the principle of justice and the ethics of consequences. It is designed to provide treatment free at the point of use regardless of income, wealth or status. The tax system that pays for the NHS follows from the same ethical principle.

The term 'post-code lottery' means an unacceptable difference in medical provision or standards according to location or region. Because of the links between regionality, patterns of disease and class, a post-code lottery often becomes an over-allocation of healthcare resources to the fortunate and the relative deprivation of the less well off.

A strict enforcement of the principle of justice would lead directly to the prohibition of private healthcare – if the principle of freedom was ignored. More of this later.

Just and therefore ethical decisions do not have to concern budgets of billions or major political arguments. In most practical situations, the scarcest resource is professional time and manpower. A nurse behaves ethically if he or she allocates time according to need. This clearly needs personal judgement and implies the risk of a wrong or inappropriate decision.

Justice in theory and justice in practice are difficult or perhaps impossible to reconcile if a wider or world perspective is substituted for local situations and decisions. Taking a global view, the 'country lottery' results in much more harm than the UK's post-code lottery. A child born in Eritrea or the back streets of Haiti is treated much less fairly than one from Plymouth or Huddersfield.

The principle of honesty

Ethics without communication is impossible and communication is much more than words and language; communication cannot be sustained without honesty and truthfulness. This principle is the most difficult to maintain and the one that often produces the starkest ethical dilemmas – 'Tell me nurse, am I going to die?'

Again, attitudes have altered. Withholding the diagnosis of a terminal illness used to be commonplace, but in most cases this would now be seen as unethical. Many patients say they can cope with bad news, but not with uncertainty and not with deception.

Lack of honesty can only be ethical if telling the truth does more harm than not doing so. Paternalism is always involved, but who is being protected?

Three possibilities

The patient or client may be judged not capable of accepting a diagnosis. Traditionally, this kind of decision was justified with expressions like 'let him spend the time he has left in peace and comfort'.

Relatives and the family of a patient sometimes ask that he or she 'should not be told'. A carer accepting this wish may be protecting the family rather than the patient.

A doctor or nurse delivering bad or very bad news is inevitably volunteering for stress, difficult questions and heartbreaking conversations. Personal fears, anxieties and insecurities can surface. Lack of honesty offers protection to the health professional.

A decision not to be truthful sets up a contest between doing good by withholding bad news and the patient's right to know. Avoiding the truth may imply lack of respect for the client.

Truth delivered at the wrong time, in the wrong circumstances or with inappropriate language can never be ethical. It is also very unlikely that a direct lie in response to a calm rational question put by a client or patient can be ethical. Delivering false hope or optimism is always unethical.

We have concentrated on the most difficult ethical dilemmas of all – those concerning terminal diagnoses. In most other circumstances, lack of honesty is always unethical. Truth telling may involve probabilities rather than certainties – 'This operation has an 85% success rate'; 'There is a 25% chance that your child will be born with cystic fibrosis.'

Information cannot be truthfully delivered if it is wrapped up in impenetrable medical jargon. The ethics of honesty also includes the duty to explain and translate.

The principle of freedom

Some philosophers argue that there are only four ethical principles because the fifth, that of autonomy or personal freedom is limited by the first four. In real life, the distinction makes little difference. People are free to act in any way they please, provided they respect life, try to do good, act justly and are truthful.

UK law restricts the autonomy of children and some adults who are not judged competent to handle their own affairs. Societies value autonomy very highly. Law-breakers are punished by imprisonment – the greater the crime, the longer autonomy is forfeited.

Medical procedures and therapies lead to a temporary loss of autonomy. This becomes permanent in some cases. The word 'institutionalised' is used to describe the acceptance or even the welcoming of reduced personal freedom – hospitals, nursing homes and prisons are all institutions.

In healthcare, ethical actions are those that maximise the autonomy of patients and clients, while recognising that complete autonomy may not be possible. Informed consent and its withdrawal is based on the principle of personal freedom. Treatment may not be imposed; options, choices and consequences have to be explained.

The traditional regimented hospital ward of the past limited patient autonomy largely for the benefit of doctors and nursing staff. Visiting hours were restricted, there was a fixed timetable for waking, eating and sleeping; inconvenient behaviour was discouraged.

Autonomy increases the workload – for nurses in particular – but within acceptable limits it must be accommodated or encouraged. Almost all patients are capable of some autonomy, deciding what to wear and when to drink, for instance.

6 Ethical codes

Traditionally, a professional was a self-employed person paid via a variable fee structure rather than as an employee on a fixed salary. Many barristers, solicitors and architects are still professionals using this definition – as were the majority of doctors before the NHS.

In its more usual modern meaning, a profession is defined by its characteristics.

Professions

A profession is different from a job or an occupation because:

- Its members have a body of knowledge and experience not possessed or available to the general public.

- The group has a monopoly. Non-members are not allowed to practise.

- Membership is restricted to those with appropriate education, experience and training.

- The group decides who may be admitted, how members should be disciplined (if need be) and, in some circumstances, who should no longer be allowed to practise.

Because professions have specialist knowledge and power, professionals can do harm as well as good. Good is defined by reference to a set of rules devised by the professional group. These rules or ethical codes go beyond what is right or legal. Entry to the profession is conditional on acceptance of the code.

Statutory organisations

All professions have ethical codes or codes of conduct of one sort or another. Medicine and healthcare in the UK are rigidly controlled by a number of statutory and professional organisations.

Statutory organisations are government-funded and largely concerned with legislation, its enforcement, amendment and development. The General Medical Council (GMC), for example, is a statutory body. It was formed in 1858 and is responsible ultimately to parliament. There are about 25 health-related statutory bodies, and reform in the NHS or the law often creates new organisations or merges existing ones.

Professional and voluntary organisations

Voluntary organisations represent the full range of specialisations within medicine and healthcare in the UK. These are generally described as the Royal Colleges and Faculties. They are responsible for training, education, examinations, and the writing and enforcement of ethical codes. The Royal Colleges and Faculties also offer protection and advice to their members in the same way as more conventional trades unions. The table lists the larger voluntary organisations.

The Royal Colleges of:

Anaesthetists	Psychiatrists
General practitioners	Radiologists
Obstetricians and gynaecologists	Surgeons
Ophthalmologists	Midwives
Pathologists	Nursing
Paediatrics and childcare	Speech and language therapy
Physicians	

Other organisations:

Faculty of Occupational Medicine	British Medical Association
Faculty of Pharmaceutical Medicine	Royal Pharmaceutical Society
Faculty of Public Health Medicine	Medical Defence Union
Chartered Society of Physiotherapy	Medical Protection Society

The code of professional conduct for nursing and midwifery

As an example of ethics in action, we will look at the code of professional conduct published by the Nursing & Midwifery Council in April 2002. This came into effect on 1 June 2002.

From start to finish, the code is written in straightforward, clear, non-technical English. The introduction states its purpose and the duties and responsibilities of registered nurses and midwives. In summary:

- The code defines the standards of conduct required of registered professionals and makes these standards known to the public, employers and other professions.

- A registered nurse or midwife must protect and support the health of individual patients and clients, and that of the wider community.

- A registered nurse or midwife must act in a way that justifies public trust and confidence and must uphold and enhance the reputation of the profession.

- Registered practitioners are personally accountable. This means they are answerable for their actions and omissions, regardless of advice or direction given by other professionals.

- A registered professional has a duty of care to patients and clients.

- Registered nurses and midwives must adhere to the laws of the country in which they are practising.

Shared values

At the outset, the code lists seven values that are shared by all UK regulatory bodies and organisations in healthcare. In caring for patients and clients, health professionals must:

1 Respect the patient or client as an individual.

2 Obtain consent before any treatment or care is given.

3 Protect confidential information.

4 Cooperate with other team members.

5 Maintain professional knowledge and competence.

6 Be trustworthy.

7 Act to identify and minimise risk to patients and clients.

As a class exercise, you may be asked to consider and discuss this or a similar ethical code point by point and line by line. Here we highlight the most important obligations that the code places on nurses and midwives.

Respect for the patient or client as an individual

Patients and clients are part of a team along with carers and practitioners, not a thing apart or an object of study. Wherever possible, the nurse or midwife should meet the patient's preferences for care and treatment.

The nurse or midwife must promote and protect health regardless of an individual's ability, race, sexuality, economic status, lifestyle, religion or lack of religion, and political beliefs.

Individuals and groups must be helped to gain access to health services, social care, information and support relevant to their needs.

The code allows conscientious objections on the part of the practitioner, but this must be reported to the relevant person or authority and care continued until alternative arrangements are made.

Informed consent

This is the longest and most detailed section of the code. It recognises consent as a potentially difficult issue and obliges the nurse or midwife to seek the guidance of colleagues, and legal advice, in some situations.

All patients have the right to receive accurate, truthful and easily understood information about their condition, but the wish not to be told or the inability to receive information must also be respected or acknowledged.

Individuals have the right to refuse treatment, even where refusal may result in harm or death to themselves or a foetus. In some circumstances, this right can be removed or limited by a court order. Guidance and legal advice may be required.

Consent must be given voluntarily and on an informed basis by a legally competent person. All patients and clients should be assumed to be legally competent unless assessed otherwise by a suitably qualified practitioner.

Those who are legally competent may give consent in writing, orally or by cooperation. They may also refuse consent. All conversations and discussions regarding consent must be documented in the patient's healthcare records.

Consent and legal competence

When patients are no longer legally competent and have therefore lost the capacity to consent to or refuse treatment:

- Preferences indicated in an advance statement, sometimes called a living will, must be respected – provided that these decisions are clearly applicable to the current circumstances and there is no reason to believe the patient or client has changed his or her mind.

- If there is no advance statement, the patient's wishes – if known – should be taken into account.

- If these wishes are not known, practitioners must act in the patient's or client's best interests.

No one has the right to give consent on behalf of another competent adult.
The principles of consent apply equally to sufferers from mental illness, but the process of obtaining or confirming consent may involve a psychiatrist and those close to the patient or client. Nurses and midwives caring for those detained under the Mental Health Acts must be aware of the circumstances and safeguards needed before treatment can be given without consent.

In emergencies where treatment is necessary to preserve life, care may be provided without consent if the patient or client is unable to give it – provided the client's best interest can be demonstrated.

Consent and children

Parental responsibility and involvement in consent for the care and treatment of children is usually necessary, but the guiding principle is the degree of understanding possessed by the child – not chronological age. If a child is under 16 in England and Wales, 12 in Scotland or 17 in Northern Ireland, local protocols may apply and legal advice should normally be sought.

Teamwork and cooperation

The healthcare team is very widely defined. It includes the patient or client, their family, informal carers, health and social-care professionals in the NHS, their equivalents in the private sector and the relevant voluntary organisations.

Nurses and midwives are expected to cooperate with and respect the skills and contributions of all members of the team. Knowledge, skill and expertise must be shared for the benefit of the patient or client. Communication between members of the team should be efficient and again in the patient's best interest.

Healthcare records are a vital communication tool. They must be an accurate account of treatment, care, planning and delivery. The nurse or midwife is personally accountable for inaccuracies and omissions. Records must be consecutive and, wherever possible, completed as soon as possible after the event concerned.

Nurses and midwives may delegate some aspects of care to non-professionals but only in the client's best interests. A registered professional remains accountable for the work delegated and must ensure appropriate supervision and support.

Nurses and midwives have a duty to cooperate with internal and external investigations.

Confidentiality

Patient and client information is confidential and must only be used for the purposes for which it was given. Patients and clients must be made aware that some confidential information may be shared with other professionals. Information must be protected from improper disclosure at all times.

Clients' wishes regarding the sharing of information with their families must be respected. Disclosure of information to others outside the team must involve client or patient consent unless:

- Disclosure is in the public interest or is essential to protect the patient or another from the risk of significant harm.

- It is required by law or by order of court.

- Where there is an issue of child protection. In these cases, action at all times must be in accordance with national and local policies.

Maintaining knowledge and competence

Nurses and midwives should ensure that their knowledge and skills are constantly updated. There must be a commitment to lifelong learning and regular formal activities that develop competence and performance.

The limits to professional competence must be recognised and not exceeded. Procedures and practice beyond these limits, or outside the appropriate area of registration, must involve help and supervision from a competent practitioner.

Registered nurses and midwives have a duty to assist students of nursing and midwifery to develop their competence.

There is a responsibility to deliver care based on current evidence, best practice and, where applicable, validated research.

Trust, character and financial exploitation

Nurses and midwives must behave in a way that upholds the reputation of the profession. Disreputable behaviour, even if it is not directly connected with the health sector or professional practice, may result in withdrawal of registration.

Professional status must not be used for commercial gain. Any financial interest in a company or organisation providing goods or services to the health sector must be registered and declared. Products and services must never be endorsed or recommended if personal financial advantage might result. A specific product or service may, however, be recommended, based on freely available, properly documented evidence.

Health professionals must refuse gifts, favours or hospitality that might now, or in the future, be taken as an attempt to secure preferential treatment.

Health professionals must not ask for or accept loans from patients, clients, their relatives or friends.

Risk identification

Health professionals have a duty to promote environments that encourage and support safe, therapeutic and ethical practice.

A timely and rapid response may be needed to reduce the risk to patients and clients of actions taken by those who may not be fit to practise for reasons of conduct, health or competence.

Where a remedy is not immediately available, a written report must be made to a person with sufficient authority to effect a remedy.

When working as a manager, with accountability for others, there are duties towards patients, clients, the organisation and the wider community. In conflict situations, the interests of patients and clients must come first.

In emergencies, inside or outside the workplace, health professionals have a duty to provide the help and support that might reasonably be expected from an individual possessing their knowledge, skills and abilities.

Theories, principles and rules

We have now outlined the series of steps that have produced one particular ethical code, starting with theories that were first proposed very many years ago. This process is ongoing and it is applied in all aspects of all professions. The greater the possible consequences of a professional decision, the greater the need for guidance and a set of rules. Starting with Thiroux's five principles, all professions have put together ethical codes. These have many features in common – above all that a professional must always act in the best interests of his or her patient, client or customer.

Some ethical codes have been devised to guide decisions in particular circumstances and situations. These impose an extra layer of duties and responsibilities on top of general codes of conduct. Specific codes are invaluable where the law is ambiguous, untested or absent.

For instance:

- Perhaps the most difficult ethical decisions concern defining the point of futility and hence the withholding or withdrawal of life-prolonging treatment.

- Medical and healthcare research is closely controlled by national and local ethics committees. These bodies, not the researchers themselves, make final ethical decisions.

- There are detailed ethical codes governing the care and treatment of the mentally ill. Here the central issues are informed consent and the dangers of paternalism.

- The diagnosis of HIV/AIDS and other sexually transmitted diseases raises difficult issues of confidentiality and public protection.

- The law in England and Wales changed in 1985. In the so-called *Gillick* case (*Gillick* v *West Norfolk and Wisbech Area Health Authority* [1985] 3 All ER 402 (HL)), the House of Lords ruled that people under the age of 16 who are fully able to understand a proposed treatment and its implications, may give consent regardless of age.

The *Gillick* decision is open to different interpretations, in particular if the wishes of children and their parents differ or if the child's rights to confidentiality are uncertain.

7 Legal issues and client rights

A complete description of the UK legal system's influence on medical and healthcare decision making is clearly beyond the scope of this unit. However, a general understanding of the relationships between the law, ethical codes and ethical choices is essential background for health professionals.

The UK has three legal systems, not one. The law differs in England and Wales, in Scotland and in Northern Ireland. Some of these differences, in particular between English and Scottish law, are directly relevant to medicine and healthcare. EU legislation also regulates some aspects of healthcare in the UK.

Nothing described or explained in this topic should be construed as legal advice or opinion.

Criminal and civil law

The law in the UK is divided into criminal law and civil law. Criminal law is concerned with the rules laid down by the state; civil law regulates relationships and transactions between citizens. Civil law is the main area that affects and controls the interaction of patients, clients and professionals in the health sector.

A tort is a breach of duty that may result in a liability for damages. Tort law is the basis for most negligence claims. In England and Wales, the plaintiff must show that a duty of care existed, that this duty was breached and that damage followed as a direct consequence.

The burden of proof rests with the allegedly injured party in negligence cases. Civil courts may decide on the balance of probabilities, but English criminal justice requires proof beyond reasonable doubt. This system involves considerable financial risks for most complainants but the introduction of no win no fee litigation has increased the number of negligence claims.

The sources of law

Primary legislation is that which is made and approved by parliament. New laws may be introduced and old ones repealed or amended. Some primary legislation also originates from the European Union.

Secondary legislation is law made by bodies empowered by parliament.

Common law or case law is made by custom or by precedent. In essence, judges may interpret law in given situations and these decisions hold until or unless a new or overriding precedent takes its place.

The courts

The UK's court structure has developed over centuries. Its detail is bewilderingly complicated and would need many hundreds of pages for a full explanation. For this unit, you only need an outline of the main concepts:

- The court structure differs in England, Wales, Scotland and Northern Ireland.

- Civil and criminal cases are tried in different kinds of courts.

- The system is hierarchical. There is a progressive appeal procedure from lower to higher courts.

- Magistrates', Crown and County Courts are widely spread around the country. The High Court and the Court of Appeal are based in London.

- The High Court has three specialist divisions.

- The final court of appeal for the UK is presently the House of Lords, although this system may alter in the foreseeable future. Some exceptional cases are referred to the European Court of Justice, which decides matters of European law. Appeals to the House of Lords are about the meaning of law rather than the evidence of a particular case.

- The decision to prosecute in most English criminal cases is made by the Crown Prosecution Service.

- Tribunals are specialist organisations set up to resolve disputes and hear appeals against decisions made by bodies with powers delegated from parliament. The Mental Health Review Tribunal, for example, hears appeals from patients compulsorily detained under the Mental Health Acts. Amongst other things it can discharge patients, delay their return to the community or recommend transfers to different hospitals.

- In England and Wales, Coroners' Courts investigate violent and unnatural deaths or sudden deaths where the cause is unknown. A local coroner is usually a senior lawyer or a doctor. Cases may be presented to coroners by the police, doctors, a number of other authorities or by members of the public. A coroner may order a post-mortem examination to establish a cause of death rather than hold an inquest in court.

The diagrams summarise the criminal and civil court structures in England and Wales. Much detail is omitted; they show only the most important functions and interrelationships.

The English criminal court structure

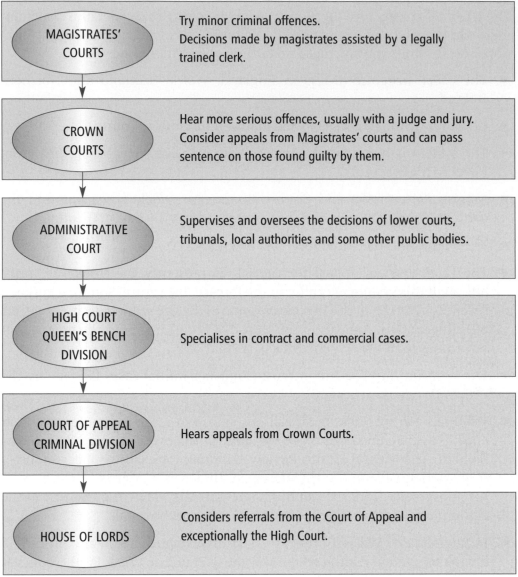

MAGISTRATES' COURTS	Try minor criminal offences. Decisions made by magistrates assisted by a legally trained clerk.
CROWN COURTS	Hear more serious offences, usually with a judge and jury. Consider appeals from Magistrates' courts and can pass sentence on those found guilty by them.
ADMINISTRATIVE COURT	Supervises and oversees the decisions of lower courts, tribunals, local authorities and some other public bodies.
HIGH COURT QUEEN'S BENCH DIVISION	Specialises in contract and commercial cases.
COURT OF APPEAL CRIMINAL DIVISION	Hears appeals from Crown Courts.
HOUSE OF LORDS	Considers referrals from the Court of Appeal and exceptionally the High Court.

Source: The Department for Constitutional Affairs

Client rights – the theory

Questions of rights, responsibilities and duties have been a major and general area of research. These are issues for all interrelationships amongst people in modern societies, they are not confined to the health sector.

Fordham (1992) suggested that rights were especially concerned with freedom and justice and that they always imply corresponding duties – you cannot have one without the other. Fordham also said that rights could be divided into positive or subsistence rights, and negative or option rights.

The English civil court structure

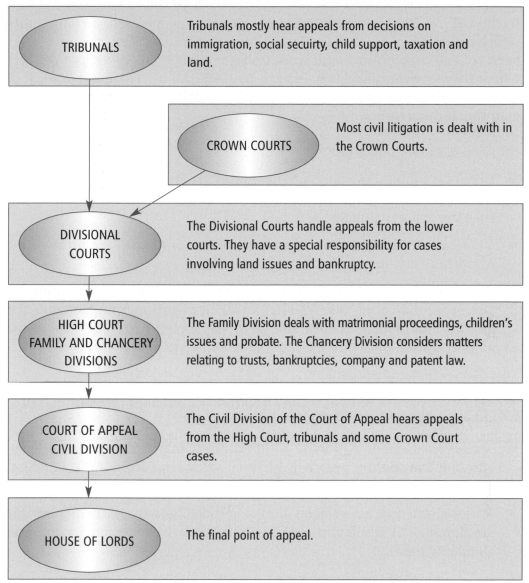

TRIBUNALS — Tribunals mostly hear appeals from decisions on immigration, social secuirty, child support, taxation and land.

CROWN COURTS — Most civil litigation is dealt with in the Crown Courts.

DIVISIONAL COURTS — The Divisional Courts handle appeals from the lower courts. They have a special responsibility for cases involving land issues and bankruptcy.

HIGH COURT FAMILY AND CHANCERY DIVISIONS — The Family Division deals with matrimonial proceedings, children's issues and probate. The Chancery Division considers matters relating to trusts, bankruptcies, company and patent law.

COURT OF APPEAL CIVIL DIVISION — The Civil Division of the Court of Appeal hears appeals from the High Court, tribunals and some Crown Court cases.

HOUSE OF LORDS — The final point of appeal.

Source: The Department of Constitutional Affairs

Negative and positive rights

Negative rights are the rights to be free from interference. They are based on the principle of autonomy and lead directly to the right of informed consent in healthcare. These are also called option rights because they allow individual choice and freedom.

Positive rights are the rights to receive food, clothing, shelter, healthcare and education – at the public expense if need be. These are the rights to subsist or exist. Not all societies guarantee subsistence rights.

Nurses as guardians of human rights

In the UK, we have become used to the idea that people have certain innate rights, irrespective of social, legal or political institutions. This has not always been so, and many nurses still work under undemocratic or violent regimes where they face formidable challenges. In 1983, the International Council of Nurses (ICN) produced a statement that tried to define the nurse's role in safeguarding human rights.

The rights of those in need of care:

- Everyone should have access to healthcare, regardless of financial, political, geographic or religious considerations. The nurse should seek to ensure such impartial treatment.

- Nurses must ensure that adequate treatment is provided – within available resources – and in accord with nursing ethics.

- A patient or prisoner has the right to refuse to eat or to refuse treatments. The nurse may need to verify that a patient or prisoner understands the implications of their actions, but he or she should not participate in the administration of food or medications to such patients.

The rights and duties of nurses:

- Action and lack of action can have a detrimental effect. Nurses are accountable for both.

- Nurses have a right to practise within the code of ethics and nursing legislation of the country involved. Personal safety and freedom from abuse, threats or intimidation are the rights of every nurse.

- National nursing associations have a responsibility to participate in the development of health and social legislation relative to patients' rights and all related topics.

- It is a duty to obtain the informed consent of patients' relatives to having research done on them as part of treatments. Such informed consent is a patient's right and must be ensured.

Patient and client rights under the NHS

UK society no longer automatically accepts paternalism from those in positions of power and authority. For instance, the general assumption that doctors, policemen and judges always know best has been replaced by increasing demands for greater autonomy and personal freedom. The NHS has been in the front line of this dramatic behavioural and attitudinal shift. There is increasing focus on the rights of patients and clients as citizens and consumers.

In 1991, the then Conservative government published the NHS Patient's Charter – a detailed policy statement of rights and expectations. This was abolished in 2000 and replaced with another formal statement of patients' rights. This forms part of the present government's 10-year reform plan for the NHS.

The full text of the current statement is available on the NHS website. Here we outline and summarise its main provisions.

Patients' rights	Limitations to these rights
For UK residents – to be registered with a GP	A GP may refuse to register a patient without giving reasons. There is no right to choose a particular GP
Immediate emergency treatment from a GP, even if not registered with them	
Treatment outside surgery hours	'Out of hours' care can be provided, by locums, GPs or a telephone service. There is no right to home visits
Appropriate medication on prescription but no prescription charge for emergency treatment	The GP decides what is appropriate
	There is no automatic right to a second opinion from another GP or specialist
Basic GP treatment is free	Overseas visitors may be charged. Some non-essential treatments may have to be paid for
A patient can change GP at any time without giving a reason	GPs can remove patients from their register without reason. Violent behaviour that has been reported to the police is grounds for immediate delisting
Access to free confidential medical advice from experienced nurses by telephone 24 hours a day – the NHS Direct service	Currently only available in England and Wales. The Scottish equivalent, NHS24, is planned for the end of 2004
To receive maternity services and hospital ante-natal care, and to give birth at home	Services may be provided by midwives, GPs or hospital ante-natal care, and specialists according to medical need and local conditions
To receive free hospital treatment in emergencies and a free, prompt ambulance service	Non-emergency treatment is not available without referral by a GP. There are exceptions for some specialist clinics
Violent or abusive patients suffering from severe mental health problems or life-threatening conditions will not be refused hospital treatment	In other circumstances, violent and abusive patients may be refused treatment. The decision to refuse is made by the local NHS trust
There is a right to see a doctor competent to deal with the condition concerned	There is no right to be treated by any particular doctor, consultant or specialist

▶

Patients' rights	Limitations to these rights
To receive hospital treatment or a first out-patient appointment within published waiting-time standards	Other than in emergencies, there is no right to immediate hospital treatment. Medical need determines priorities, not 'first come, first served'
To be assessed immediately on admission to an accident and emergency department	Casualty 'waiting times' are subject to published standards, but there is no right to immediate or prompt treatment
If an operation is cancelled, an alternative date should be offered	Timings and priorities for operations are decided on medical need within available resources
	Nobody has the automatic right to visit a patient in hospital
	There is no right to be cared for in a single-sex ward
If a patient dies in hospital, his or her relatives and GP must be informed as soon as possible	
There is a general right not to be examined or treated without consent. Information concerning the nature, consequences and risks of the treatment must be given. Consent for an initial procedure does not imply consent for further treatment	Treatment without consent may be given to: (i) Carriers or sufferers of notifiable diseases (ii) In some cases, those detained under the Mental Health Acts (iii) People in life-threatening situations who are unconscious (iv) A child who is a ward of court, subject to court approval (v) A child, if there is parental consent Consent does not have to be given in writing
In England and Wales, a young person over 16 but under 18 can give consent without parental involvement	A young person can be overruled by court order
In England and Wales, a child under 16 can give consent, provided he or she is judged capable of understanding the treatment and its consequences	Capability is judged case by case on its individual merits. There is no general test
There is an absolute right, for competent people, not to have to take part in experimentation, research or teaching. No one can consent to research being carried out on another person	Parents may consent to their children under 16 being the subjects of experimentation, research and teaching – provided the child is not judged capable of consent

Patients' rights	Limitations to these rights
Any treatment or procedure can be refused	There is no right to a treatment that a doctor or specialist thinks inappropriate
	Parents who refuse consent for their children to have urgent or life-saving treatment may be overruled by a doctor and may be prosecuted for neglect

Rights to confidentiality

The keeping of accurate, complete and fully updated reports and health records is part of the ethical code of all branches of the health sector and all of its specialist professional groups. Without documentation, teamwork would be impossible and the risks of failing to treat or of mistreating would rapidly become intolerable. The list of formally stated NHS patients' rights includes:

- The right to see most health records held about you, subject to certain safeguards.

- The right to know who has access to your medical records.

- The right that your medical information should be kept confidential and not released to people not involved in your medical care without your consent. Relatives have no rights to see your medical records.

Rights to confidentiality generally in the UK are guaranteed by law as well as by ethical codes.

The Data Protection Act 1998

The Data Protection Act 1998 updated and amended previous legislation made in 1984. The Act places responsibilities on data controllers (people or organisations that collect, process or store information), and it protects data subjects (the people described or identified by the information). In the health sector, data subjects are patients or clients; data controllers are organisations like NHS trusts or, in theory, any health professional.

The 1998, a new legal definition of sensitive personal data was introduced. This is information concerning:

- Racial or ethnic origin.

- Political opinion.

- Religious or spiritual belief.

- Membership of a trades union.

- Physical or mental health condition.

- Sexual history.

- Records of alleged or actual criminal activity or sentencing.

Medical records count as sensitive personal data under the 1998 Act.

Eight sections

The Data Protection Act can be divided into eight sections or eight different obligations that the data controller must meet. Most of these are directly relevant to health records.

1   Sensitive personal data must be processed fairly, lawfully and with the subject's consent. Consent is not required if the data controller has a legal obligation to process employee information – for example, to calculate tax and National Insurance payments. Exceptions to consent are also lawful in the vital interests of the subject or another person – for instance in accidents and emergencies. Government, acting through the appropriate minister, may also examine sensitive personal data in monitoring some kinds of equal opportunities legislation.

2   Sensitive personal data may be obtained only for one or more specified and legal purposes. It must not be further processed in any way incompatible with the specified purpose(s). The specified purpose must be notified to the data subject or to the Data Protection Commissioner.

3   Sensitive personal data must be adequate, relevant and not excessive in relation to the purpose(s) for which it is processed.

4   Sensitive personal data must be accurate and kept up to date.

5   Personal data processed for any purpose(s) must not be kept for any longer than is necessary.

6   A data subject may ask to be given details of their data. A fee is payable, the request must be written and the data controller has 40 days to comply. The information provided must include the purpose(s) for which it is being processed, to whom it is disclosed and the name of the organisation that actually does the processing.

7   Precautions must be taken to ensure that data is properly processed and is protected from loss, damage, distortion or corruption.

8   Data must not be transferred to countries outside the European Union unless that country has legislation offering the same rights and protections as the UK Act.

Chapter 5
Interpersonal skills

National unit specification
These are the topics you will be studying for this unit.

1 Group dynamics

2 Verbal and non-verbal communication

3 Communication – psychology and sociology

4 Reflective listening

5 Private and professional confidentiality

There are significant overlaps between this and several other units. Communication as a core skill is usually taught in the early weeks of the course. *Interpersonal skills* is one of the specialist subjects that make up the nursing, midwifery and health professions pathways.

Communication in the health sector often involves ethical choices and ethical decisions. You should read or reread *Introduction to ethics* before you begin this unit.

1 Group dynamics

Given an unlimited supply of money and qualified staff, it would be possible to organise an Access course as a series of one-to-one lectures. There would never be more than two in a class – one student and one lecturer. Access does not work like that, but not just for financial reasons.

A group cannot work together unless its members communicate effectively. We begin to learn interpersonal skills in a family. These grow as we become members of many different groups – at school, then at work, and in our leisure time.

As a health professional, the ability to communicate with patients, clients, their families and your colleagues is an essential skill.

There are no written exams for this unit. Your skills will be continually assessed by the contributions you make to class discussions, in role play and in case studies and scenarios. Part of your work will be videoed and some exercises will involve smaller groups rather than the whole class.

Group formation and development

Few groups are permanent and with a fixed membership. You will, for instance, keep in touch with some but not all of your classmates when the course finishes. Another group of students will be sitting in your chairs next year.

Groups usually have a life cycle with five stages:

- Formation: You did not choose your classmates and you start the course as strangers. In the beginning, there is no group identity or cohesion. The first concern is to establish personal identity. Early impressions are based on body language and non-verbal signals more than spoken communication.

- Bargaining and negotiation: This is often a stressful but brief period. Differences in ambitions and personality are identified. Degrees of distance or intimacy are negotiated. Pairs and trios begin to form and verbal communication becomes more important.

- Norming: The group works out a set of rules, standards or norms. Some behaviour is encouraged; some is more or less prohibited. Larger groups form as pairs and trios recognise common interests and attitudes. The group's norms may or may not be the same as those imposed from outside.

  Rules and standards are not debated or documented. There is no vote taking – a majority decision emerges by constant interaction and communication.

- Clumping and splitting: The majority view of psychologists and sociologists is that the most effective groups have more than five but fewer than

15 members, and that 10 is roughly the optimum number. Very large organisations work because smaller groups cooperate.

Typically, a class of 15 can become one group or about three. There is constant clumping and splitting between sub-groups. The most cohesive classes sort out their sub-groups in the first weeks. Constant admission, rejection and reshuffling makes for conflict.

- Performing: Group norms and standards are reinforced by behaviour that is seen as appropriate and productive.

Groups tend to last through the course unless external conditions change significantly. Late entrants and early leavers can trigger another cycle of formation and development.

Empathy and sympathy

These definitions are taken from the *Concise Oxford Dictionary* (Eighth edition):

Sympathy – the state of being simultaneously affected by the same feeling as another person; sharing an emotion with another.

Empathy – the power of identifying oneself mentally with, and so fully understanding, another person.

Sympathy may be learned or it might be innate. Wherever it comes from, sympathy is one of the basic human emotions. People who cannot show sympathy are rare. Groups who share attitudes, experiences, values and backgrounds have few problems showing sympathy to one another.

On day one of week one, an Access class starts with a level of mutual sympathy, if only because everybody has arrived at a particular point at the same time. However, this may be no more developed than that of a dozen people waiting in a bus queue. If sympathy was all there was, then no disparate group of more than say three or four could come together to make a coherent, mutually supportive unit.

Empathy is almost certainly not innate – it has to be learned and it has to be practised. Too much sympathy and not enough empathy reduces performance. Health professionals need to learn how to handle constant stress. Burn-out and exhaustion happen when health workers continually personalise the fears and doubts of their clients day after day, week after week.

Professional empathy is in the best interests of client and carer. Ethical codes often prohibit the treatment of close friends and relatives. A surgeon would not usually operate on his or her partner or child because sympathy would cloud empathy.

Rapport

Using the *Concise Oxford English Dictionary* again, this defines **rapport** as '**a relationship or communication, in particular when useful and harmonious**'.

Rapport (pronounced 'rapp-ore') is difficult to pin down in English. This is why we borrowed the word from the French. Rapport is a combination of empathy, courtesy, respect and flexibility. It does not happen by accident or without effort.

A safe environment

Respect for difference is at the centre of a safe environment. A cohesive productive group has many norms or rules in common. To promote a safe environment, group members should:

- Acknowledge that personal beliefs and values differ.
- Not 'get defensive' when questioned.
- Remain flexible in attitude.
- Not try to dominate or remain withdrawn and isolated.
- Express feelings as well as facts.
- Recognise all ideas as worth discussion.
- Not blame or accuse, and use moderate or mutually acceptable language. Raised voices are counterproductive.
- Focus on areas of agreement, not disputes and differences – but remember that not all disagreements can be resolved.

Every member of every group breaks at least one of these rules every day. Perfection is impossible but targets should remain.

Assertive behaviour

Like criticism, the phrase 'assertive behaviour' has negative associations. It should not – assertive behaviour encourages rapport and leads to good communication. Assertive behaviour is very different from aggression.

Assertive behaviour gives people the right to:

- Make mistakes and change opinions.
- Not understand or know something.
- Feel and express emotions.
- Refuse demands made by others.
- Judge their actions and take the consequences.

Assertive behaviour allows open, honest and direct communication.

My views are worth little.
I cannot contribute very much.
I will do everything to avoid conflict.
I will agree with the majority or dominant view.

My views are important, but so are everyone else's.
I can usually make a contribution.
I will speak up for myself.
I will not bully, or be bullied.

My views are very important.
I have a great deal to offer.
Other people's opinions can be ignored.
People will accept my view if I am sufficiently dominant and aggressive.
Conflict is normal and inevitable.

Assertive people are not manipulative. Passive or aggressive behaviour always means 'playing one group off against another'. It follows that assertive behaviour is low risk and sustainable.

Role play

Empathy can be taught. Role play comes as light-hearted relief in the middle of a busy day, but it is also an effective and powerful teaching technique. Typically, a small group of students is asked to act out a real-life situation while the rest of the class observes and takes notes. Then the exercise repeats until everybody has been both watcher and player.

No acting skills are required. There are no scripts, costumes, theatrical makeup or props. The point of role play is to practise 'thinking yourself into somebody else's head'. This is a good practical definition of what empathy is all about.

Discussion groups

A discussion is communication between two or more people. It can take many forms.

CHAT OR CONVERSATION	Brief, informal, unsupervised. No agenda.
SMALL GROUP DISCUSSION	Longer, may be more structured with an agenda or fixed purpose. No supervision, typically three to six members.
WHOLE CLASS DISCUSSION	Whole class involved, time-limited, stated purpose, written summary and notes often required.
SUPERVISED WHOLE CLASS DISCUSSION	As above, but with a lecturer or student in the chair or in charge.
SEMINAR	Discussion group devoted to a pre-stated issue. Time-limited, written summaries needed.
FORMAL DEBATE	The most formal discussion. Speakers for and against a motion. Strict rules enforced by the chair. Vote taken, majority decision results.

2 Verbal and non-verbal communication

The central point of this unit is to show that communication is far more complicated than is commonly recognised. An understanding of these complications is important in all working and social situations – it is essential knowledge in the health professions.

Healthcare is about teamwork, and professional practice often involves communication and interaction in larger groups. However, most of the rest of this topic discusses interpersonal skills in smaller groups – typically one or two carers and a single patient or client.

A simplistic communication model

The diagram shows the simplest possible model of communication between a patient and a carer.

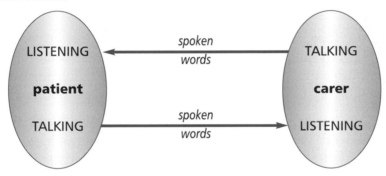

Here we are looking at just two people. Let us suppose that the spoken words were brief and straightforward, something like, 'Good morning, how are you?' with the reply, 'I'm fine thank you'. Let us also imagine that the patient and carer are native English speakers and that both have perfect speech and hearing.

The diagram does not begin to explain or describe this simple interaction. Many essential elements are missing and it gives no answers to a long string of vital questions.

A more realistic description

The patient and carer had to decide what to say, and how to say it, before any words were spoken. Our choice of words and how they are delivered is based on an accumulation of experiences, attitudes, assumptions and beliefs.

The simple diagram says nothing about the accent, dialect, tone of voice, speed, pitch or volume of the spoken words.

Assuming that the conversation did not take place remotely or by telephone, then the patient and client would have been exchanging an additional layer of hugely complex non-verbal signals together with the spoken words. What body language and facial expressions were involved? Did the exchange include any touching or physical contact?

Where did the conversation take place? What was the context? Was anyone else present? Are we describing a fit young woman asking her GP for contraceptive advice or a chat between a nurse and a desperately ill patient?

Where had the carer come from, and where was he or she going? What else was happening during the conversation, for instance was the nurse plumping up pillows? Was the patient reading?

Are the carer and patient talking for the first time or have they known each other for days, weeks or months? What is the history of their relationship?

The patient might be the prime minister and the carer a junior nurse on the first day of her first job. Alternatively, the carer could be an internationally famous neurosurgeon talking to a homeless elderly woman. Communication is greatly influenced by the differences and similarities of the people involved – this includes gender, class, age, wealth, income, race, education, social status and language.

Did you assume that the carer said, 'Good morning, how are you?' and the patient replied, 'I'm fine, thank you'? It could easily have been the other way around. Communication, especially in healthcare, usually involves unequal status and power, or at least an assumption of inequality that may be temporary or permanent.

Most of all, the words we use are not straightforward, unambiguous building blocks that always link together to form universally understood and accepted messages. The expression 'I'm fine, thank you' may mean nothing of the sort – in all probability, these words are delivered because they are thought appropriate and acceptable. The patient, or the carer, might be feeling dreadful.

Four principles of communication

So far we have described, in general terms and only with a very straightforward example, the basic components of communication. Many researchers have studied these elements and components in great detail. The most useful analysis is probably that proposed by Watzlawick (1967) as the four principles of communication.

Communication is inevitable

Watzlawick said that it was impossible not to communicate. Any action or behaviour that can be detected by one or more of the five senses delivers a message. Absence of communication is often a more powerful signal than attempts to communicate. We can turn our backs on others – literally and metaphorically. Sulking is withdrawal of communication but it is not lack of communication.

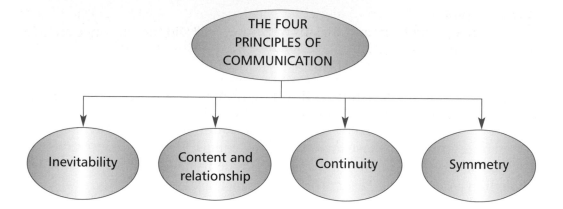

If communication is inevitable, it is also irretrievable. Once delivered, a message cannot be taken back or erased. An apology is an explanation or justification after the event. We often forgive, but we rarely forget.

Content and relationship

Communication is more than the simple delivery or exchange of objective information. There is always a message within the message that defines the relationship, or perceived relationship, between the parties involved. We often do not recognise these relationship signals. At other times, the choice of words or gestures is deliberate and designed to send a second, coded or more subtle communication along with the main content.

The relationship defined is usually to do with power and authority, but it may also include emotions like affection, approval, dislike or distaste. Messages within messages are almost universally used to show that one or more of those concerned wants to extend, limit or end communication. Tact and courtesy depend on choosing the right mix of content and relationship signals.

For example, one person says to another, 'It's past your bedtime'. The content of this message is precisely defined by looking at a clock, but it also implies status. It might be appropriate for a mother talking to a child, but inappropriate for a nurse talking to a patient. The words are the same; the relationship is different.

Continuity

It is impossible for a communication to be a single isolated event. This point is obvious if we are describing an ongoing relationship because what has gone before influences the next interaction. We avoid people we dislike, or who seem to dislike us. Expectations are based on history.

At a different level, it can also be argued that a new interaction not influenced by previous events only occurs rarely. A history of poor communication with, say, policemen or maths teachers, will alter the signals sent whenever we interact with a new or unknown member of these groups.

Symmetry

The fourth principle of communication follows from the second – interaction is influenced by relationships of power.

Two work colleagues may have the same rank and status in theory but not in practice. What Watzlawick called symmetrical relationships are rare, usually temporary and determined by context. Most communication is altered or distorted by asymmetry – those involved are not equals. Virtually all interaction in the health sector is asymmetric. Patients and clients have less specialist knowledge than practitioners. Disease or disorder increases vulnerability.

Non-verbal communication

Human interaction is dominated by two of the five senses – hearing and sight. Touch is important in some relationships, smell and taste are the least used. We all think we understand 'body talk' but the language is not universal.

Some non-verbal signals are physiologically determined and therefore common to all cultures. Crying or screaming to register pain or distress and laughing or smiling to indicate pleasure are the best examples.

Innate or physiological responses can, however, be suppressed or exaggerated by cultural pressures. In many societies adult men are not allowed to cry in public; other societies see this as normal acceptable behaviour. The severity of pain cannot be judged by a patient's reaction to it – there are individual as well as cultural differences in what signals may or may not be transmitted.

Most non-verbal communication is variable and potentially confusing. Moving the head from left to right does not always mean 'no' and nodding need not always mean 'yes'. The same hand gestures may have dramatically opposed meanings in different societies.

In apparently integrated and homogenous cultures, like the UK, non-verbal codes and signals also differ according to region, gender, age and class. In the same way as vocabulary changes and develops over time, non-verbal communications can become fashionable or outdated.

Face

The contraction or relaxation of the muscles of the iris in response to changing light conditions cannot be consciously controlled, and some other responses like sneezing, coughing or gagging are difficult to control. With these exceptions, nearly all humans can arrange eyes, eyebrows, mouth, nose, tongue and facial expression in combinations to deliver a vast range of non-verbal signals. The word 'supercilious' denotes disdain or arrogance – literally translated, it means 'with raised eyebrows'.

Hands

In the UK we shake hands on meeting and perhaps wave goodbye when we part. Hand gestures vary considerably amongst individuals and societies, but they are very powerful non-verbal communication channels. Signing replaces spoken words altogether in special circumstances, for instance among the hearing-impaired and in very noisy workplaces.

Personal space, posture and touch

Personal space is partly determined by status and power. Attempts to invade it are hostile acts unless permission is granted or taken for granted. Touch is the only non-verbal communication channel that needs physical proximity – 'invasion' is essential – and touch is an inevitable part of healthcare.

In all settings, personal and professional, touch involves difficult choices. Expectations and acceptability differ markedly, even among individuals with very similar backgrounds.

Posture delivers signals. For example, criminologists have found that people with an upright confident posture and a purposeful walk tend not to be victims of muggings or random violence. Again, the coded signals differ from one society to another. In conversation, the English tend not to adopt confrontational stances but hold their bodies at a slight angle, one to another.

A more realistic model

The diagram on the next page tries to summarise the main points discussed in this topic.

You will see that we show a 'private person' inside the 'public person'. Intercommunication describes the public interaction between two or more people. Intracommunication can be defined as the processes that take place inside an individual. How we communicate, and what we communicate, is determined largely by our past experience, attitudes, assumptions and beliefs. Communication cannot be effective without understanding the importance of intracommunication – in ourselves and in others. These issues are outlined next.

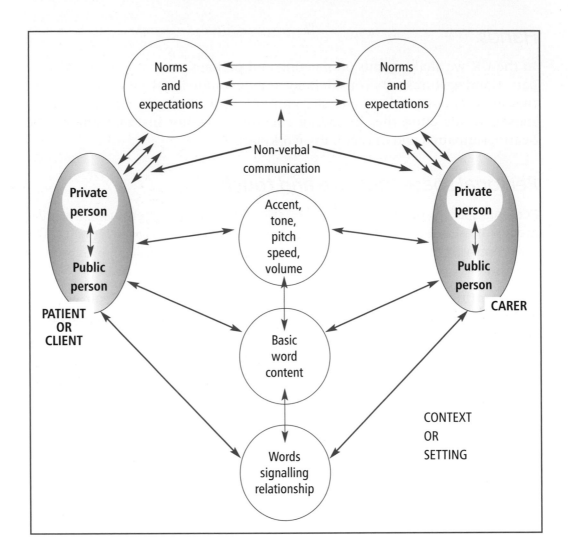

3 Communication – psychology and sociology

Previously we have described the communication that could be recorded using audio and video equipment. Any human interaction might then be analysed and studied in great detail after the event. The experiment, if properly designed, would capture all of the detail of vocabulary, accent, intonation, facial expression, body language, touch, proximity and so on.

However, this kind of research could not explain the behaviour observed.

The behavioural or social sciences make essential contributions to understanding and then improving communication.

Assumptions and predictions

No two human interactions can be the same, but nobody has the time – least of all a busy health professional – to analyse the content, real meaning and motives of every single communication from first principles. We all make assumptions about others, and these assumptions are used to predict how people will behave. Sometimes assumptions are well founded; sometimes they are false or partly false, and misunderstandings or conflict follow.

We choose our friends and, to a more limited extent, our colleagues, but health professionals and the next patient or client start their relationships as strangers.

Barriers and distortions

No single psychological theory can explain completely how the 'private person' inside all of us was produced and developed. Similarly, the interactions between the private person and the public one must be complex and, in their full detail, unique.

Perhaps the most surprising fact is that effective communication is usually possible, not that it is sometimes difficult, frustrating and confusing.

According to Watzlawick's first principle, complete barriers to communication cannot exist – because any interaction involves a communication of one sort or another. Turning this argument around, it must also be true that completely effective, unambiguous communication is unusual. In some instances, one channel of communication may be completely blocked. The female dress codes of some cultures, faiths and beliefs are designed to prevent women transmitting messages that are thought to be improper, unwise or inappropriate.

More commonly, communication is sent and received through many channels but it is distorted or filtered in some way. These sieves and filters are the product of the interaction between the private and public person.

Barriers and filters to communication are usually considered under three headings.

These categories are not mutually exclusive. It could be argued that all communication filters originate from differences in the belief and value systems of those involved.

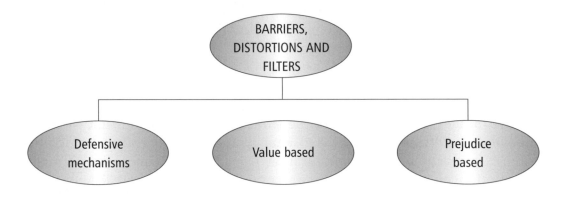

Defence mechanisms

Defence mechanisms are states of mind leading to communication distortions that protect the individual's dignity, self-worth or self-image. Put differently, these mechanisms also eliminate or reduce shame, guilt, fear, doubt, anxiety and regret. This definition can be usefully enlarged to include filters that protect others from negative emotions.

Defence mechanisms can be deliberately employed or they may result from unconscious or unrecognised drives and emotions. Freud would have argued that most are unconscious; the humanists and the cognitive school would take the opposite view.

Filters are an essential part of tact, courtesy, diplomacy and sensitivity – in particular where communication is asymmetrical and involves people with differing status, knowledge and power.

At a deeper level, the most common filters are repression, denial and inappropriate justification. To a limited extent, we all use these devices to reduce stress and anxiety, but they are constant dangers in healthcare communication. A patient may deny or repress symptoms until forced into doing so by a medical emergency. A busy or harassed nurse might have ignored a patient's needs because, at that moment, she was 'busy' tidying the linen cupboard.

Value-based filters

The words belief, value, norm, standard, expectation, attitude and assumption describe different ideas, but all have three factors in common:

- They are learned or acquired.

- They are culture-specific not universal.

- They result in a definable pattern of behaviour.

Many attitudes and assumptions are so deeply rooted that we do not recognise their influence on communication. These filters produce stereotypes and categorisations that range from the humorous to the sinister, and all distort communication.

Prejudice

Prejudice, considered objectively, is no more than a learned attitude or set of values, but the word is reserved for states of mind that result in negative, destructive, cruel or perhaps illegal behaviour. At its most extreme, prejudice becomes bigotry.

Prejudice stems from ignorance and isolation. Note that ignorance and stupidity are not the same thing. Travel really does broaden the mind because it shows the illogicality of most prejudice. Travel in this sense need not involve trains and boats and planes. A health professional travels between one set of values and another every time he or she meets a new patient or client.

Labels are the foundation of prejudice. The word 'gay' has replaced its unpleasant or offensive ancestors as prejudice towards homosexuals has decreased. In 1917, the name of the British royal house was changed from Saxe-Coburg-Gotha to Windsor and, at about the same time, German Shepherd dogs became Alsatians. The dogs and the royal family still had significant German ancestry, but the new labels gave a different impression.

Learning to recognise and then cope with prejudice is one of the most valuable interpersonal skills.

Place, time and participants

A policeman documenting an interview that may later be used in a criminal trial is obliged to record, amongst other things, the place, time and people involved. These minimum requirements recognise the importance of sociology in communication – two or more individuals are involved and context or setting are critical influences.

In Chapter 3, we looked at social structures and personal identity. The principles outlined for that unit are directly relevant to this one. Communication cannot be neutral, value-free and objective, because it cannot take place in a neutral or value-free social environment – and no two people are the same.

Personal identity and personal difference

Our language and culture recognise personal identity and difference as pivotal factors in communication.

'I felt like I'd known her all my life – we were soul mates.'

'He may as well have come from a different planet – I couldn't get through to him at all.'

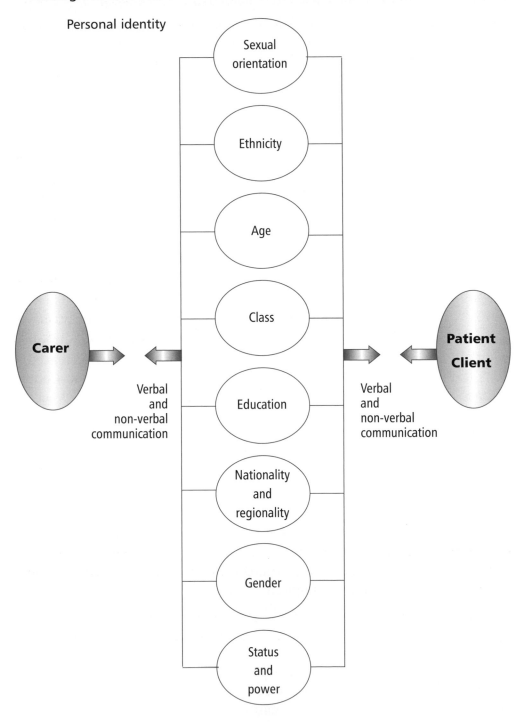

Personal identity

Sexual orientation

Ethnicity

Age

Class

Carer

Patient Client

Verbal and non-verbal communication

Education

Verbal and non-verbal communication

Nationality and regionality

Gender

Status and power

Personal identity is a two-way street. It describes not just the way we see ourselves, but also how others see us.

The diagram shows how personal identity might influence communication between a patient or client and a carer.

Language and ethnicity

The *Annual Abstract of Statistics 2003* (Crown copyright) gives government estimates of the UK population by ethnic group for 2001. This showed that 51.3 million people described themelves as 'white British', equivalent to 87% of the population. Other self descriptions were as shown in the table.

Self-ascribed ethnic group	2001
	'000s
Asian	2,375
White non-British	1,690
Black	1,196
Mixed ethnic origins	511
Total	5,772

© Crown copyright

There are no reliable figures for first language or fluency in English that would add valuable detail to these numbers. Most Asians, black Africans and African-Caribbeans are second or third generation UK citizens whose first language is English, but these figures illustrate the scale of likely differences in factors like accent, vocabulary, grammar and speech patterns.

Of the 53 million people who described themselves as white – either British or non-British – there will be language and cultural differences as great as those originating from ethnicity. This group includes all of the dialects and accents of the UK, plus significant numbers who define themselves as Irish, rather than British, and many other Europeans and North Americans, for instance.

Language, class, age and gender

Personal identity can be used as a marker for the different ways people use and interpret language. Class, age and gender are perhaps the most important in healthcare. As a very broad generalisation, men use more aggressive language forms, concentrating on status, power and factual information. Women are more passive and better able to express feelings, emotions and anxieties.

There are ongoing debates concerning the use of language and class. Attribution of class by accent or dialect is no longer the generally accepted prime indicator that it once was in the UK, but accent is still widely used as shorthand for socioeconomic status.

Language, and especially vocabulary, evolves and changes. We would not expect grandparents to use the same word forms as their grandchildren.

Roles, expectations and first impressions

First impressions are largely based on prejudice because we only pick up an incomplete range of signals, many of which may be false or misleading. We see or hear what we expect to see or hear using an initial and very brief assessment of personal identity. Dress, physical appearance and accent are the first indicators.

Personal identity defines a role. Unconsciously we act out these roles in our working and personal lives. Nurses wear uniforms because this is part of their role as carers. Doctors often wear white coats and carry stethoscopes – this is part of role play. The white coat is another kind of uniform and the stethoscope is part medical instrument and part badge of office.

A multiplicity of personal identities is the normal human condition. Your identities might include those of student, parent, child, part-time care worker and amateur musician, for example. We each play different roles with different expectations in different settings.

The sick role

The sick role is not officially documented, for example, in a leaflet given to patients on hospital admission. Nonetheless it is a central feature of healthcare communication.

Society grants concessions and makes allowance for those that are unwell. The sick person is excused his or her responsibilities at work and in care for the home and family. If need be, financial and other support is provided. The fit and the healthy are expected to show sympathy and empathy towards the patient.

In turn, sick people agree to their half of the unspoken bargain. They are required to do their best to recover as rapidly as possible and above all to comply with and accept treatment. This implies a temporary loss or yielding of independence and autonomy – identity is altered or modified.

Breaking the rules of the contract leads to disapproval. Malingerers are not respected; difficult or disobedient patients are seen as a nuisance, selfish or perhaps a danger to themselves or to others.

The sick role excuses the patient or client from blame – it defines the unwell as innocent victims or as unfortunate. In some groups and societies, the sick role is being subtly redesigned. Ill health brought about by poor lifestyle choices can be seen as breaking the sick-role contract. How much empathy, care, attention and money should society spend on looking after those that will not care for themselves?

4 Reflective listening

Words like reflection, reflective practice and reflective learning have become very fashionable in adult education. We need to explain what reflection is – and its value – before we can discuss reflective listening.

Academic and vocational education

Academic education traditionally focuses on pure learning or learning not directly applicable to any predefined purpose. A vocation is literally a calling, but it has come to mean a job, occupation or profession – often one that requires dedication and public service. Vocational education is preparation for further training or direct entry into an occupation.

Access is an unusual, intensive mix of academic and vocational education. Pathways define vocation, but a general academic foundation is also given. This unit is called *Interpersonal skills* – it is not called 'Interpersonal theory' and its end product is vocational. There are special responsibilities associated with vocational education for the health professions: an ineffective nurse can do more harm than a bad tailor, for instance.

Reflection is an invaluable technique in teaching, learning and improving practical skills.

Active learning

Reflective learning is best described as development and improvement based on a conscious or determined examination of experiences. It is more than learning from mistakes, because there is nothing haphazard, casual or informal about the exercise. Reflective learning has several stages:

- Past events are recalled or documented in detail. Setting, purpose, participants and outcome are equally relevant. This is the start point for reflective learning, not its final objective.

- The learner then honestly assesses their reactions to these events. Actions taken are less important than the thoughts, feelings and emotions generated in the learner and in others. How the feelings of others are judged or observed is a vital part of reflective learning.

- Special attention is given to consequences or reactions that are unexpected, apparently illogical or seemingly irrelevant.

- An attempt is made to rank or evaluate the experience as a success or failure. What went wrong? What went right? What do you mean by wrong and right?

- Making prompt mental or written notes is essential. Review or revision, say 24 hours after the event, can be equally profitable. Perspective and conclusions may alter.

- Finally, the student is asked to think about what could be done differently when the event, or a similar one, happens again.

Empathy and self-awareness

A Johari window (named after its first users, Joseph Luft and Harry Ingham) is a diagram that explains, at a glance, the links between empathy, self-awareness and reflective learning. It is based on the ideas of the public and the private person that we outlined at the beginning of this unit.

	Known to self	*Unknown to self*
Known to others	PUBLIC SELF What everybody knows	BLIND SELF What others know about you, but you do not
Unknown to others	PRIVATE SELF What you know but other do not	UNKNOWN SELF What nobody knows

'Not recognising' or 'not acknowledging' has the same outcome as 'not knowing'. Your friends and colleagues might all agree that you are maybe arrogant or short-tempered. If this characteristic is not personally accepted or recognised then the reactions you generate in others will constantly cause surprise, confusion and disappointment. Perfect self-awareness is an impossible ideal, but it would imply the complete absence of blind self – an empty top right-hand box, together with full knowledge of the private self – and its influence on interactions with other people.

Empathy means trying to understand and then allow for the private and public selves of those you interact with. Clearly, perfect empathy is also an impossible ideal.

Reflective learning cannot happen without some initial level of empathy and self-awareness. However, all three grow and develop in parallel. The point of reflection is to set up a self-reinforcing virtuous circle.

Reflective listening

It is impossible to treat the whole person without reflective listening. This skill sits at the centre of the biopsychosocial model of healthcare if you prefer a different set of words.

A conversation includes at least two people. To listen, you have first to stop talking.

Context and setting are clearly important. Every attempt must be made to ensure privacy and to minimise intrusions, interruptions and distractions.

Reflective listening cannot be combined with ward or clinical routines. A promise to 'come back later when I have more time' should not be made if it cannot be honoured.

Information and feedback

Reflective listening encourages patients and clients to organise, release and then discuss feelings, thoughts and emotions. This in turn leads to greater understanding and improved care. Feedback or responses and replies pass through a series of filters. There are always messages within messages. What you are hearing may not be what the patient is thinking.

Reflective listening is a continuing process, not an isolated or one-off event.

Getting started

Somebody has to start a conversation. Mutual agreement to begin talking is nearly always signalled non-verbally with the help of a few ritualistic words, perhaps 'Hello, how are you?' or simply 'Good morning'. Non-verbal signals are nearly always the best indicators of consent or unwillingness to start or to continue a conversation.

Body language and facial expressions are powerful ways of showing attention, commitment and respect for the patient as an individual. Attention and confrontation are easily confused because both may include close proximity and direct eye contact. Personal space has to be negotiated.

Questions and answers

Questions and answers are the framework of a conversation, but also of an interrogation. There may be an urgent or essential need to give or to receive factual information, but a quick-fire series of questions cannot be reflective, productive or respectful.

Closed questions look for precise and brief answers – they should be avoided if possible. Open questions invite a range of responses and they allow people to express and acknowledge their real feelings and concerns.

Funnelling is a technique that uses a series of open questions to arrive at some productive or positive conclusions. A leading question is not an open question – the conclusions must be genuine, not the views and opinions of the carer imposed on the patient. A series of open questions is a journey with an unknown destination. Unexpected or seemingly irrational responses must not be seen as wrong, misplaced or unjustified.

Open questions often trigger unrecognised or deeply hidden emotions – this is stressful and a reflective listener will learn to spot when enough is enough, or when the conversation is best continued at another time.

Silence and turn-taking

In English, there are expressions like 'an embarrassing silence' and 'a pregnant pause'. We feel the conversation must be kept moving ahead at all costs. It is also considered discourteous to interrupt another's word flow, to 'talk over' or to finish somebody else's sentences.

The rules of silence and turn-taking are influenced by age, class and gender and are also heavily culture-specific. In Japan, relatively long periods of silence between alternative contributions to a conversation are marks of respect. A listener may also close their eyes to signal attentiveness – precisely the reverse of the English or British convention. In southern Europe, the culture, as a generalisation, is different again – overlap and 'talking over' show interest and commitment.

Speed of delivery can be mistaken for eloquence, intelligence or confidence, and vice versa. Turn-taking and the use of silence in reflective listening is difficult to judge at first meeting. Not allowing time for thought and reply is verbal aggression. Too much silence can be read as loss of interest or reluctance to give a straight or honest answer.

Carers routinely have to make adjustments for the distortions and changes in speech patterns caused by illness, stress or confusion. The inability to find or formulate words in ways that we have come to take for granted always causes frustration, fear, isolation and anger.

Paraphrase, repetition and summary

A caring listener can mirror or reflect the other's conversation using paraphrases, summaries or partial repetition of key words and sentences. Combined with positive gestures and facial expressions, these methods are amongst the most valuable interpersonal skills.

Words have to be chosen with care. For example:

Positive, empathetic and reflective	Negative, ill-chosen and counter-productive
Let me try to understand how you're feeling.	I know exactly how you feel!
You're afraid that your husband isn't coping well at home alone?	What you really mean is that your husband isn't managing.
What's worrying you most? Let me try to help.	You mustn't worry so much!

Notice the difference between sensitive open questions and insensitive statements of opinion.

Names and naming

Names are badges of personal identity. Using them wrongly, inappropriately, without permission or not at all signals disrespect in all societies. Labels like 'dear', 'ducks', 'love', 'angel', 'darling', 'sweetie' or 'pops', may be entirely appropriate, but they may also cause deep offence and irritation. The carer's difficulties are greater than the patient's. You will probably be called nurse, sister, doctor, or whatever at first – these labels are neutral and therefore not a barrier or a distortion to communication.

Informed consent is a fundamental principle of ethics. It applies to names and naming. A patient may be called Mrs Jennings, and then Angela, then Angie and finally sweetie as the relationship develops, but only if Mrs Angela Jennings signals her permission.

By wearing a name badge, a carer gives automatic and general consent for the name on the badge to be used.

5 Private and professional confidentiality

In this final topic, we discuss the kinds of communication that can never be in the best interests of patients or clients. Irretrievability is the central issue – once a message has been transmitted it cannot be taken back or erased.

We consider confidentiality at three levels: first in terms of what most people would describe as common decency, then as controlled by ethical codes, and last as regulated by law.

Gossip

We are cooperative social animals with extraordinary communication skills. People have an irresistible urge to talk, and the most fascinating subject has always been other people. Information is power – those that are 'in the know' expect and receive status and attention. Gossip may be another way of describing good conversation, but malicious gossip can cause life-changing harm.

It helps to think through the motives for and the characteristics of malicious gossip:

- The prime motive is attention-seeking or a wish to be socially promoted within a particular group.

- The content usually involves sexual or financial relationships, health or any combination of the three.

- There is a value judgement which comes as a message within the message – usually of disapproval or disgust. The sender of the message feels relatively more moral than the subject of the gossip.

- There is no regard for fact, evidence or sources.

- Empathy and malicious gossip are incompatible. Consequences are not considered or, if they are considered, they are ignored.

The dividing lines between innocent and malicious conversation are difficult to draw. We all have to make our own decisions.

There are parallels between gossip and infectious disease. The more shocking or scandalous the message, the more virulent the pathogen becomes. Individuals can immunise themselves and others by avoiding the infection or by refusing to pass it on.

Civil law recognises slander, libel, defamation and rights to privacy, but these are extreme remedies of little use in regulating everyday behaviour.

Private dilemmas

If you knew for sure that your 16-year-old niece was using cocaine on a regular basis, would you tell her parents? You find out that your best friend's partner is having an affair – what do you do?

These are true dilemmas because both preserving and breaching confidentiality will have negative consequences. Difficult as they are, these kinds of decisions are private matters – there is no rule book or guide to tell you what to do or how to do it. Somebody else faced with the same choices might reach completely different conclusions.

Ethical codes

A private person in a private situation is free to decide what is, and what is not, confidential information, provided no law is broken. Decisions are guided by conscience.

As a member of a profession, you are no longer a private person – in the workplace or outside it. Previously we discussed ethical codes in detail. Here we give the sections of the current Nursing and Midwifery Council's code of professional conduct that relate to confidentiality.

As a registered nurse or midwife you must protect confidential information.

- You must treat information about patients and clients as confidential and use it only for the purposes for which it was given. As it is impractical to obtain consent every time you need to share information with others, you should ensure that patients and clients understand that some information may be made available to other members of the team involved in the delivery of care.

- You must guard against breaches of confidentiality by protecting information from improper disclosure at all times.

- You should seek patients' and clients' wishes regarding the sharing of information with their family and others. When a patient or client is considered incapable of giving permission, you should consult relevant colleagues.

- If you are required to disclose information outside the team that will have personal consequences for patients and clients, you must obtain their consent. If the patient or client withholds consent, or if consent cannot be obtained, for whatever reason, disclosures may be made only where:
  - they can be justified in the public interest (usually where disclosure is essential to protect the patient or client or someone else from the risk of significant harm)
  - they are required by law or order of a court

> – where there is an issue of child protection, you must act at all times in accordance with national and local policies.

The need to know

All ethical codes restrict the sharing or transmission of confidential information to those who need to have it to further the patient's, client's or customer's best interests. The convenience or curiosity of other practitioners or professionals are not grounds for disclosure.

Improper disclosure

The code says you must guard against improper disclosure at all times. There are implications that may not be immediately obvious.

To comply with the code, practitioners must recognise the difference between public and private spaces. A patient-related conversation between two nurses (who are members of the same team) in a wine bar at the end of a shift, for instance, cannot be ethical. There can be no guarantees that their conversation will not be overheard by other customers or staff – the social networks of strangers or acquaintances, and equally of patients or clients, are unknown.

Coding or limiting information discussed in public is no defence or excuse. It is often possible to identify somebody from the tiniest scrap of seemingly innocent anonymous information.

A hospital, clinic, office or GP's surgery has some private and some public spaces – the same rules apply.

It also follows that all written records must be protected. This is a legal as well as an ethical requirement.

Informed consent

The ethical code treats the spouses, partners, relatives and friends of a mentally competent adult as strangers. Without the informed consent of the patient, they have no rights to be given confidential information.

Children and child protection

Confidential information must be disclosed if not to do so might endanger or continue to cause harm to a child. If an issue of child protection is suspected, guidance from colleagues must be sought immediately.

The law in the UK does not precisely define the relationships of confidentiality between parents or guardians and children. Similarly, a child's ability to give or to withhold informed consent is judged by competence and understanding, not chronological age. Again, guidance must be sought – assumptions may lead to improper disclosure.

Public interest disclosure

In exceptional circumstances, the ethics of confidentiality shifts into reverse. Regardless of consent, it becomes improper not to disclose.

Some diseases are notifiable in the interests of public health. As the name suggests, these diagnoses must be notified or disclosed to the appropriate authorities. It is worth noting that, in the UK, HIV/AIDS is not a notifiable disease.

The Mental Health Acts sometimes require disclosure if this is considered in the best interests of the patient or client and the wider community.

There is also a general duty to disclose when not to do so may expose the patient, client or others to significant harm. Difficult judgements are involved, but as usually interpreted, a health professional must not withhold information from the police or other authorities if a serious crime might not then be investigated or prevented.

Whistle blowing

A whistle blower is an individual who exposes a colleague or another professional because their behaviour has become a risk or a potential risk to patients, clients or customers. These are professional dilemmas – is loyalty owed to the team or to those at risk?

The nurses' and midwives' code of conduct gives clear instructions. The first consideration must be the best interests and the safety of patients and clients. The code of conduct also includes a duty to act without delay.

Heavy burdens

The duty to protect confidentiality goes beyond common sense and common decency. It places heavy burdens on practitioners. It should be remembered that confidentiality cannot be fragmented or subdivided. Conversations that start with words like 'All I can tell you is …' are as unethical as full disclosure.

Denial is also improper, even to prevent the spread of obviously false or malicious information. The teenage daughter of a friend of a friend may or may not be pregnant. This is information confidential to her – confirmation or denial is unethical.

Spouses, partners and close relatives of a health professional do not have a need to know.

Confidentiality in law

Legal issues and client rights are discussed in topic 7 of Chapter 4. The Data Protection Act 1998 makes the disclosure of confidential information illegal as well as unethical.

Under the Act, health records are defined as sensitive personal information. It imposes legal duties to protect them from improper disclosure, theft, loss, distortion and inaccuracies.

The consequences of improper disclosure can be catastrophic for all concerned. They may result in permanent damage to a patient's or client's happiness and well-being, the withdrawal of professional registration and criminal prosecution in some cases.

Chapter 6
Methods in psychology

National unit specification
These are the topics you will be studying for this unit.

1   The five schools of psychology

2   Psychological research in healthcare

3   Quantitative and qualitative research

4   Interviews

5   Questionnaires

6   Observational research

7   Results analysis and presentation

Topic 7 of this unit describes the methods most often used to analyse and summarise research results. For some pathways, students may need to extend the basic techniques. These topics are covered in Chapter 7.

1 The five schools of psychology

There are several acceptable definitions of psychology. The briefest is 'the study of the behaviour of individuals and their mental processes'.

Psychology is a diverse discipline and alternative definitions are often used in an attempt to describe the full scope of the subject, for example it has been called 'the study of mankind's interactions with his social and physical environment'.

No science exists in isolation, but psychology, more than most, sits at the centre of a network of related subjects. Clearly, any discipline that can explain, or partly explain, differences in behaviour makes a contribution.

Psychology in context

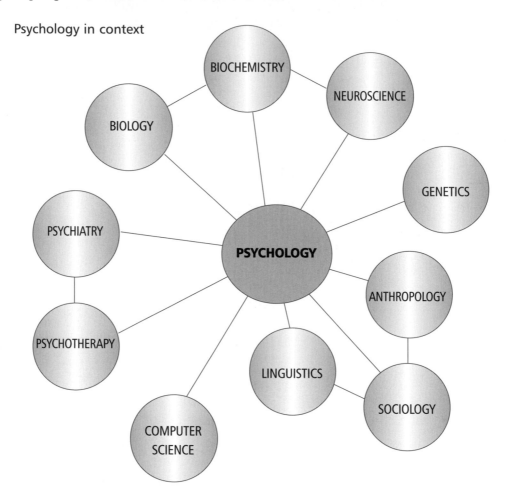

Psychology was a late developer as a separately identified field. Until around 1850, it was seen as part of theology or philosophy.

This changed in 1879 when Wilhelm Wundt opened a psychological laboratory in Leipzig. His work was the first attempt at investigating the mind and human behaviour under controlled conditions. Psychological investigation is more difficult than experiments in natural science. Wundt had many critics and the challenges of proof and validity continue to this day.

Psychology versus common sense

It is vital to distinguish formal psychology from informal observation of human behaviour. A large part of psychology is an attempt to explain intuitive or 'gut' reactions. Common sense is a poor guide because it varies amongst individuals and across societies. Folklore and proverbs are dictionaries of common sense. However, they are sometimes contradictory, for example:

Look before you leap	– He who hesitates is lost
Spare the rod and spoil the child	– A loved child is a loving child
Birds of a feather flock together	– Opposites attract
A problem shared is a problem halved	– Keep yourself to yourself
Many hands make light work	– Too many cooks spoil the broth
The hand that rocks the cradle rules the world	– Women are the weaker sex

Five schools

Five schools of psychology are recognised. No single theory is generally applicable. The five schools are best regarded as different approaches to the same set of problems, not a model of irreconcilable differences.

The five schools of psychology

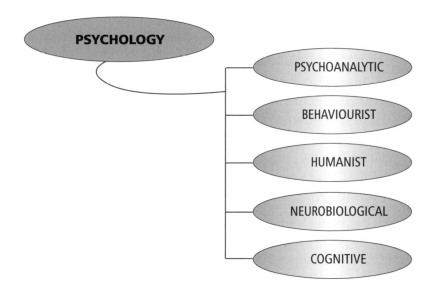

The psychoanalytics

Sigmund Freud was born in 1856 and did most of his work in Vienna. In 1900, he published *The psychoanalytical theory of personality*. Freud's major contribution was to realise that much of our behaviour is determined unconsciously and that many basic drives and motives are difficult to acknowledge or to accept. He also believed that personality is largely formed in childhood. Freud identified three components in the development of behaviour.

- The id is the primitive, pleasure-seeking or pain-avoidance principle. In the beginning, for instance, infants crave food, warmth, attention and comfort with no recognition of the needs of others.

- The ego, or reality principle, emerges when children start to acknowledge the limits to permissible behaviour and the consequences of their actions.

- The superego develops as a control system – managing the excitability of the id and the activity of the ego. Control and censorship is unconscious, but the superego is the source of emotions like guilt and shame.

Freud thought interactions and conflicts between id, ego and superego continued into adulthood. Psychoanalysis was introduced as a treatment, or at least a method for understanding psychoses and neuroses. Typically the analyst and patient are involved in many hours of conversation and close contact. Freud's methods, and the psychoanalytic school generally, divide opinion amongst psychologists and health professionals. Its reliance on the interpretation of dreams has been heavily criticised. Also, it is, of course, impossible to prove the existence of the id, ego and superego. Freud concluded that repressed sexual desire dating from childhood was the trigger for most abnormal behaviour in later life. Other schools of psychology think this approach is too simplistic.

Carl Gustav Jung (1875–1961) was a Swiss psychologist and initially a follower of Freud. Between 1910 and 1915 their views steadily diverged. Jung said that all humans shared basic values – a collective unconscious set of motives and desires.

The behaviourists

Pavlov (1849–1936) was an eminent physiologist and a Nobel Prize winner. He made major advances in our understanding of the digestive system and blood circulation. His best-remembered work involved conditioned responses or reflexes in laboratory animals. Pavlov's most famous experiment concerned dogs, food and a bell. For a period he rang a bell every time his dogs were fed. He then noticed that they salivated in response to the bell without food being offered. This is conditioning – salivation was a conditioned reflex.

Pavlov was the first behaviourist. The theories were greatly extended by John Watson in the early part of the 20th century. B F Skinner later advocated scientific or radical behaviourism.

The behaviourist school has variants, but in essence it says that:

- Only behaviour that can be observed or measured is valid or relevant to psychological understanding. The mind may not exist, or may as well not exist.

- Behaviour that is rewarded, or that leads to some beneficial outcome, will be repeated and becomes part of a complex set of responses. The reverse is also true – punishment, or an unwanted outcome, discourages and eventually eliminates the behaviour that causes it.

- We also learn to time or delay responses to give the desired effect or to avoid unpleasant results.

- By implication, the behaviourists believe that the results of experiments with laboratory animals, such as mice, rats, dogs and monkeys, are directly transferable to human behaviour.

At first glance, behaviourism looks like common sense wrapped up in jargon. We are all behaviourist to some extent – children learn that fires and knives are dangerous because cuts and burns are painful. However, the theory does not explain widespread patterns of self-destructive behaviour.

Imprisonment is supposed to be a mixture of punishment, exclusion and re-education. Behaviourist psychology cannot easily explain why the majority of prisoners reoffend.

Preventative medicine and health education campaigns are never completely or rapidly effective. They should be if behaviourism really is the complete explanation of human psychology.

Radical or scientific behaviourism has no place for free will.

The humanists

Abraham Maslow (1908–1970) is generally reckoned to be the founder of humanistic psychology, although humanism itself traces its roots back at least to the early 19th century. Secular humanism was a reaction against some aspects of organised religion. The traditional Christian view of mankind as weak, sinful and flawed was refuted. Instead, humanists believe that individuals are unique, free willed, rational and logical. Humanism implies that society is improvable and perhaps even perfectable – in time.

Maslow suggested that we all have a hierarchy or pyramid of needs. The foundations of the pyramid are the requirements for basic survival – food, clothing and shelter. As these needs are met, we then seek out intimacy and social contact with others. The hierarchy extends – at its peak we all look for self-esteem, self-fulfilment and ways to achieve our true potential.

Humanist psychology rejects most of the alleged similarities between men and other animals assumed by the behaviourists. The humanist school is essentially optimistic and seen by many as directly relevant to many modern societies where religion is no longer a dominant force.

Humanists recognise the importance of childhood socialisation but they also believe that experiences throughout life can alter behaviour patterns.

The neurobiologists

The neurobiological school of psychology sees the discipline as a branch of human biochemistry – not as a social science. We have known for thousands of years that drugs and infections alter behaviour. For example, alcohol diminishes social inhibition, many plant materials are sedatives, and the bites of rabid animals and some insects cause extreme or irrational actions. Medical research has shown that some mental illnesses have a biochemical origin. Sometimes, abnormal behaviour is associated with unusually high or low levels of a biological molecule like an enzyme or a hormone.

The human central nervous system is an incredibly complicated structure, but we are beginning to have some grasp of the changes in the brain that are associated with perception, learning and memory. Advances in scanning technology, for instance, may eventually reveal a great deal concerning normal brain function.

There is no doubt that some behavioural patterns 'run in families'. However, it is difficult to distinguish between genetic inheritance and similarities caused by a shared social environment. We know for sure that some physical conditions, or vulnerability to some diseases, have a genetic component – it is illogical to assume that behaviour is entirely determined by social and environmental pressures.

A greater understanding of the human genome has led to misleading or oversimplified reporting in the mass media. There is very unlikely to be 'a gene for homosexuality' or a 'gene for musical ability' because human inheritance almost always involves the interaction of very many different genes and a huge variety of environmental influences.

Neurobiology and therefore neurobiological psychology is an infant science. Few dispute its potential; however, even fewer think it will ever give a complete understanding of human behaviour.

There are links between the radical behaviourist school and the neurobiologists. The strongest defenders of these two different theories both minimise the role of free will: 'I am aggressive because my aggressive behaviour was constantly rewarded rather than discouraged in childhood.' Or at some point in the future a lawyer might perhaps be able to claim: 'My client is aggressive because he has inherited 31 of the 49 genes known to cause aggression in human males.'

The cognitive school

Cognition is the word that describes thinking or the thought process, as distinct from emotion or irrationality. Cognitive psychology is the newest of the five theories – it has grown in parallel with computer science.

Cognitive psychologists argue that computer systems are a useful and accurate model of how the mind works. The diagram shows cognitive psychology at its simplest.

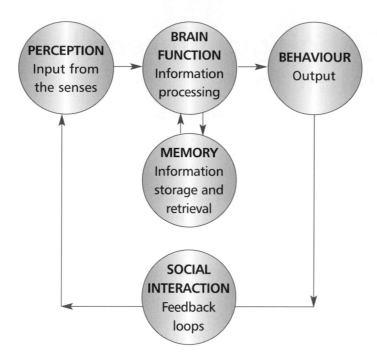

Cognitive theories become more persuasive and plausible as the processing speeds and memory capacities of computer systems increase.

The distinction between intelligence, or processing power, and speed of processing, or calculation, is hard to define. The ability to identify the billions of possible solutions to a problem and then to select the right answer from these alternatives may be the best definition of intelligence. If this is so, then the creation of genuine artificial intelligence is just a matter of time and engineering.

The links between brain and senses are only beginning to be understood. We have invented devices like microscopes, telescopes and microphones, but there is a huge difference between detecting signals and processing and using the information they contain. Comparing a sophisticated modern camera to the human visual sense is a bit like confusing a piece of steel tubing with an aircraft carrier or a brick with a cathedral.

2 Psychological research in healthcare

Most of us make three assumptions about medicine:

- First, that medical science will always improve.

- Second, that the rate of advance will accelerate.

- Third, that the medical profession will be able to solve very nearly all of our healthcare problems, given time.

These assumptions are false – progress is not guaranteed.

Taking the UK since 1945, medicine and healthcare has met more of the needs of more people because:

- We have become more prosperous. Individuals, families, companies and governments, via taxation, have more money to spend.

- As citizens, voters, taxpayers and consumers, our expectations have risen. In an educated democracy, politicians are obliged to meet these expectations, or at least to try to meet them.

- Science, technology and engineering have made spectacular advances.

These factors are interrelated but research in the broadest sense is the most important of the three. In an ideal world, greater understanding and an ability to solve more problems generates increased wealth and prosperity. This then drives a virtuous cycle of expenditure, expectation and the satisfaction of these expectations.

The object of study

Large complex societies depend on microdivision of labour. There are thousands of different jobs and professions. Each has its own objects of study, body of knowledge and expertise. Healthcare practitioners and a few other specialists study living organisms. Their body of knowledge can only be expanded through experimentation, but to what extent, if any, should this be allowed? If it is to be permitted, how should it be controlled?

These are major challenges for medicine.

Natural and social scientific research

Modern medicine is evidence based. Procedures and therapies have emerged and improved following experiment and observation. Put differently, healthcare is built on scientific foundations. The importance of chemistry and biology is self-evident, but the social sciences also make essential contributions. Take the following simple example of a series of linked investigations.

A blood test will show normal or abnormal levels of a number of organic molecules like cholesterol or lipids. In the very short term, the client cannot influence the results of this experiment. This investigation is largely based on the natural science of biochemistry.

This test might be followed by a routine blood pressure measurement. For some clients, this experiment has much more to do with social than natural science. White-coat hypertension is a widely recognised condition – blood pressure increases because blood pressure is being measured. The experimenter and the object of the experiment interact to deliver a false reading. In contrast, if you measure the temperature of a beaker of hot water, the water does not give a false reading because it does not interact with the experimenter holding the thermometer.

Next, you might question the client concerning his or her lifestyle – smoking, diet, exercise and so on. You will certainly get answers and you will certainly be able to tick boxes on a form – but are the answers correct? Is the experiment reliable? This investigation is pure social science – there is very significant human interaction.

Experience has shown that experiments of this type can be virtually meaningless. We give the answers we think the investigator is looking for; we tell white lies to protect our dignity.

A final social science experiment to test the reliability of the lifestyle questionnaire could take many forms – nearly all of them absurd and unethical. You might question the client's friends and relatives, you could follow at a distance and take notes, you might even collect supermarket till receipts to check on fat and alcohol consumption.

Codes of conduct

All aspects of medicine and healthcare are regulated by codes of conduct. Next, we summarise the ethical principles for conducting research with human participants as currently laid down by the British Psychological Society.

Participants in psychological research should have confidence in the investigators. Good research is only possible if there is mutual respect between all of the parties involved. Members of the society are responsible for the ethical conduct of students and research assistants under their supervision as well as their own personal conduct.

As a general principle, an investigation should be considered from the standpoint of its participants. Foreseeable threats to their psychological well-being, health, values and dignity should be eliminated. Investigators should recognise that they may not have enough knowledge of the background of some participants. In these circumstances they should take advice from those that do have this specialist knowledge.

Consent

In psychological research, whenever possible, the investigator should inform the participants of all aspects of the research that might reasonably influence their willingness to take part.

Research with children or with vulnerable adults who have limited understanding or communication skills requires special safeguards. In addition, work involving children under the age of 16 should not proceed without parental consent or consent from those *in loco parentis*. In circumstances where consent is difficult or impossible to obtain, research should only follow approval from an appropriately constituted, independent ethics committee.

Investigators are often in positions of authority or influence over participants, who may be their students, employees, subordinates or clients. This relationship must not be used to pressurise the participants to take part in, or remain part of, the investigation.

The payment of participants must not be used to encourage them to risk harm – beyond that which they risk in their normal lifestyles – without payment.

In multi-stage experiments, the participants' consent must be obtained for each stage of the investigation.

Deception

The code of conduct recognises that, in some circumstances, it is impossible to design reliable investigations if the participants have full prior knowledge of the purpose of the experiment. The withholding of information or the misleading of participants is unacceptable if the participants are likely to object or show unease once debriefed at the end of the exercise.

Intentional deception should be avoided whenever possible. Participants should not be misled without extremely strong scientific or medical justification. In these circumstances, prior approval from an ethics committee is essential.

Debriefing

At the end of an investigation, participants should be debriefed as fully as possible and at the earliest opportunity. The investigator should provide the information needed for participants to complete their understanding of the research.

Debriefing does not justify or excuse any unethical aspect of an investigation.

Withdrawal

Participants must be made aware of their rights to withdraw from the investigation at any stage without having to explain or justify their reasons. When testing children, avoidance of the testing situation should be taken as withdrawal of consent.

Following debriefing, participants have the right of retrospective withdrawal of consent. In these circumstances, data and records relating to the participants must be destroyed.

Confidentiality and protection

All information collected should be assumed to be confidential unless otherwise agreed in advance. It should not be possible to identify individuals from published research.

Investigators have a primary responsibility to protect participants from physical and mental harm during the investigation. Participants must be asked about any factors, such as pre-existing medical conditions, that may pose particular risks.

There should be no concealment or deception when seeking information that might encroach on privacy.

Observational research

Studies based on observation must respect the privacy and psychological well-being of the individuals concerned. Unless prior consent is obtained, observational research is only acceptable in situations where those involved would expect to be observed by strangers. Particular account should be taken of local cultural values.

The scientific method

Research in the natural and social sciences is based on the scientific method. The point of the method is to eliminate subjective judgements, personal opinion, guesswork and narrowly based intuition.

In a positive way, the scientific method also places little value on common sense. For thousands of years, for example, it seemed obvious that the sun revolved around the earth. The scientific method disproved this common-sense view.

Medical research has shown that much of the folklore relating to health is erroneous. It has also found that some customs and traditions are beneficial and should be encouraged. Without the scientific method, it would be impossible to tell one from the other.

The diagram summarises the three main kinds of research.

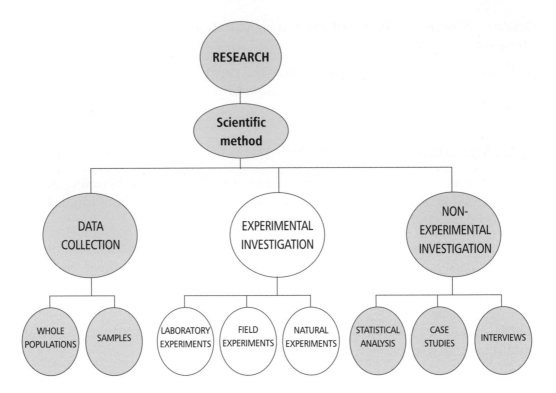

Data collection

The simple collection of descriptive data is the bedrock of medical research. In the UK, there are formalised and legally enforced systems for data collection. For instance:

- Total UK population is measured by a 10-yearly census. This also shows population by region, county, city, town and district.

- Births, deaths and marriages have to be registered.

- Place, date and cause of death must be recorded. This gives data on life expectancy, infant mortality, birth rates, trends in diseases and disorders and so on.

- The NHS and private health providers are legally obliged to collect, record and process a mass of health-related information. This includes admissions, procedures undertaken, length of stay, drugs administered and so on.

Hypothesis and experimental investigations

A meaningful experiment is not a hit-and-miss affair. Prior thought and planning is always involved. Generally, experiments follow the same pattern:

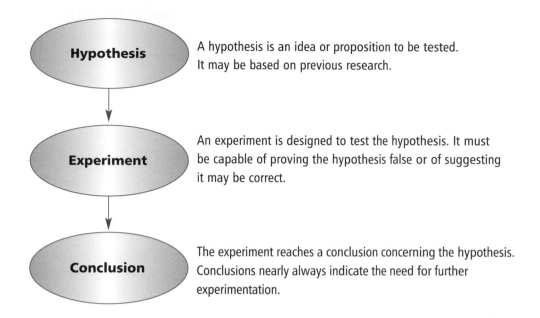

Hypothesis — A hypothesis is an idea or proposition to be tested. It may be based on previous research.

Experiment — An experiment is designed to test the hypothesis. It must be capable of proving the hypothesis false or of suggesting it may be correct.

Conclusion — The experiment reaches a conclusion concerning the hypothesis. Conclusions nearly always indicate the need for further experimentation.

Experimental design

An experiment usually involves the investigation of two variables. Psychological and natural science investigations follow identical principles, but the details often differ. Psychological experiments are more difficult to design. Consider these two illustrations.

	Natural science investigation	Psychological investigation
Hypothesis to be tested	Resting pulse rate increases with age	Memory declines with age
Independent variable	Age	Age
Dependent variable	Resting pulse rate	Memory capacity

The independent variable can be manipulated by selecting appropriate samples. The hypothesis defines the dependent variable – we are proposing that pulse rate and memory capacity depend on age.

Extraneous variables

Our first hypothesis is going to test the proposal that pulse rate depends on age. The many other influences on pulse rates – those outside the scope of our experiment – are known as extraneous variables. The experiment must be designed to minimise or eliminate their ability to confuse or invalidate the investigation. In the pulse rate trial we can identify a long list of complicating factors, for instance:

- Recent physical exertion or psychological stress. 'Resting' has to be defined or standardised for all participants. We may know that prolonged stress causes prolonged elevated pulse rate, regardless of physical exercise.

- Pulse rate is known to depend on general physical fitness.

- Pre-existing medical conditions can have a major influence.

- Many drugs have been developed to control and regulate heart function. Some of these affect pulse rate directly and significantly.

- Most of all, the test itself may alter pulse rate.

Reliability and validity

All experiments involve measurement, so this has to be reliable. In the pulse rate investigation, reliability would not be a major problem. For our chosen variables, a birth certificate could prove age and a good watch would be a reliable measure of pulse rate.

Validity is a more complicated idea, but again, this is not often an issue in natural science. For example, it would be difficult to confuse a pulse rate with another variable.

However, validity and reliability are major challenges in psychological trials.

Designing psychological investigations

In our illustration, the second hypothesis to be tested is that memory declines with age – the independent variable is the same but the dependent variable cannot be measured directly. It may not even be capable of precise definition. Without this precise definition, the investigation might be invalid. For instance, should we measure short-term memory or long-term memory? Also, what aspect of memory are we interested in – names, faces, places, numbers, dates, or something else?

An investigation of short-term memory is reasonably easy to put together but it should be immediately obvious that this kind of trial may be less reliable than the age/pulse rate research.

Participants could be asked to study a series of flash cards for, say, 30 seconds. Each card might carry a two-digit number. After a break of, say, five minutes the participants could be asked to write down the numbers they can remember.

The experimental conditions are arbitrary. Different results might be obtained with different examination times – say, two minutes instead of 30 seconds. The delay between examination and recall could be reduced or extended – for example, when does short-term memory capacity shade into long-term ability? There is also no obvious way of grading the results of this experiment. Is five correct out of 10 only half as good as 10 out of 10? Should a number remembered with the digits reversed count as half a mark?

Validity is a more serious issue. We may not be testing short-term memory at all. We might be investigating intelligence; we could also be testing interest in puzzles. Some people always want to win or succeed, others are more laid back. This investigation may really be testing competitiveness or aggression.

Long-term memory

A reliable and valid experiment to investigate long-term memory is very difficult to design. Test questions could be general or personal, for example: 'What was the name of your first teacher at infant school?'. There are two possible replies: 'I can't remember' or a name which is almost certainly impossible to check or verify. You might then ask, 'Who was Prime Minister in 1975?'. Although the correct answer is easily verified, this question is as much a test of the participant's interest in politics as it is of memory.

A reliable and valid investigation of long-term memory capacity and its possible association with age would involve tracking and regular testing of the same group for maybe 10 or 20 years.

Field versus laboratory

Human behaviour is extremely sensitive to surroundings and environment. We all act differently in different situations. A laboratory investigation does not have to happen in a laboratory – it is a general term used to describe research which takes place under closely controlled conditions. Similarly, field research means investigation of behaviour in real-life environments.

A psychologist researching crowd behaviour at football matches could simulate a real game by collecting 30 or 40 fans in a laboratory and showing them a video of an emotional hard-fought FA Cup semi-final. The alternative would be to buy a ticket and go to the ground to watch a real football match.

In this case, the field experiment is more valid but the laboratory investigation ought to be more reliable. Psychological research often involves compromise and the use of both techniques.

Factor	Field investigation	Laboratory investigation
Environment	Natural	Artificial
Independent variable	Controlled	Controlled
Sample selection	Inevitably random or whole population	Random by design
Extraneous variable	Very difficult to control	Easier to control
Equipment	Complex equipment cannot usually be used	Trial can be designed around equipment use
Cost	Usually higher	Usually lower

Non-experimental investigations

Some of the most valuable medical research takes place away from laboratories and without direct patient or client contact. The NHS employs many medical statisticians. Their work is to compare sets of descriptive data in an attempt to find correlations or associations between two or more variables.

Most of our knowledge concerning the influence of lifestyle on health started with statistical analysis. Statistical analysis is a vital tool in the attempt to disentangle the contributions of inheritance and environment in very many diseases and disorders.

Natural experiments

Some psychological experiments are impossible to design; some may be possible but utterly unethical.

Sometimes, the right people are in the right place at the right time to observe human behaviour under exceptional stress. During the 1930s, most psychologists thought that the mass aerial bombing of cities would cause large-scale panic and a complete breakdown of social order. This theory was disproved during the early part of the Second World War, when cities like London and Coventry were attacked for months on end. Most people were remarkably resilient and, if anything, social order and cohesion increased, rather than collapsed. This was a natural experiment.

Case studies

Case studies are widely used as teaching aids in medicine and healthcare. Typically, the progress of a particular client or group of clients is closely monitored from first presentation, through a course of treatment and then on to some final conclusion. Particular note is made of turning points observed or important decisions made by the practitioners involved. The case study is then documented or 'written up' in considerable detail and used as a model or simulation to train practitioners who are likely to face similar challenges in the future. Cross-comparisons of case studies are an important tool in research.

The research process in summary

Research is a continuing process. Scientists communicate and cooperate with each other by publishing their results and inviting peer review. A peer is an equal – in science this means a specialist working in a similar or related field. Peer review can involve support for or confirmation of somebody else's research – sometimes, work can be refuted or criticised. In most instances, publication, peer review and peer group discussion produce new hypotheses and new research proposals. In this way, the research cycle continues.

Research in practice

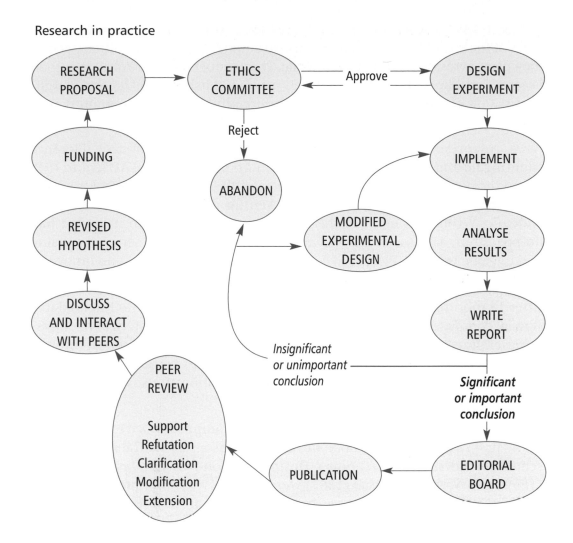

Florence Nightingale (1820–1910)

No account of research in healthcare can be complete without acknowledgment of the work of Florence Nightingale. After Queen Victoria, Florence Nightingale is generally recognised as the most influential British woman of the 19th century. She is best remembered as the founder of modern nursing, but few know that she was also the first to use healthcare statistics and documentation on a major and consistent basis.

Florence Nightingale was born into a privileged family. Her father was a politician and landowner, her mother was active in the movement to abolish slavery. Unlike many Victorian women, Florence was well educated and she showed a particular aptitude for mathematics. Her vocation was for nursing, but initially her father would not allow her to train for the profession – at that time, nurses were regarded as little better than kitchen maids. Her father relented and at the age of 33, Florence worked for a year as the unpaid superintendent of the Hospital for Invalid Gentlewomen in London.

In March 1854, Britain joined with France to resist Russian attempts to occupy parts of the crumbling Ottoman or Turkish empire. Most of this military action took place across the Crimean peninsula. The conduct of the Crimean War soon became a public scandal. *The Times* newspaper published daily reports of military incompetence and in particular of the dreadful conditions in military hospitals.

As a response to public outrage, the Secretary for War sent Florence Nightingale and a team of 38 nurses to Scutari in the Crimea. At Scutari they found the hospital was a converted barracks with straw mats, no cooking facilities, polluted water and no sanitation. Vermin, dysentery and cholera were endemic. Within six months, the death rate amongst British wounded had dropped from 47% to 3%. As well as implementing a whole series of nursing and hygiene reforms, Florence kept meticulous records. She was an innovator in the use of tables, graphs and charts.

After 18 months in the Crimea, she was invalided back home to England in a state of complete physical and emotional exhaustion. This pattern of relentless never-ending hard work, followed by periods of collapse, was to repeat through most of her life. She spent her last 50 years confined to a sick room, but nevertheless masterminded many of the reforms and innovations we now take for granted.

Florence Nightingale's contributions to a Royal Commission led to the creation of the first Army Medical School. In 1860, she was instrumental in founding a school for nursing at St Thomas' Hospital in London. Her *Notes on Nursing* (1859) and *Notes on Hospitals* (1863) were the first texts that properly defined the rules of hygiene, competence and conduct that are still seen as the essentials of the nursing profession.

The sentimental image of Florence Nightingale as the 'lady with the lamp' has little connection with the truth. By today's standards, she would have been judged obsessive, overbearing and ruthless. History shows that progress often follows the efforts of difficult and unreasonable people – Florence Nightingale is an excellent example of this generalisation.

3 Quantitative and qualitative research

People have two kinds of characteristics – those that can be measured directly using tools and instruments, and those that cannot be measured but can be judged, ranked or assessed.

Quantitative research produces results which can be expressed as quantities or numbers. For example, about 700,000 babies were born in the UK in the year 2000. Each was weighed at birth and their weights recorded. An arithmetic mean of these 700,000 numbers could be calculated to give an average birth weight accurate to, say, the nearest gram.

Another example is the considerable amount of ongoing qualitative research investigating women's views of the service provided by the NHS during pregnancy and childbirth. The results of these studies cannot be summarised by a single number; nonetheless, it is essential and genuine research.

Qualitative investigation in healthcare is concerned with thoughts, feelings and emotions. It has to be based on social interaction – through question and answer – because there is no instrument that can measure things like anxiety, confidence, optimism or depression.

On the borderline

Interviews and questionnaires are the basis for nearly all psychological research in healthcare. The dividing line between qualitative and quantitative investigation becomes blurred if a questionnaire is closely structured and used to study the views, opinions or behaviour of a large number of participants.

Work of this sort is essentially qualitative but it can be analysed in ways similar to pure quantitative research.

In-depth unstructured interviews with small numbers of participants are qualitative research.

Measurement

There are four kinds of measurement:

- By category.
- By order or rank.
- By interval.
- By ratio.

The differences are important if we are trying to compare quantitative and qualitative research.

Category

Category measurement is straightforward and familiar. You might find that a patient or client was female, pregnant, AB blood group and a resident of Northamptonshire. For gender there are only two possibilities, likewise for pregnancy – you are either pregnant or not. There are four categories in the ABO blood-group system, and you can only be one of these.

The fourth category – in this case residence – can be manipulated by the investigator. An experiment might divide participants into two categories – those resident in Northamptonshire and all of those that live elsewhere. The number of residence categories could be extended significantly if this was relevant to the investigation.

No hierarchy is presumed in category information. For example, being female and blood group AB is not better than being male and blood group O.

You cannot calculate averages for category data, but you can produce frequency information. For example, we know that in England about 46% of individuals are blood group O and only around 3% are AB.

Order, rank or sequence

Many measurements are expressed as a sequence or rank.

Ranking is a popular technique in consumer and market research. You might be asked to arrange ten TV programmes or eight brands of soft drink into an order of preference. The word 'preference' is important. Market research tries to identify the most popular product – not the one that is best in any absolute sense.

In healthcare investigations, rank measurements usually try to establish some genuine hierarchy rather than just grade preferences. Patients are often asked to rank pain on a scale of 0 to 10, where 0 is freedom from pain and 10 is unbearable or excruciating. This technique is valuable but far from foolproof.

For any particular respondent we can be reasonably sure that a rating of 8 would be far worse than a rating of 2 given on a previous occasion, but this does not mean that 8 is four times worse than 2.

Following the same surgical procedure, a group of similar patients would very probably report different pain ratings. We have no way of knowing if these differences are genuine. It is also likely that, in these circumstances, the word 'genuine' does not mean very much – because response to pain is hugely variable. All of the pain ratings could be different and all could be genuine.

Interviews and questionnaires often use words instead of numbers to produce orders or ranks. The principles are identical. For example:

Question: Do you think that the accident and emergency service at Hospital X has improved over the last three years? Tick the box that most closely corresponds to your view.

Answer:

Strongly agree	Slightly agree	Do not agree or disagree	Slightly disagree	Strongly disagree

Interval and ratio measurements

Measurements by category or rank are difficult to analyse. Statistics like average, maximum or minimum values cannot always be calculated and comparisons between different sets of categories or ranks may have little meaning.

'Real' numbers and quantities do not present these problems because all of the common units of measurement work with fixed intervals. This may seem like a pointless glimpse of the obvious but it is the foundation of all quantitative measurement.

The difference between 101 g and 100 g is the same as the difference between 4 g and 3 g. Also, the mass measurement scale has a zero point – zero mass is zero grams. This means that mass calculations always give precise and definitive answers: 400 g is exactly twice as much as 200 g, 1 kg minus 300 g is precisely 700 g, and so on.

You cannot add, subtract, divide or multiply the results of psychological experiments whose measurements involve categories or rankings.

Zero points and logarithmic scales

You need to know that very occasionally you will come across units of measurement that do not work with fixed intervals or that have two different definitions of the zero point.

A temperature of 80 °C is not twice as hot as 40 °C because 0 °C is not the coldest temperature there is. We use 0 °C as a false zero for convenience – this is the freezing point of pure water.

A fixed-interval scale can also be called a linear scale. Some scales are logarithmic rather than linear. The only logarithmic measure you are likely to meet in healthcare is pH, which describes the acidity or alkalinity of a solution.

A solution, which may be a sample like blood or urine, is neutral if it has a pH of 7.0. Figures below 7.0 denote acidity; those higher than 7.0 describe an alkaline solution. Each change of one unit of pH corresponds to a tenfold change or acidity or alkalinity. The diagram explains.

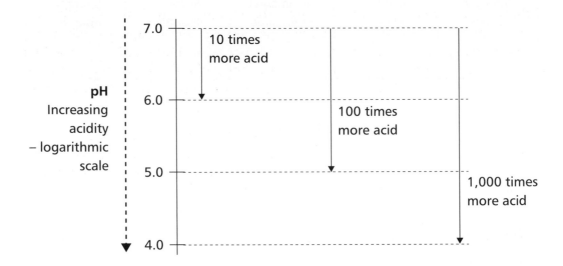

There are medical implications. A change in blood pH from 7.35 to 7.05 may seem trivial but it is in fact significant and an important factor in diagnosis.

Objectivity, subjectivity and bias

Measurements in healthcare do not always produce true or real values. The characteristic being measured may be highly variable, so that a quantity recorded at any particular time may not be representative or typical of the client's true condition. Instrument accuracy varies, as does the skill and experience of the person doing the measuring.

Some measures are more objective than others and less likely to be influenced by human error or expectation. The most objective measurements are those involving simple or purpose-designed instruments like weighing machines or automated blood analysers.

Interviews and questionnaires work with subjective measures so human bias is always a factor. Both the investigator and the participant can show bias.

The investigator may expect a certain set of responses based on the client's appearance or manner. Unexpected responses can be seen as errors or of no significance.

Social desirability bias is common. Participants typically under-report behaviour like smoking, excessive alcohol consumption and unsafe sexual habits, but over-report desirable characteristics like exercise and good diet.

A third kind of bias involves recall. Asking a participant to remember or describe past behaviour gives less reliable results than investigation of what the client did today or yesterday, for example.

Blind trials

Blind or masked trials are attempts to eliminate subjectivity and bias. Techniques vary, but all investigations of this sort are designed to minimise complicating interactions between investigator, participant and the individual or group analysing the results of the experiment. Blind trials are impossible in interview-based research, but triple blind experiments are usually essential in drug development.

A triple blind trial is one in which the health practitioner, the patient and the research staff have no knowledge of the treatment the patient is receiving. This information is only available, usually in coded form, to an independent uninvolved research director.

Populations and samples

Research begins with a hypothesis. For example:

1   Regular exercise increases cardiovascular efficiency.

2   Wheelchair users have limited access to the NHS.

3   General practitioners working in the London Borough of Newham are more stressed than GPs working in the London Borough of Bromley.

The target population for the first hypothesis could be everybody in the UK or even the entire population of the world.

The population for the second hypothesis is a smaller group with two shared characteristics – they are wheelchair users and potential clients of the NHS. It may, however, be difficult to define 'wheelchair user' – does this include infrequent or temporary use?

The third hypothesis is different. It precisely defines two groups and a total population of a few hundred.

All research has to operate within limited resources. There is never enough money, equipment or trained people to support all of the experiments and trials that might give valuable results. Most research works with samples selected from target populations. The word 'population' has a special meaning in statistical theory – it describes the entire group from which a sample is chosen. A population need not be a collection of people. A mechanical engineer might select a sample of bolts from a population of bolts for strength and safety testing.

It is not usually possible to test a whole population regardless of its size. In our third hypothesis, many of the London GPs would be too busy to spare time for a non-essential research project.

Sampling methods

Statistical analysis is used to infer conclusions about populations based on sample measurements. Statistical theory breaks down if the sample is not representative of the population. A biased sample is the opposite of a representative one.

It is sometimes difficult to select a representative sample and even more difficult to confirm that the sample is representative. Returning again to the GP stress hypothesis, those that volunteered to take part are likely to be less stressed than the population overall. Special methods would be needed to select representative samples from both groups of GPs.

Random sampling is the most statistically reliable method. A sample is truly random if every member of a population has an equal chance of selection and if the choice of one member does not influence the chances of another member being chosen.

Many populations have some kind of identifying number – typically a patient number or a National Insurance code. Special computer software has been designed to select random samples from these large populations.

Primary and secondary sources

Information gathered via your own research, or by others conducting an experiment that you have designed, is called a primary source. Everything else is a secondary source.

Because research is a continuing process, secondary sources are always used in the development of new hypotheses and new original-research projects.

4 Interviews

As commonly used, the word 'interview' describes a process with a certain level of inbuilt stress and tension. Police interview suspects, job candidates are sometimes outnumbered by a large panel of interviewers, TV commentators interview or 'grill' politicians in front of audiences of millions.

In psychological research, interview techniques are designed to minimise stress. They are private in all but the most exceptional circumstances and only rarely include more than two people – the interviewer or researcher and the interviewee or participant.

Interviews are used to investigate behaviour that cannot be observed, or at least not ethically observed. The technique can also be used to research reasons for particular behaviour patterns or to reconstruct significant past events.

There are three kinds of interview:

- Unstructured.

- Semi-structured.

- Structured.

Unstructured interviews

Viewed from a distance 'with the sound turned down', it would be impossible to tell the difference between a good unstructured interview and a friendly conversation. Unstructured interviews have no formal agenda and, within reasonable limits, no fixed time frames. They allow a great deal of freedom for both parties and opportunities to develop any relevant issue. Participants are likely to feel relaxed and to talk with fewer inhibitions.

Unstructured interviews place considerable burdens on the investigator. Experience, sensitivity and some background knowledge of the participant and the issues are needed.

Semi-structured interviews

In a semi-structured interview, the investigator starts with a list of general headings or topics for discussion – the interview has a predetermined goal or objective. Some freedom is allowed, but the interviewer does not depart for long from a defined schedule. Semi-structured interviews are less demanding for the researcher than unstructured techniques.

As a disadvantage, valuable information may be lost if it does not fit readily into the chosen framework. Bias is also a risk, because the extent to which questions may be reworded or resequenced is difficult to decide once the interview has started.

Structured interviews

Aside from privacy, there is very little difference between a fully structured interview and a questionnaire that is delivered through face-to-face meeting. A number of questions are usually printed in full on a pre-prepared form. The investigator asks the questions precisely as written and in a sequence that should not be altered. Only a limited number of responses are catered for – often the researcher will tick one of several boxes that best matches the participant's response. Structured interviews are usually time-limited and shorter than the semi-structured or unstructured alternatives.

The results of structured interviews are easy to analyse. Cross-comparisons amongst groups of participants can be straightforward because all have been asked the same questions in the same way. The investigator need not be highly skilled.

Structured interviews are not useful, and are usually not ethical, as tools to investigate sensitive or complex issues. The interviewer may misinterpret replies and the participant may not understand some questions. There are no opportunities to correct misunderstandings in most structured interview designs.

Closed and open questions

Two kinds of questions can be included in interviews and questionnaires.

Closed questions demand definitive answers or a restricted choice of replies. These are used in quantitative research like structured interviews and in most questionnaires.

Closed questions may force respondents into inappropriate or inaccurate choices – with a consequential loss of valuable information. As an advantage, closed questions are time efficient and easy to document and analyse.

Open questions are commonly part of qualitative research – answers are not pre-specified in any way. They give freedom of response, allowing a much wider range of replies.

Open questions are more difficult for both the investigator and the participant. They have to be devised with care and replies usually require much thought and effort.

5 Questionnaires

A questionnaire is a list of questions designed to collect information from a relatively large group. As previously discussed, there are overlaps and similarities between some interview and some questionnaire techniques. Interviews and questionnaires may be combined and targeted at large audiences – this research is one kind of survey.

Survey methods

A survey need not involve face-to-face contact. Questionnaires can be delivered by post, by electronic means like email, or they may be circulated among defined groups like the employees of an organisation, students at a school or college, or members of a particular occupation or profession. Some market research is conducted via telephone surveys.

The physical separation of investigator and respondent has benefits. Postal surveys can be much cheaper than transporting teams of investigators around the country, and they eliminate the possibility of investigator bias. However, postal and circulated surveys have many disadvantages:

- You cannot be sure that the addressee – the carefully selected participant – actually completed the survey. It might have been answered by a friend, partner or relative.

- It is impossible to judge the truthfulness of any response. This is a general problem for psychological research, but some interview techniques and some interviewers can spot and eliminate lies, half-truths and fantasy.

- The participant can read all of the questions before choosing replies. Sequenced or structured questioning to investigate an issue in greater depth is impossible.

Low or unpredictable response rates are the greatest disadvantage of postal surveys. There are two problems:

- A survey becomes very costly if only a small percentage of questionnaires are returned. Market research companies offer incentives, but even so, typical response rates can be less than 1%.

- More importantly, low response rates produce biased samples. People that always return surveys are not usually representative of most target populations.

Designing a survey

As part of the assessment for this unit you may be asked to design and conduct a survey. This will be rewarding, provided you tackle the project in a logical sequence.

- You need to start with a formally written hypothesis. What proposition are you testing? What information are you looking for?

- The hypothesis defines the target population. How will you contact them? How will you confirm the validity of the survey sample?

- At the outset, you need to decide how the survey results will be processed and analysed.

- You next need to devise a set of draft questions. It is always a good idea to run a preliminary trial of these with fellow students or colleagues. This will identify problem areas.

- All questionnaires have to be supported by a checklist, a form or a document of some kind. Once questions have been finalised, the form can be designed.

We will now look at these stages in detail.

Hypothesis and target population

The hypothesis may be general, specific or comparative. In the first case, no special precautions are needed to identify the respondents for a survey – almost anybody will do. The more general the survey, the less valuable its results are likely to be – usually this kind of research is only descriptive.

Most hypotheses are specific and are aimed at slices or subsets of the overall population, for example mothers with young children, retired men or car mechanics.

Sometimes your survey will want to compare two different groups, such as smokers and non-smokers or men and women.

From the beginning you need to have a firm idea of sample size – too small and its results will be unreliable, too large and you will not have time to complete the exercise. There are no hard and fast rules, but 50 respondents is the minimum sample size for most hypotheses. Similarly, you ought to have a target interview time. This translates into the number of questions you are going to ask. Most surveys have between 10 and 30 questions. The fewer the better, provided the questions are well designed.

Processing and analysis

This aspect must be considered before the work begins, never once you are faced with a pile of completed questionnaires. The replies to closed questions are relatively easy to handle. Usually these are coded or ranked to produce percentages or some measure of average and range. Open questions are more difficult. Often these can only be summarised using a qualitative commentary.

Question design, identifiers and quotas

Again, you must start with the hypothesis. What information is essential and what secondary information might be useful? If your hypothesis is selective or comparative, the first one or two questions need to be identifiers or quota questions. For instance, a survey on car preference ought to start with '**Do you own or have use of a car**?'.

Comparative surveys need to establish quotas. A survey comparing male and female behaviour would obviously be unreliable if you interviewed 48 women and six men. Gender is usually self-evident but some quotas may not be as easy to define.

The framing, phrasing or wording of the questions themselves is never easy. There are many traps and pitfalls for the inexperienced. The keys are clarity and brevity.

Questions not to ask

Vague questions are useless. For example, '**Do you eat fruit regularly**?' leaves the respondent to decide what regularly means – is it once a day, once a week, once a month or every Christmas? Better alternatives would be: '**Do you eat at least one portion of fruit a day?**' or '**On an average day, how many portions of fruit do you eat**?'.

Double questions should be avoided because accurate replies might be impossible. For instance: '**Do you like watching football and cricket on television?**'. Participants might like one or the other, both or neither.

Some single questions can have double answers. These should also be avoided. A respondent might be asked if she is an employee, self-employed, part time, full time or unemployed. Most of us could tick two boxes in answer to this question.

Leading questions are the commonest fault in questionnaires. By accident, a question can be worded so that one type of answer is more likely than another, regardless of the participant's real views. '**What is it that you like about your Access course**?' is a leading question. An alternative might be '**What part of your Access course do you most enjoy**?'.

Hypothetical questions usually give meaningless answers. For instance: '**If you were a surgeon, what would you regard as an acceptable salary**?'.

Questions including jargon, technical terms or those that require calculations should only be included if the target population is certain to have the appropriate skills or background to understand them. Surveys aimed at nurses can safely use words like hypertension and spontaneous abortion. For a more general audience, high blood pressure and miscarriage would be better.

Social desirability bias is a big problem in question design and one that cannot always be overcome. The more sensitive the question, the more neutral and unbiased the wording must be. Any hint of judgement or criticism must be eliminated.

Unethical questions

Even as a student, your research survey must conform to the codes of the appropriate or local ethics committee.

Offensive questions are not permitted under any circumstances. More importantly, the person designing the research might be a poor judge of what is likely to cause offence. Some areas are obviously inappropriate for public survey research, but other issues can cause unexpected problems. Age and income are good examples. Questions concerning income should not be included if at all possible, and many respondents will refuse to divulge their age, even within five- or ten-year brackets.

You should always discuss with teaching staff and supervisors any potential ethical problems. Sensitive questions give biased results, especially if sample size is reduced by many refusals.

Question sequence

The ordering of questions is important. There are some general rules.

The simplest closed questions, including the identifiers and quota questions should come first. Sequence is vital for linked questions. The more complex issues and open questions should be saved for the end of the list. If you are asking participants to choose one of a number of options, these should not be placed in what you think is the likely order of preference.

Many surveys are designed so that not all respondents are required to answer all the questions. Make sure that instructions like 'If the answer to question 4 is no, please go to question 10' are clear and accurate.

Designing the forms

A traditional survey involves an interviewer asking questions of a participant with the interviewer completing a form or document. Two people are present and interacting but only the interviewer needs to be able to understand and navigate his or her way around the form.

In postal surveys, no interviewer is present, so it follows that the form – the questionnaire itself – must be clear, precise and user friendly.

Other variants are possible. The participant might fill out the questionnaire and the interviewer may offer help and assistance as needed.

Therefore, first you have to decide if the interviewer or the participant will be filling in the form.

The document has to be prepared and presented to a high standard. Grammar, punctuation and spelling must be perfect and questions have to be clearly numbered; there must be enough space allocated for any reasonable reply. The questionnaire should be word processed. Remember, many people have trouble reading font sizes smaller than 11 point – 12 point is better. It is false economy to cram 20 questions onto two A4 pages when three or four pages would give a cleaner, clearer layout.

Be creative with lines, borders, tick boxes and font sizes. Sometimes arrows can help to indicate sequence, but the end result should not look fussy or cramped.

At the beginning of the survey, explain its purpose clearly and briefly. Where possible, guarantees of confidentiality and privacy should be given. A postal survey should show a completion or closing date for last returns.

At the end of the questionnaire, you should thank participants for their time and trouble.

The questionnaire itself is not the only piece of paper you will need to design. You will also need a control document of some kind. For traditional interview and questionnaire surveys, this shows:

- Date, time and place where participants were interviewed. Often a time period is sufficient rather than precise details for each interview.

- Quota tallies if needed – for example, running totals of male and female respondents.

- A record of the number of refusals and the numbers, if any, who refused to complete the survey or parts of the survey after initial agreement.

- A note of any exceptional conditions.

Safety and security

As part of an assessment you may have to act as an interviewer to collect responses for the survey you have designed. This is a fascinating experience, but you need to take some sensible precautions. We are describing here the traditional 'clipboard' interview-based survey where researchers stop passers-by and ask for 'a few minutes of their time'.

- You have the right to refuse to be an interviewer if you feel the experience would be too daunting or intimidating. Interviewers often work in pairs but three or more is unacceptable.

- Always choose a busy pedestrian location. Do not start interviewing before 9 am and do not continue after 6 pm, or after dark in winter months.

- Carry your student ID card or some other current proof of identity.

- Limit each work period to an hour, or 90 minutes at most. Accuracy declines rapidly after this.

- Some shopping centres and retail precincts are private property. You will need permission to work in these locations. Railway stations, bus stations and airports are not suitable sites for surveys – people are always in a hurry.

- Do not cause an obstruction. Always move on if asked to by security staff, traffic wardens or the police.

- Do not attempt a survey in poor weather conditions and abandon work for the day if the weather deteriorates. Nobody wants to stand in the rain asking or answering questions.

- Dress cleanly, tidily, modestly and comfortably. Do your best to look cheerful, friendly and approachable.

- When approaching potential respondents, be courteous at all times. Always take 'no' for an answer – never try to persuade a reluctant passer-by to take part.

- Do not get disheartened by many consecutive refusals – this often happens.

- Always let a friend, relative or colleague know where you are and what time you are expected home or back at college. Carry a mobile phone if you have one.

6 Observational research

In one way or another, all research is observational because it is an essential part of the experimental design sequence.

In psychology, observational research has a narrower meaning. There are two categories – non-participant and participant observation.

Non-participant observation

Here, the observer takes no part in the behaviour being observed. Ideally, the observation should not be detected by the subjects of the research. The investigator merely watches, listens and takes notes.

These experiments can give valuable insights into normal or natural behaviour.

Non-participant observation is used to study behaviour in circumstances that would be difficult or unethical to simulate. In a large general hospital, for example, simply sitting in an out-patient waiting room or in an accident and emergency centre might reveal a great deal about individuals in stressful or irritating situations.

Non-participant observational techniques do, however, have many drawbacks:

- It is often impossible to avoid detection for more than brief periods. Abnormal or unrepresentative behaviour is virtually guaranteed if people think they are being watched.

- This research is qualitative, difficult to analyse and difficult to duplicate or verify. Two different observers often reach different conclusions.

- There is major scope for misinterpretation and error. It is, for instance, impossible to prove cause and effect. You could observe or hear raised voices, but this might be usual behaviour for the subjects concerned and not a response to a three-hour wait in casualty.

Participant observation

With this technique, the observer becomes part of the group or situation under study. Deception need not be involved – a lecturer might ask to 'sit in' on a discussion or debate between two groups of students, for instance.

Deception or pretence must, however, be used if a research project is not to be influenced by the presence of an 'outsider'. A researcher wanting to understand how a building site works might get a job as a bricklayer's labourer and observe from the inside, not revealing his or her true profession.

The degree of involvement in participant observation can vary. Ideally, the observer should have the smallest possible influence on the group under study, consistent with an ability to make and record meaningful observations.

A health researcher might decide to join a smoking cessation self-help group posing as a non-expert. Clearly, this researcher should avoid being elected chairman or secretary of the group.

All of the problems of analysis, reliability and misinterpretation apply more or less equally to participant and non-participant observation. Participant research can be conducted in greater depth, but its results are always biased, unless the researcher is exceedingly competent and experienced.

Observational research ethics

Many research supervisors and ethics committees take strong positions against observational research, especially participant experimental designs. It is difficult to deny the argument that the more valuable the results become, the more unethical the investigation is likely to be.

There can be little objection to simple anonymous observation in public spaces or situations, but anything more needs careful consideration. As a generalisation, an alternative technique should be chosen if at all possible. The dividing lines between observation, snooping and spying are very narrow and difficult to define.

7 Results analysis and presentation

Every measurement or observation made during an experiment should be recorded and documented.

A long list of disorganised raw data is pointless because it transmits very little meaning to an external observer. In this topic we show how data is summarised or presented so that outsiders can immediately grasp the results and significance of a research project.

Pictorial and numerical presentations

The pictorial presentations you need to understand are:

- Tables.

- Graphs.

- Pie charts.

- Bar charts and histograms.

The numerical presentations you need to understand are:

- Average or arithmetic mean.

- Median.

- Mode.

- Range.

Tables

Tables are familiar but often badly used and presented. There are some basic rules:

- A table must have a title so that it can be extracted from your report and used by somebody else.

- Every row and column should have a heading.

- You should show totals for each row and column and a grand total at the bottom right-hand corner if appropriate.

- Very large tables are difficult to read. Split or divide into several smaller ones if possible.

- Often tables make more sense if values are given as percentages rather than absolute numbers. Sometimes it helps to show both.

- Always check additions and subtotals.

See the following example.

Table 4 An investigation of attitudes towards smoking by age
Question: 'Smoking should be banned in all public places.' Location: Exeter, May 2002

Age / *View*	15 to 24	25 to 34	35 to 44	45 to 54	55 to 64	65+	Total
Strongly agree	10	21	12	7	12	8	70
Slightly agree	8	9	8	9	20	17	71
No strong view	5	3	8	7	5	2	30
Slightly disagree	12	10	4	4	6	11	47
Strongly disagree	6	6	2	4	7	12	37
Total respondents	41	49	34	31	50	50	255

These numbers are much easier to understand if they are further summarised and turned into percentages, as follows.

Table 4a *'Smoking should be banned in all public places'*

Age bracket	Strongly or slightly agree (%)	No strong views (%)	Strongly or slightly disagree (%)	Total (%)
15 to 24	44	12	44	100
25 to 34	61	6	33	100
35 to 44	59	23	18	100
45 to 54	52	22	26	100
55 to 64	64	10	26	100
65 plus	50	4	46	100
Total	55	12	33	100

Graphs

A graph is a picture of some information. It is often the best way of summarising a complex set of results.

The starting point for a graph is a two-column table showing the observed relationship between two things or variables, as in the following example.

Average ambulance response times to emergency calls in region X during 2003, by month

2003, month	Averaged response time* in minutes
January	15
February	15
March	10
April	11
May	8
June	7
July	6
August	9
September	9
October	11
November	12
December	14

*Response time is defined as the time elapsed between receiving an emergency call and the arrival of the first ambulance at the accident or emergency scene

Note that we are already working with summarised or condensed information. A response time of, for example, 15 minutes in January would be an average of many call-outs.

A pattern is detectable from the table, but a graph gives a clearer and quicker idea of what really happened.

Axes, origins and scales

You can draw a graph using a computer package or by hand. In both cases, the rules are the same:

- The horizontal line or axis is called the *x* axis – remember 'x is across'.

- The vertical line or axis is called the *y* axis – remember 'wise up'.

- The point at the bottom left-hand corner of the graph where the two axes meet is called the origin.

- By convention, time is always shown on the horizontal or *x* axis because most of us imagine time as flowing forward. In other graphs there are no strict rules governing which variable should be shown on which axis. Choose the clearer or more logical layout.

- Each axis has to be labelled and divided into equal intervals.

- Each point on the graph is called a plot or a plot point. These are usually marked with a small cross, dot or circle.

- In most presentations, the plot points are joined together. This is the plot line.

The graph below shows the results of the ambulance investigation. Abbreviated labelling is perfectly acceptable provided the abbreviations are clear (in this case Jan for January, and so on).

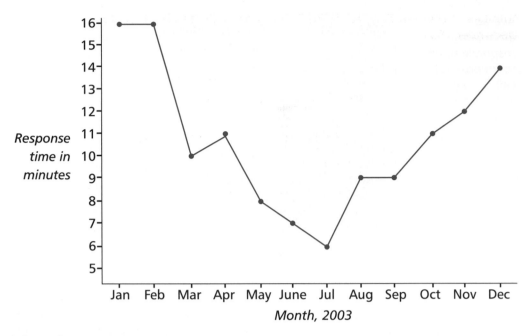

Month, 2003

Pie charts

Pie charts are by far the best way of presenting most category information. They are frequently used in newspapers and magazines because they are so easy to understand. Again, the start point is tabulated information, for example:

Family size in region A, December 1991

Women who have given birth to	Number of women
No children	180
1 child	213
2 children	593
3 children	298
4 children	92
5+ children	51
Total respondents	1,427

Percentages and angles

A pie chart is a circle divided into a number of slices. A full circle has 360°, so we have to calculate the angle for each slice. For example:

Category	Number	% of total	% of 360° 'slice angle'
No children	180	13	47
1 child	213	15	54
2 children	593	42	151
3 children	298	21	76
4 children	92	6	22
5+ children	51	3	10
Total	1,427	100	360

The calculations only need to be accurate to the nearest degree and percentage point.

Number of children born to mothers in region A. Research conducted December 1991

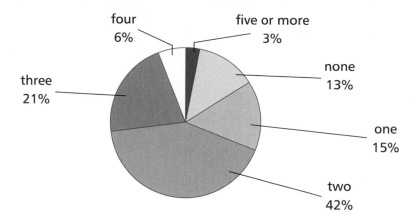

You cannot tell from this chart or the table how many women have five, six or more children because these large families are grouped together under one heading. Summary presentations always sacrifice some detail for the sake of clarity and easy understanding.

Bar charts and histograms

Graphs and pie charts are not suitable for presenting the results of large investigations. Bar charts and histograms are better, in particular for continuous variables – things that are measured rather than counted. Take the following illustration.

An out-patient clinic treats anorexia nervosa sufferers. It is thought that weight after six months from first attendance is a good indicator of progress. Over a period of years, the clinic has collected 4,216 six-month weight recordings. Clients are weighed very accurately so nearly all of the recordings are different.

Classified information

Bar charts and histograms work with classified data. In our example, each of the 4,216 measurements would be allocated to a class or category.

Heaviest patient	59.3 kg
Lightest patient	32.1 kg
Range	27.2 kg

The data is first examined to find a maximum and minimum value and then the range or difference between the two.

This range of 27.2 kg can be accommodated within 10 weight bands, each of 3 kg. Each weight band has to be the same size. The clearest bar charts have between eight and about 15 classes – there are no strict rules. The table shows the 4,216 measurements grouped into 10 classes.

Eating disorders clinic, Hospital B, 1996 to 2003

Class	Six-month weight (kg)	Number of patients in each weight class
1	32–34.9	48
2	35–37.9	107
3	38–40.9	499
4	41–43.9	692
5	44–46.9	1,042
6	47–49.9	989
7	50–52.9	570
8	53–55.9	201
9	56–58.9	56
10	59–61.9	12
		4,216

Finally, the table of classified information is used to draw the bar chart or histogram – the two presentations are very similar. A bar chart uses simple vertical lines; a histogram shows the same information as adjacent or adjoining rectangles.

Often the class information can be shown in full detail on the horizontal scale – if not, an explanatory key must be given.

Bar chart   Histogram

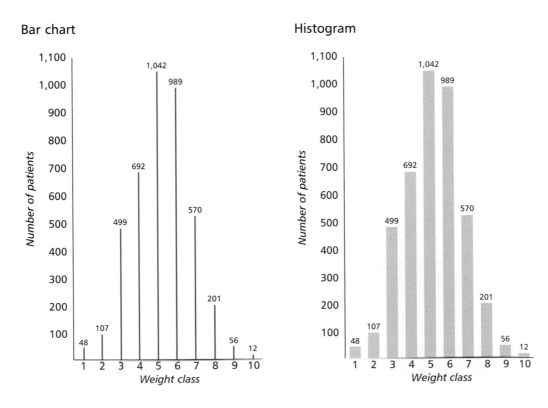

210

Averages or arithmetic means

The average, properly called the arithmetic mean, is the most commonly used statistic. It can, however, be misleading.

Three groups of five-year-old boys had their heights measured to the nearest centimetre. The results were as follows.

Boy number	Set A cm	Set B cm	Set C cm
1	107	104	96
2	108	105	96
3	108	106	98
4	108	107	99
5	108	107	105
6	108	110	119
7	108	110	119
8	108	111	119
9	109	112	121
Total	972 cm	972 cm	972 cm
Average	**108 cm**	**108 cm**	**108 cm**

The sets of numbers have the same average.

If these were the results of a trial into the influence of diet on growth, then the average height, used in isolation, would miss some important differences between the three groups – it does not take account of variation or spread.

You can tell just by looking that Set C is much more varied than Set B, which in turn varies more than Set A.

Median

The median is another kind of average that makes some allowances for variation. It is simply the middle number of a set once it has been arranged into ascending or descending order. In this example, the median height is that of boy number five. Therefore:

	Median height cm
Set A	108
Set B	107
Set C	105

The median is calculated slightly differently if the group has an even rather than an odd number of members. Say we removed boy 9 from Set C:

Boy number	Set C minus boy 9 cm
1	96
2	96
3	98
4	99
5	105
6	119
7	119
8	119

There are now two middle boys, number 4 and number 5. The median is the average of their two heights.

	Height cm
Boy 4	99
Boy 5	105
Median height	102

Mode

The mode of a set of numbers is the commonest number or the one there is most of. All groups of numbers must have an average and a median, but they need not have a mode, or there might be two or more modes or modal values.

	Mode or modal height cm
Set A	108
Set B	107 and 110
Set C	119

Range

Range is very easily calculated if a set of numbers is placed in order. It is the difference between the maximum and minimum values. For instance:

	Maximum height	Minimum height	Range
	cm	cm	cm
Set A	109	107	2
Set B	112	104	8
Set C	121	96	25

Range is a useful measure of variation for small groups of numbers that are very widely spread – like the example. For larger samples, perhaps with less variation, a more reliable statistic called the standard deviation is often used.

Chapter 7
Statistics

National unit specification
These are the topics you will be studying for this unit.

1 The uses and misuses of statistics

The words 'statistic' and 'statistics' are often used just to mean a number or a large group of numbers. In mathematics, the word 'statistic' has a different and more precise meaning – it is one number that describes or summarises a larger group of numbers.

The most familiar statistic is the average or arithmetic mean. A table showing the heights of 100 children is properly called data or raw data – their average height, of say 4 feet 8 inches, is a statistic.

Statistics, in the plural, also means the specialist branch of mathematics that you are now studying. At the outset, it is important to understand the difference between descriptive statistics and inferential statistics. The diagram explains.

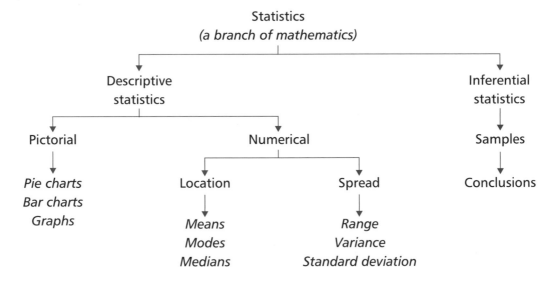

A list of, say, half a dozen numbers gives a message without the need for any rearrangement or further processing. The longer the list becomes, the more the message gets confused. A large table or array containing hundreds or thousands of numbers is meaningless.

Descriptive statistics

Descriptive statistics is the name given to techniques used to reduce, distil or summarise the information 'hidden inside' a large array of raw data.

Descriptive statistics can be further subdivided into types. Pictorial statistics are numbers turned into pictures – pie charts, bar charts and graphs. You do not have to use pictures; numerical statistics are numbers calculated from the raw data or sometimes a sample of the raw data.

Numerical descriptive statistics can be subdivided again. The difference is best explained using four sets of numbers as an example.

Set A		**Set B**	
	5		102
	5		97
	5		103
	6		98
	4		100
average $= \dfrac{25}{5} = 5$		average $= \dfrac{500}{5} = 100$	
range $= 6 - 4 = 2$		range $= 103 - 97 = 6$	

Set C		**Set D**	
	12		221
	1		41
	2		109
	3		68
	7		61
average $= \dfrac{25}{5} = 5$		average $= \dfrac{500}{5} = 100$	
range $= 12 - 1 = 11$		range $= 221 - 41 = 180$	

Measures of location

Set A is clearly very different from set B, because the average of A is 5 and the average of B is 100 – a much bigger number. In the same way, set C and set D are also very different.

A statistic like the average is called a measure of location or sometimes a measure of central tendency. These words seem difficult, but nobody has yet come up with better labels.

If you drew a number line from zero to 110, set A would be located at one end of the line and set B at the other – hence 'location'.

Put another way, the centre of set A would be a long way from the centre of set B – hence 'central tendency'.

The average, or arithmetic mean, is not the only measure of location. The mode and the median are more useful statistics in some situations.

Measures of spread

Set A and set C both have averages of 5; set B and set D both have averages of 100. However, the numbers in set C are more widely spread than in A. Similarly, set D is more widely spread than B. The range is a statistic showing the extent of the spread. The range for set D is much wider than the range for set B, even though both groups have an average of 100.

The range is a measure of spread. This kind of statistic may also be called a measure of variation, a measure of scatter or a measure of dispersion. This time, the names make immediate sense.

Inferential statistics

Going back to the diagram, you will see that the second major branch of the subject is inferential statistics.

A sample is taken from a population and a statistic is calculated from the sample. This is then used to reach a conclusion – a conclusion inferred from calculations based on the sample, not the whole population.

The word 'population' is used here to mean the total number of things or measurements under investigation. It does not only apply, for example, to the population of a town or a country. The weights of all the pigeons in Canada is a population, as is the total number of cars made at a factory in a year.

Two populations cannot usually be directly compared because measuring or counting the whole population would be impossible, time consuming or expensive. However, conclusions can be reached by comparing two samples taken from the two populations.

It is vital to realise that inferential statistics infer a conclusion – they cannot prove that a conclusion is correct. This branch of statistics works with probabilities not certainties.

A medical statistician might conclude that there is a 95% chance or a 99% chance that drug A is more effective than drug B, but he or she could not say with total certainty that A is better than B.

Cause and effect

Statistics says nothing about cause and effect. A statistical study might show that children who eat sugary foods and drinks get tooth decay. This study might also show that the association was simple and proportional – that the more sugar in a child's diet, the more tooth decay occurs. A straight line on a graph does not prove that sugar causes dental problems, nor does it prove that bad teeth cause a craving for sweets and soft drinks.

Statistics is a cornerstone of research but only because it gives pointers and clues to causes. Statistics plus a mechanism can, however, provide conclusive proof or a conclusion that is unlikely to be wrong. Dietary sugars in combination with oral bacteria produce acids which attack tooth enamel – this is the mechanism in our example.

Mechanisms may not always be this obvious, and it is all too easy to reach false or dangerous conclusions if statistics are used wrongly.

Inferential statistics are especially important in multi-factorial problems. Over the last 50 years, there has been a dramatic increase in cardiovascular disease, diabetes and some cancers in most developed countries. There are a number of possible causes for this trend – too much food, the wrong kind of food, too little exercise, smoking, excessive stress, pollution and so on. Statistics can help unravel this highly complex puzzle – it can infer which are likely to be major risks and which might be minor ones. Statistics can also infer that some combinations of risk factor may be more dangerous than others.

Nothing personal

In the true meaning of the words, there is nothing personal about statistics. We can describe the characteristics of a population but not the characteristics of any individual chosen from that population. For example: if you compare their average heights, men are taller than women. However, not all men are taller than all women – if this was so, you could identify a person's sex just by measuring their height. Statistics can, however, give probabilities. An adult measuring 6 feet 7 inches is very much more likely to be male than female.

Sampling theory

Sample theory gets complicated. For this unit, you only need a basic understanding of sample size and the precautions taken to make sure a sample is random and representative. We can use voting behaviour and election result predictions as examples of how samples are selected.

At the moment, in the UK, about 44 million people are entitled to vote. At general elections, we choose 659 MPs in 659 separate constituency elections, so in each constituency around 67,000 people have the vote.

In statistical terms, the total population is around 67,000 if you are trying to predict the result of a constituency election, or 44 million if you are trying to predict who will form the government.

Political opinion polls have to be based on samples because there is not enough time or money to interview more than a fraction of potential voters.

Common sense is not always a good guide to sampling theory. How the sample is selected is far more important than the absolute sample size. Very small samples are unreliable but properly chosen samples of a few thousand can give accurate predictions of national election results. Increasing the sample size from, say, 4,000 to 40,000 delivers very little increase in accuracy or reliability.

Random samples

The theory behind inferential statistics breaks down if samples are biased. A random sample is a familiar idea and we can define it precisely.

A sample is random if each individual in the population has an equal chance of being included in the sample and if the selection of one individual does not alter the chances of selecting another from the population.

Voting behaviour is known to depend on age, gender, class and region, amongst many other things. Samples chosen to predict a national election result would be biased if any one of these groups was over- or under-represented.

Samples can become outdated if the characteristics of a population change over time. This is a major issue in political opinion polling. A random sample of voting intentions taken in January would probably not be representative of the actual votes cast in a May election.

Which population?

It is often difficult to define the population that needs to be sampled.

In an election

$$\text{Percentage turnout} = \frac{\text{number of people actually voting}}{\text{number of people eligible to vote}} \times 100$$

In the 2001 UK general election, turnout was 59.4%, so two different populations could have been sampled – the 44 million who might have voted, or the 26 million who actually did.

As we said earlier, statistics infer conclusions but it cannot give total proof. Even the best-designed surveys and samples cannot predict the results of a very close election.

2 Pie charts and graphs

You should already have a basic understanding of pictorial data representations. In this topic, we look at pie charts and graphs in more detail. You need to know how to produce and use each of these, starting with a table or a list of raw data. To draw a pie chart you will need a protractor, a compass and a calculator.

In this first example, we show how to put together a simple pie chart and a series of charts that can be presented together to describe more detailed information.

The table lists part of the results of the 1990 US Census. It shows answers to the question 'What language do you most often speak at home?'.

Rank	Home language	Total replies
1	English	198,600,798
2	Spanish	17,339,172
3	French	1,702,176
4	German	1,547,099
5	Italian	1,308,648
6	Chinese	1,249,213
7	Tagalog*	843,251
8	Polish	723,483
9	Korean	626,478
10	Vietnamese	507,069
11	Portuguese	429,860
12	Japanese	427,657
13	Greek	388,260
14	Arabic	355,150
15	Urdu	331,484
16	Russian	241,798
17	Yiddish*	213,064
18	Thai	206,266
19	Farsi*	201,865
20	French Creole*	187,658
	All others	3,015,328
	Total	230,445,777

Source: US Census Bureau, 2001

*Tagalog is the main language of the Philippines. Farsi is the language of Iran, also spoken by other peoples in Asia. Yiddish is a German dialect incorporating many words from Hebrew. French Creole is spoken in the southern US.

Drawing pie charts

A single pie chart, even a very large one, would be a poor way of presenting all of this census data. There would be 21 slices – one very large one and many very thin slivers. No amount of shading, colouring or labelling would produce a clear picture. We can, however, construct a linked set of pie charts to make more sense of the figures.

We could use this information to draw a three-sector pie chart.

Language	Rounded raw data (millions)	%	Pie chart sector angle
English	198.6	86.2	310°
Spanish	17.3	7.5	27°
All others	14.5	6.3	23°
Total US	230.4	100.0	360°

We work with rounded raw data numbers because we only need to draw the pie chart angles to about the nearest degree.

Now we can draw a second pie chart with seven sectors, as follows.

Languages other than English or Spanish	Rounded raw data (millions)	%	Pie chart sector angle
French	1.702	11.7	42°
German	1.547	10.7	39°
Italian	1.309	9.0	32°
Chinese	1.249	8.6	31°
Tagalog	0.843	5.8	21°
Polish	0.723	5.0	18°
Other minor languages	7.133	49.2	177°
Total	14.506	100.0	360°

This process might be repeated a third time, but at some stage clarity gets lost as detail increases.

If space permits, a table of the raw data is often shown alongside a pie chart or a group of pie charts. The reader can then choose between a summary and a detailed presentation.

Pie charts should always have a heading giving the source of the data, its collection date and the total number or quantity represented by the whole pie.

Graphs

Graphs are a very common and effective way of presenting information.

Example

This table shows the number of women under the age of 21 who were married in the UK during the years 1985 to 1995.

This is how to draw a graph starting with this raw data:

(i) You have to decide whether to show the numbers of women on the vertical or horizontal axis. Sometimes the choice of axis makes no difference to clarity, but for this kind of data, the decision is easy. Time is always shown on the horizontal axis.

Year	Number of women
1985	82,209
1986	72,466
1987	68,629
1988	59,284
1989	54,256
1990	45,626
1991	38,305
1992	32,618
1993	26,839
1994	22,903
1995	20,643

Source: Office for National Statistics. © Crown copyright

(ii) You need to work out how best to show the numbers of women on the vertical axis. The origin does not often have to be the point where both variables have a value of zero. For this data, the lowest number of women is 20,643 and the highest is 82,209. A vertical scale starting at 20,000 and ending at 90,000 will accommodate all 11 figures.

Next, you label the vertical axis from 20,000 to 90,000 using equal intervals of 10,000 women. In the same way, you label the horizontal axis from 1985 to 1995. The axes of the graph should look like this:

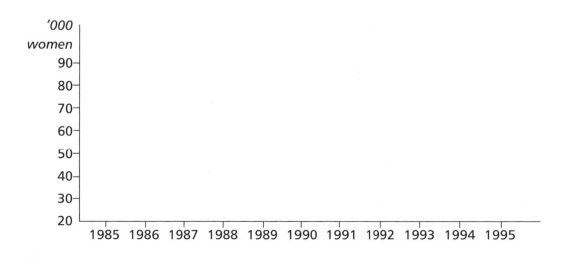

You will see that the labels are abbreviated. A key should always explain the abbreviation – in this case '000 women. You could also abbreviate the labels on the horizontal axis to '85, '86, '87 and so on.

When this graph is completed there will be an empty square at its bottom left-hand corner around the origin. Alternatively, the two scales could be shifted so that the origin marked the point corresponding to 20,000 women and the year 1985. Choose whichever method gives the clearest picture.

(iii) You can now plot the graph. Unless you are working with a very large piece of paper, with this scale you will only be able to plot rounded numbers on the vertical axis, for example plotting 82,209 as 82,000 or at best 82,200.

It usually helps to show the plot points as well as the plot line, like this:

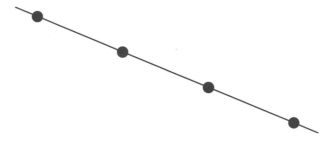

Extrapolation

Sometimes you can estimate, using graphs like this, what might happen in the future, based on an historical trend. Extrapolation is never more than an educated guess. It is reasonable to assume that the marriage rate fell again in 1996 and 1997 but a dramatic further decline to, say, 5,000 or 10,000 marriages might be an unreasonable prediction.

Big changes in external factors can make nonsense of all extrapolations. For example, there might have been a major income tax change in 1996 which discouraged or encouraged early marriage.

Extrapolations far into the future are usually completely unreliable – there is no way, using this graph, of predicting the early marriage rate for the year 2030, for example.

3 Bar charts, histograms and frequency polygons

Some observations or experiments produce thousands of readings. Organisations like the NHS and the Inland Revenue work with databases containing millions of numbers. Large arrays of raw data are difficult to describe pictorially – it would take a long time to plot 10,000 pairs of figures on a graph for example.

Extensive lists or tables of raw data are usually summarised using bar charts or histograms, but first the data has to be compressed or classified.

Data classification

These figures came from a study of the effect of diet on growth in young children. Some 1,033 12-month-old boys had their heights measured to the nearest 0.1 of a centimetre. The shortest was 70.1 cm, the tallest was 80.9 cm. The table shows how these 1,033 measurements can be classified.

Class	Class limits (cm)	Class frequency
1	70–70.9	4
2	71–71.9	24
3	72–72.9	90
4	73–73.9	115
5	74–74.9	321
6	75–75.9	223
7	76–76.9	135
8	77–77.9	58
9	78–78.9	47
10	79–79.9	14
11	80–80.9	2
Total		1,033

The overall size range of 10.8 cm – the tallest boy's height minus the smallest boy's height – is divided into a convenient number of classes. The clearest bar charts have between six and 15 classes, all of which must be the same size. This data happens to divide neatly into 11 classes, each of one centimetre.

The middle column on the table above shows the class limits. Each boy was measured to the nearest 0.1 cm – therefore the class limits have to be arranged so that there is no doubt about which height measurement goes into which class. A child measuring 70.9 cm belongs to class one, a boy of exactly 71.0 cm is counted in class two, and so on.

Each child on the list of 1,033 is placed into one of the 11 classes. The number in each class is called the class frequency.

Drawing the charts

The classified information can now be turned into a bar chart or a histogram. A histogram is commonly called a bar chart – a chart showing a number of adjacent or adjoining vertical rectangles. Using the correct terminology, a bar chart is one where the 'bars' appear as vertical lines. The diagrams show a bar chart and a histogram produced from some simple classified data.

Classified data:

Class	Class frequency
1	10
2	30
3	70
4	30
5	10
Total	150

Histogram

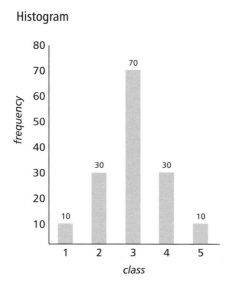

Bar chart

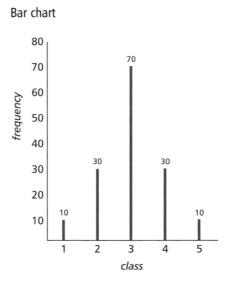

The actual class frequency is usually written at the top of each bar.

Frequency polygons

A frequency polygon is a histogram with a bit more added detail. A dot is placed at the centre of the upper edge of each vertical bar and the dots are joined together to give something very much like a graph plotline.

Frequency polygon

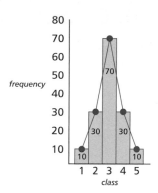

Data classification makes large arrays of numbers easier to understand. However, classification destroys detail. More often than not, the person using classified information has never seen the full array of raw data. How do we calculate medians and means if we only have classified data?

Median of classified data

The median is the middle number of a list of numbers arranged in ascending or descending order. Turning back to the first example, we saw classified information showing the heights of 1,033 one-year-old boys, arranged in ascending order. The median height is the height of the middle boy. The middle boy is boy number 517 because

$$\frac{1033}{2} + \frac{1}{2} = 517$$

or, put another way:

Shorter boys	516
Median boy	1
Taller boys	516
All the boys	1,033

We can work out which class includes the median:

- Adding the first four classes together, there are 233 boys.

- Adding the first five classes together, there are 554 boys.

- The median boy, number 516, must be in class 5 and therefore he must be 74 cm or taller, but not bigger than 74.9 cm.

This is all we can be certain of because class 5 might include 321 boys of 74 cm, 321 boys of 74.9 cm or any other combination that fits inside the class limits of 74 cm to 74.9 cm.

Averages, or arithmetic means, can be estimated from classified data but the calculation is time consuming and rarely used. A good statistician will always calculate a precise arithmetic mean from his or her raw data before passing the numbers on to somebody else for classification.

227

4 The standard deviation

Statistics uses a system called summation notation. The word 'sum' is informally used to mean any kind of calculation; each of these might be called a sum:

$$\sqrt{x} = 3, \quad ab = 15, \quad \frac{4b}{3} = x$$

To be totally accurate, a sum or summation should only be used to describe addition, for instance the sum of 6, 7 and 3 is 16.

The symbol Σ is the Greek capital letter sigma. Used in a formula it means 'add these numbers together'.

A summation can be shown algebraically using small subscripts, for example:

$$x_1 + x_2 + x_3 + x_4$$

This expression means 'add together four numbers, or the first four numbers in a set'. You would say 'x one plus x two plus x three plus x four'.

This way of doing things gets impossible if you are adding together hundreds or thousands of numbers. An instruction to add up 1,033 heights can be written more briefly as

$$x_1 + x_2 + x_3 + x_4 \ldots x_{1,033}$$

with the row of dots meaning 'carry on adding until you have included the last value' – in this case number 1,033.

An even better shorthand uses sigma, Σ. This says 'add together values of x'.

$$\Sigma x$$

However, this expression is unclear, because it does not tell you where to start adding and when to stop. To solve this problem, start and stop instructions are added to the sigma symbol, for example:

$$\sum_{n=1}^{n=1,033} x_n$$

Here, the term x_n is a general way of describing any number in a list or table. The expression means 'start with the first number and carry on adding until you have included the 1,033rd number, then stop'.

Usually, the summation symbol is written more simply, for instance as

$$\sum_{1}^{1,033} x_n$$

Summation examples

Statistical calculations would be difficult or impossible to explain without summation notation. Make sure you understand these:

(i) $\displaystyle\sum_{1}^{4} x_n$ = 10   because $1 + 2 + 3 + 4 = 10$

(ii) $\displaystyle\sum_{4}^{9} x_n$ = 39   because $4 + 5 + 6 + 7 + 8 + 9 = 39$

(iii) $\displaystyle\sum_{1}^{5} 2x_n$ = 30   because $2 + 4 + 6 + 8 + 10 = 30$

In this summation, $2x_n$ is an instruction to double the numbers 1 to 5 before summation. It is telling you to add together a string of even numbers.

(iv) $\displaystyle\sum_{1}^{6} (2x_n - 1)$ = 36   because $1 + 3 + 5 + 7 + 9 + 11 = 36$

In this summation, $(2x_n - 1)$ produces a list of odd numbers.

(v) $\displaystyle\sum_{1}^{8} x_n^2$ = 204   because $1 + 4 + 9 + 16 + 25 + 36 + 49 + 64 = 204$

You can see that summation notation is exceedingly powerful. The expression below takes seconds to write but the calculation it represents would take hours to complete.

$$\sum_{27}^{1,721} (x_n^3 + x_n) = ?$$

Averages or arithmetic means

Most statistical calculations include averages or, to use their correct label, arithmetic means. A horizontal bar placed above an algebraic term means that this number is an average of a group of numbers. So

$$\bar{x} = \text{the average of } x_1 + x_2 + x_3 \ldots x_n$$

$$\bar{a} = \text{the average of } a_1 + a_2 + a_3 \ldots a_n$$

You call this '*x* bar' or '*a* bar'.

You can use summation notation as part of a formula.

$$\bar{x} = \frac{\sum_{1}^{n} x_n}{n}$$

This is a general formula for calculating an average. It looks intimidating, but an example shows that it is no more than a set of simple instructions:

What is the average of 45, 107, 32 and 204?

(i) $x_1 = 45, x_2 = 107, x_3 = 32, x_4 = 204$

the order or sequence makes no difference

(ii)   n = 4 because there are four numbers in total. $x_n = x_4$

(iii) $\sum_{1}^{4} x_n = 45 + 107 + 32 + 204 = 388$

(iv)
$$\bar{x} = \frac{\sum_{1}^{4} x_n}{n} = \frac{388}{4} = 97$$

(v) $\bar{x} = 97$, the average of the four numbers.

Here, you could easily calculate an average, even if you had no idea what Σ means. In practical statistics, calculations are usually more complicated than simple averaging and you might have to handle thousands of numbers. Summation notation is the only way of showing precisely what steps are needed in any particular operation.

Location and spread

Means, medians and modes are measures of location. They are also called measures of central tendency – they all show where the centre of a group of numbers is located.

So far, we have only used one measure of spread or scatter – the range – that is, the difference between the biggest and the smallest numbers in a sample.

These five groups of seven numbers have the same average but different values for median, mode and range:

Notation	A	B	C	D	E
x_1	10	9	1	1	1
x_2	10	10	6	10	1
x_3	10	10	8	10	1
x_4	10	10	10	10	1
x_5	10	10	12	10	1
x_6	10	10	14	10	1
x_7	10	11	19	19	64
Total	70	70	70	70	70
$\bar{x}$ (mean)	10	10	10	10	10
Median	10	10	10	10	1
Mode	10	10	none	10	1
Range	zero	2	18	18	63

The median is the middle number – in this case, x_4. The mode is the most common number – in other words, the one there is most of. Group C has no mode because all of its members are different.

If these figures were pay rates in £/hour of five companies, each with seven employees, then it becomes obvious that the five firms are very different. For example, three of them – C, D and E – would be operating illegally in the UK, because £1 per hour is well below the statutory minimum wage. Companies A and B have slightly different pay policies; companies C and D are different but their average pay and range of pay rates are identical.

These four statistics, taken alone or taken together, cannot clearly describe how much variation there is in each group of numbers.

Standard deviation

The standard deviation is the best way of precisely describing spread – it also gives a number that can be used in further statistical analysis.

The three ideas behind standard deviation are straightforward:

- By definition, every sample of numbers has an average, although none of the numbers in the sample has to equal the average – like the pay rates for company E.

- A sample where many of its members differ from the average has a greater spread than one where only a few members are different from the average.

- A sample where many of its members differ a great deal from the average is more widely spread than one where these differences from the average are smaller.

The standard deviation is a statistic that combines and measures both of these different kinds of spread. The standard deviation calculation produces a single summary number.

The word 'deviation' in mathematics just means the difference between two numbers. In other words, a deviation is the answer to a subtraction calculation.

We can use a realistic example to show how standard deviations are calculated.

The table shows the heights of 12 men, measured to the nearest inch.

Man number	Height (inches)
1	61
2	65
3	67
4	68
5	68
6	69
7	70
8	71
9	71
10	72
11	72
12	74

(i) First, you calculate the average or mean height of the 12 men.

This is 828 inches/12 = 69 inches.

(ii) Next, you work out the difference between each man's height and the average – this is the deviation. These deviations are shown in inches:

Man number	x_n Height	$\bar{x}$ Average	$(x_n - \bar{x})$ Deviation
1	61	69	−8
2	65		−4
3	67		−2
4	68		−1
5	68		−1
6	69		0
7	70		+1
8	71		+2
9	71		+2
10	72		+3
11	72		+3
12	74		+5

For clarity, we have shown the height table in ascending order. However, sequence makes no difference in standard deviation calculations.

At first glance it might look as if an average of the 12 deviations would be a good measure of spread. However, when you look more closely, you can see that the deviations are a mixture of negative and positive numbers – if you add them up, the answer is zero. It will always be zero for every sample because of the way the average is calculated.

There are two ways of getting rid of the sign problem. First, you might just pretend each deviation was a positive number – you could then average the deviations to give a positive number rather than zero. This method is occasionally used, but it gives a measure of spread that cannot be used in any other statistical calculations.

One of the basic rules of number applies to the multiplication of values with identical or opposite signs. If the signs are the same, the multiplication gives a positive answer. If the signs are different, the answer is always negative.

$$+6 \quad \times \quad +6 \quad = \quad +36$$
$$-6 \quad \times \quad -6 \quad = \quad +36$$
$$-6 \quad \times \quad +6 \quad = \quad -36$$

If the 12 deviations are squared, you end up with a string of positive numbers.

The sum of the squares

Man Number	$(x_n - \bar{x})$ Deviation (inches)	$(x_n - \bar{x})^2$ Squares of the deviations* (square inches)
1	−8	64
2	−4	16
3	−2	4
4	−1	1
5	−1	1
6	0	0**
7	+1	1
8	+2	4
9	+2	4
10	+3	9
11	+3	9
12	+5	25
Total	zero	138

*All of the numbers in this column are positive

**Zero squared = zero

Using summation notation, we can say that

$$\sum_{1}^{12} (x_n - \bar{x})^2 = 138$$

Put into words, this expression means 'the sum of the squares of the 12 individual deviations equals 138'.

The sample variance

The sum of the squares of the deviations cannot be a useful measure of spread because the figure would get bigger and bigger as the size of the sample increased.

However, the average of the sum of the squares is used to compare the spread of different-sized samples.

We can express this number in two ways:

(i) For this particular sample $\dfrac{138}{12} = 11.5$

(ii) Or for all samples:

$$\text{Sample variance} = \frac{\sum_{1}^{n} (x_n - \bar{x})^2}{n}$$

where $\bar{x}$ = the arithmetic mean of a sample with n members.

The sample variance is one of the most important theoretical statistics.

At the end of all this, we have two numbers that accurately and precisely describe the location or central tendency and the spread of heights in our original sample of 12 men. These are:

Sample mean   =   69 inches
Sample variance   =   11.5 square inches

The variance is in square units because we squared all the deviations shown in inches as the first step in its calculation.

A comparison of linear and square units presents problems, so another statistic is calculated by taking the square root of the variance.

Sample standard deviation

The sample standard deviation is the square root of the sample variance.

For theoretical reasons, a slightly different average is used to calculate standard deviations:

Sample variance

$$\frac{\sum_{1}^{n}(x_n - \bar{x})^2}{n}$$

Sample standard deviation

$$\frac{\sum_{1}^{n}(x_n - \bar{x})^2}{n - 1}$$

$$\downarrow$$

$$\sqrt{\frac{\sum_{1}^{n}(x_n - \bar{x})^2}{n - 1}}$$

In our example:

Sample variance

$$\frac{138}{12} = 11.5 \text{ sq ins}$$

Sample standard deviation

$$\frac{138}{11} = 12.55 \text{ sq ins}$$

$$\downarrow$$

$$\sqrt{12.55} = 3.54 \text{ inches}$$

Our sample was 12 men, so a figure of $(n-1)$, or 11, is used as the bottom number in the standard deviation formula. For samples of around 40 or larger, this technical and theoretical adjustment makes very little difference and the standard deviation is often calculated directly as the square root of the variance.

We have found that for the heights of the 12 men in our sample:

Mean	= 69.0 inches
Standard deviation	= 3.54 inches

These two numbers give precise numerical descriptions of location and spread. Taken together, they are the most widely used of all statistics. The sample standard deviation has the symbol **s**. Algebraically, we could say:

$$\overline{x} = 69.0 \text{ inches}$$
$$s = 3.54 \text{ inches}$$
$$n = 12$$

The larger the spread or variation in a sample, the greater its standard deviation becomes. The reverse is also true. For instance, a sample of men all of identical height would have a standard deviation of zero.

5 The normal distribution

A variable is just a number that can vary – like the height of a child or the number of goldfish in a pond. In maths, the opposite of a variable is a constant – a number that never changes.

There are two kinds of variables – discrete variables and continuous variables. Discrete variables are things you count; continuous variables are things you measure. Nearly all discrete variables are positive whole numbers. In theory, a continuous variable can have any value. The following example illustrates the difference.

A Spanish fruit grower has 60 orange trees. She wants to know which ones are the most productive. At harvest time, she first counts the oranges from each tree and then she weighs them. The number of oranges is a discrete variable. The weight or yield of oranges is a continuous variable.

Measurements are continuous variables because, in theory, they can be shown to any degree of accuracy. For instance:

The yield from orange tree number 17 is 53 kg

or 53.1 kg

or 53.12749 kg and so on.

But, for example, 341 oranges is a whole number.

Distribution is shown pictorially using bar charts, histograms and frequency polygons. Classified data gives bars of different heights – if this is declassified the bar chart turns into a smooth graph.

Distribution patterns

Continuous variables, when shown graphically, can take one of several patterns.

Symmetrical distribution

Smaller standard deviation

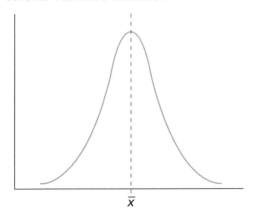

$\bar{x}$

Larger standard deviation

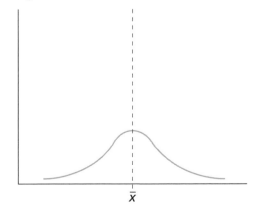

$\bar{x}$

Asymmetric or skewed distribution

More lower values

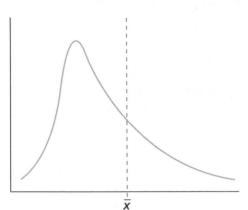

More higher values

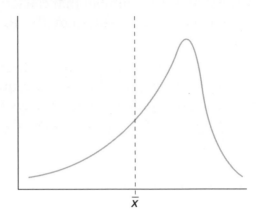

Symmetric distributions have equal frequencies of lower and higher values below and above the sample mean – the two halves of the curve are mirror images of each other. The flatter the curve, the greater the spread or scatter and therefore the bigger the standard deviation.

Lopsided curves show asymmetric or skewed distributions. A chart of the distribution of annual salaries in the UK would be asymmetric – most people earn about the average, a few are very highly paid. The frequency distribution tails off to the right because exceedingly high salaries are much rarer than high salaries. The last point of the extreme right of the UK income distribution curve would show the salary of the best-paid person in the country.

Multi-factorial variation

The normal distribution is a strange name – it does not mean that other kinds of distribution are abnormal. The description was first used in the 18th century and it has stuck. The following example explains.

Imagine a steel rod, machined to be exactly one metre long. Now ask 1,000 people to measure the length of the rod. Some will get it right, others will make mistakes. The number of overestimates will roughly equal the number of underestimates, and bigger errors will be less common than smaller ones.

This kind of symmetrical continuous distribution was originally called 'the normal curve of errors'. Nowadays it is called the 'normal distribution'.

Measurement errors have many different causes. It has been found that any variation caused by many factors, acting independently, produces normal distribution curves or curves that closely resemble the normal distribution.

Variations in plants and animals are caused by a range of genetic and environmental factors. The normal distribution often describes these variations very well. There are thousands of examples, such as:

- The weights of new-born piglets.
- The weights of potatoes.
- The heights of adults.
- Human intelligence measured by IQ tests.
- Shoe sizes.

Height variation is an idea that is familiar to everybody, so it is often used to explain the normal distribution and its uses. The shape of any normal distribution curve is determined by the mean of a continuous variable and its standard deviation. To explain, using real figures:

	Mean	Standard deviation
UK males aged 30 to 40	5 feet 9 inches	3½ inches

A bell-shaped curve

The normal distribution curve is shaped like a bell. It is perfectly symmetrical about a vertical line drawn through the mean.

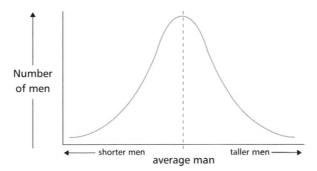

The area bounded by the normal distribution curve and the horizontal axis is directly proportional to the percentage of the sample within a particular height range. For example, for a sample of 600 men:

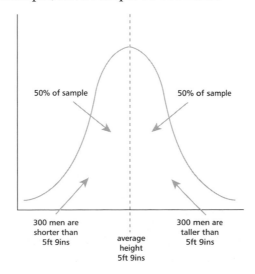

Predictions in general

Using the standard deviation, we can widen the concept to predict what percentage of a sample will be within any height range that we care to choose. This is one of the most important and most useful ideas in statistics.

Using calculus and the equation for the normal distribution curve, it has been found that:

- 68.27% of a normally distributed sample is within the mean ± one standard deviation.

- 95.45% of a normally distributed sample is within the mean ± two standard deviations.

- 99.73% of a normally distributed sample is within the mean ± three standard deviations.

The symbol ± means 'plus or minus'.

These three statements need translation – we can do this by rounding the percentages, using examples and drawing some diagrams.

For UK men aged 30 to 40, we know that the average height is 5 ft 9 ins and one standard deviation is 3½ inches.

- The mean ± one standard deviation is 5 ft 9 ins ± 3½ inches, or 5 ft 5½ ins to 6 ft ½ ins.

- The mean ± two standard deviations is 5 ft 9 ins ± 7 inches, or 5 ft 2 ins to 6 ft 4 ins.

- The mean ± three standard deviations is 5 ft 9 ins ± 10½ inches, or 4 ft 10½ ins to 6 ft 7½ ins.

The percentages are usually rounded, therefore:

% of men	are taller than	but shorter than
68%	5 ft 5½ ins	6 ft ½ ins
95%	5 ft 2 ins	6 ft 4 ins
99.75%	4 ft 10½ ins	6 ft 7½ ins

The diagram on the next page shows this same information.

The extremities

In theory, the normal distribution curve extends forever beyond the limits of ± three standard deviations; however, only a tiny percentage of a sample is very much larger or very much smaller than the average. Only one man in 33,000 in the UK is likely to be taller than the mean plus four standard deviations – this statistic predicts that only about 700 adult men in the UK are 6 ft 11 ins or taller.

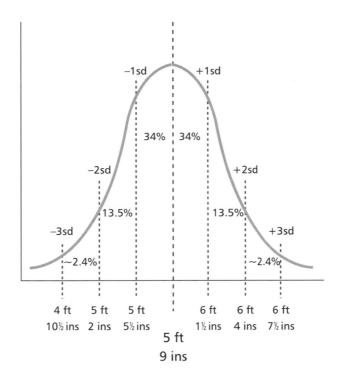

At a more practical level, the theoretical normal distribution is a bad or nonsensical predictor of extremes. Taking adult height as an example, the tallest proven height for a man is 8 ft 11 inches, but the statistical theory says it ought to be possible for a man to grow to say 12 feet or 15 feet.

More importantly, real distributions become asymmetric at the extremes. There are only one or two diseases or disorders that cause abnormal height, but many more genetic and environmental factors that restrict growth. There are more very short men than the theory predicts.

Adult weight distribution in developed countries is asymmetric because it is easier to gain weight than to lose it when food is plentiful and exercise is avoidable.

Predictions in detail

The percentages given by the normal distribution curve can be added or subtracted to give a prediction for any height range. For instance:

- 97.5% of men are shorter than 6 ft 4 ins because, using the diagram, 50% + 34% + 13.5% = 97.5%.

- 15.9% of men are taller than 4 ft 10½ ins but shorter than 5 ft 5½ ins, because 2.4% + 13.5% = 15.9%.

Statistics textbooks include tables that can be used to estimate the percentage of a sample that lies between any two limits. These can, for example, predict the percentage of men that are taller than 6 ft 2 ins. This height limit is the addition of 5 ft 9 ins + 1.43 standard deviations, because:

$$6 \text{ ft } 2 \text{ ins} = 5 \text{ ft } 9 \text{ ins} + 5 \text{ inches and}$$

$$\frac{5 \text{ inches}}{3\frac{1}{2} \text{ inches}} = 1.43 \text{ standard deviations}$$

The statistical tables show that 7.6% of men are likely to be taller than 6 ft 2 inches.

Interquartile range

A statistic called the interquartile range is sometimes used to describe spread. Like most ideas in statistics, it sounds complicated, but the concept is logical and not difficult.

A quartile is another word for a quarter. It is an alternative to dividing a normal distribution into limits marked by whole numbers of standard deviations – which give awkward percentages. It works the other way around – starting with a round-number percentage and ending up with fractions of a standard deviation.

Statistical tables show that 50% of a normal distribution lies between the mean ±0.675 of a standard deviation.

Showing this information as a graph:

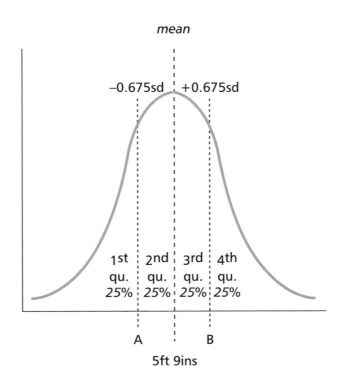

The distribution is divided into four quarters, or quartiles. Each contains 25% of the sample.

The mean of men's heights, between the ages of 30 and 40, is 5 ft 9 ins; the standard deviation is 3½ or 3.5 inches.

Point A on the diagram is the mean minus 0.675 of a standard deviation.

Point B on the diagram is the mean plus 0.675 of a standard deviation.

$$0.675 \times 3.5 \text{ inches} = 2.36 \text{ inches}$$

Point A is 5 ft 9 ins minus 2.36 inches – roughly 5 ft 6½ ins.

Point B is 5 ft 9 ins plus 2.36 inches – roughly 5 ft 11½ ins.

Referring back to the diagram, we can use the quarters or quartiles in any combination. For instance:

- 25% of men are shorter than 5 ft 6½ ins.

- 25% of men are taller than 5 ft 11½ ins.

- 50% of men are taller than 5 ft 6½ ins but shorter than 5 ft 11½ ins.

6 The null hypothesis test

Statistics works with samples because it is nearly always impossible to test or measure an entire population.

Based on samples, we can infer what a particular population statistic is likely to be, but statistical analysis alone can never give absolute proof. Statistics is based on the mathematics of probability.

Probabilities can be expressed as percentages, fractions, odds or decimals. For example:

%	Fraction	Odds	Decimal
50	$\dfrac{1}{2}$	1 in 2	0.5
90	$\dfrac{9}{10}$	9 in 10	0.9
95	$\dfrac{95}{100}$	19 in 20	0.95
97.5	$\dfrac{195}{200}$	39 in 40	0.975
99.0	$\dfrac{99}{100}$	199 in 100	0.99
99.5	$\dfrac{199}{200}$	199 in 200	0.995

This table gives probabilities in ascending order. A probability of 99.5% means that a conclusion or an inference is very likely to be correct. A probability of 50% means that an inference has an equal chance of being right or wrong.

Statistics calculations use probabilities shown as decimals. A probability – given as a percentage, a fraction or as odds – has to be converted into a decimal before it is 'plugged into' a statistics formula.

Hypotheses

Statistical tests are properly called tests of statistical hypotheses. A hypothesis is a supposition or informed guess made as a starting point for further investigations. It is based on limited or incomplete information, and we test the hypothesis by collecting more information.

Statistical tests cannot prove or disprove a hypothesis, but they can show that it is likely or very likely to be true or false.

Medical research

Medical research would be impossible without statistical testing. Healthcare improvements are nearly always gradual – miracle cures and dramatic break-throughs happen occasionally, but new drugs and new therapies are most often just a bit better than existing treatments.

No drug is completely safe. Decisions have to be made which balance advantages and disadvantages for the population as a whole. Immunisation and vaccination are good examples. A few otherwise healthy people might be damaged by a new vaccination. Very small risks can be tolerated, but at some point the dangers become unacceptable and the therapy will not be licensed or will be withdrawn from sale. Safety decisions are based on statistical tests.

Drug dose, safety and efficiency are related. Ignoring cost, the 'best' drugs are effective in small amounts and not dangerous in large quantities. The 'worst' drugs have considerable overdose risks and need frequent administration.

Vaccinations are excellent drugs. Insulin is a life saver for some diabetics but it needs very careful handling. Some drugs are safe but not very effective. It is difficult, for example, to overdose on cough syrup.

Individual reactions to the same quantity of the same drug can vary dramatically. Statistical tests are always used to establish a safe but effective minimum dose.

An extended example

In the following extended example, we show how some drug trials are conducted and how one of the commonest statistical tests is applied. Detail differs from one investigation to another. Here we outline the main concepts.

An asthma drug treatment has been on sale for five years. It works for about half of sufferers but it does not help the rest. The manufacturer develops a new drug and wants to know if it is better than the old one.

The manufacturer arranges an experiment – a clinical trial – to compare the two drugs. In most cases, a government agency will need to approve the new drug for sale. This agency has to be provided with written records and evidence of all aspects of the trial and its results.

A random sample

A random and representative sample of asthma sufferers is selected. The sample need not be very large – a few hundred to a thousand is usual. Assume the sample for this trial is 200.

On a random basis, the total sample is split into two groups – a control sample of 100 and an experimental or second sample of 100. The control sample is given the old drug and the experimental sample is treated with the new one.

As far as possible, the control and experimental trials have to take place under identical conditions, using identical doses.

In many trials, success or failure is easy to define. A blood analysis, for example, would be a direct test of success or failure for a cholesterol-reducing drug. For this example, something like freedom from asthma attacks during a trial of 28 days might be used as a definition of success.

At the end of the trial, the results are analysed. We find, as expected, that the old drug gave relief to 50 out of the 100 in the sample. Looking at the second or experimental sample, there are three possibilities:

- The new drug might have worked for 50 or fewer than 50 of the second sample. In this case, the new drug would be abandoned – probably after a second trial to confirm the first results.

- The new treatment may have worked for all or nearly all of the second sample, say for 97, 98, 99 or even 100 people. This result suggests very strongly that the new drug is a massive improvement on the old one. However, the government safety agency would still insist on statistical tests before it granted approval.

- Nearly all clinical trials give results that cannot be interpreted just by common sense or intuition. We need to know what success rate in the second trial is needed before we can say that the new drug is likely or very likely to be better than the old one. Is 51 out of 100 good enough? Or do we need 58 successes, or 71? Precisely how many do we need?

The null hypothesis test

We solve the problem using the null hypothesis test. The null hypothesis is that the new drug is no better than the old one. In other words, the probability of success of the new drug is 50% or lower. Written as a formula this is:

$$H_0 : P_e \leq 0.5$$

$\leq$ meaning equal to or less than

H_0 (read as 'H nought') is the symbol for the null hypothesis. P_e is the probability of success for the new drug, shown as a decimal.

The alternative hypothesis, called H_1, is that the new drug really is better than the old one and that a result better than 50 successes did not happen just by chance, so:

$$H_1 : P_e > 0.5$$

$>$ meaning greater than

The trials can be thought of as 100 different experiments, each with two possible outcomes – success or failure. The variation in the overall results of this kind of experiment closely follows the normal distribution. As the results of the experimental sample improve, the less likely it becomes that the success rate is better than 50 just by chance. The probability that any number of results, from 51 to 100, has happened – just by chance – can be calculated because we know how a normal distribution works.

Probability again

As we have said many times before, statistics alone cannot prove anything with absolute certainty. However, statistical analysis can show that some conclusions are much more likely to be true than others.

The English criminal justice system obliges a jury to give a guilty verdict if all or most of them believe that the case against a defendant has been proved 'beyond reasonable doubt'. This is another way of saying 'only convict if you think the probability of guilt is very high indeed'. Words are imprecise.

In statistical tests, reasonable doubt is precisely defined using numbers instead of words. Five levels of proof are commonly used in clinical trials. These are expressed as percentage probabilities:

$$90\%$$
$$95\%$$
$$97.5\%$$
$$99\%$$
$$99.5\%$$

The null hypothesis, H_0, is rejected if its probability of being wrong is very high. If you reject the null hypothesis, then you must accept the alternative hypothesis, H_1, and conclude, in our example, that the new drug really is better than the old one. We can turn this concept into a picture of the normal distribution.

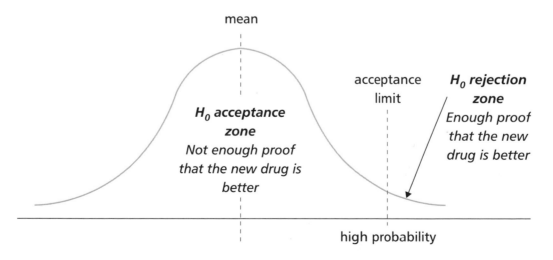

We can be more, or less, cautious. If we are happy with a 90% chance of the new drug being better than the old one, then the acceptance limit is the vertical line that separates the area under the normal curve into a 90% acceptance zone and a 10% rejection zone. If we decide to be extra careful, the acceptance limit is shifted to the right – making the acceptance zone bigger and the rejection zone smaller. To be 99.5% sure of making the right decision, the rejection zone only represents 0.5% of the area under the normal curve.

Probability and standard deviations

This next point is critical. The distance between the mean and the acceptance limit can be measured in standard deviation units.

Acceptance limit	Number of standard deviations above the mean	
90%	1.285	
95%	1.645	acceptance limit
97.5%	1.96	shifts to the
99%	2.33	right
99.5%	2.58	

These figures come from statistical tables. The diagram shows the acceptance limits for 90% and 99.5% probabilities:

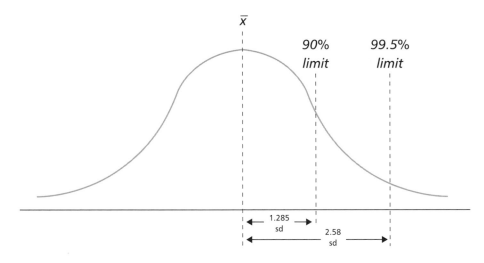

The formula

The null hypothesis formula gives the acceptance limit for any number of successes in the experimental trial – if you know the sample size and the probability of success in the control trial. You do not need to remember the formula, but you must know how to use it.

$$Z = \frac{P_e - P_o}{\sqrt{\dfrac{P_o(1 - P_o)}{n}}}$$

Z	=	acceptance limit in standard deviation units.
P_e	=	probability of success in the experimental trial – as a decimal.
P_o	=	probability of success in the control sample – as a decimal.
n	=	sample size.

In our example:

P_e	=	the number of successes in the new drug trial.
P_o	=	0.5: the old drug worked for 50 people
$(1 - P_o)$	=	0.5: the old drug did not work for 50 people
n	=	100

Note that we are comparing two trials of 100, so $n = 100$ not 200.

The calculations

The next table shows the detail of the null hypothesis calculations for success rates between 51 and 65 cures in the experimental trial.

The formula looks difficult but it is easy to handle if you split the top and bottom halves of the fraction.

The bottom half only needs to be calculated once, because P_o is always 0.5, therefore:

$$\frac{P_o(1 - P_o)}{n} = \frac{0.5 \times 0.5}{100} = 0.0025$$

$$\sqrt{0.0025} = 0.05$$

The top half of the fraction gets bigger as the experimental trial gets more successful.

Experimental trial success rate	$P_e - P_o$	$\sqrt{\dfrac{P_o(1-P_o)}{n}}$	Acceptance limit z standard deviations	H_0 acceptance zone* %
51	0.01	0.05	0.2	58
52	0.02		0.4	65.5
53	0.03		0.6	72.6
54	0.04		0.8	78.8
55	0.05		1.0	84.1
56	0.06		1.2	88.5
57	0.07		1.4	91.9
58	0.08		1.6	94.5
59	0.09		1.8	96.4
60	0.10		2.0	97.7
61	0.11		2.2	98.6
62	0.12		2.4	99.18
63	0.13		2.6	99.53
64	0.14		2.8	99.74
65	0.15		3.0	99.865

*The percentages shown in this column can be read directly from statistical tables of the normal distribution.

It can be easy to get the meanings of acceptance and rejection the wrong way round. Remember, we are testing the null hypothesis, H_0. Null means something like nil, nothing or no improvement.

If we accept the null hypothesis, we are saying that the new drug is no better than the old one.

If we reject the null hypothesis, then we are saying – beyond reasonable doubt – that the new drug is better than the old one. The detailed calculation table defines reasonable doubt.

- 51 new drug successes is only a bit better than the control sample. There is a 58% chance that the new drug is an improvement, but the evidence is not very strong.

- For new drug success rates of 57 or better, we can be more than 90% sure that it would be a good idea to carry on developing the new drug.

- If the success rate is 65 or more then we can be practically certain that the new drug is better – because 99.865% is very close to 100%.

We can work the formula backwards to show the number of new drug successes that would be needed to give various levels of proof expressed as round-number percentages.

Level of proof %	Number of successes needed
90	57
95	58
97.5	60
99	62
99.5	63

The burden of proof

In medical research, different levels of proof are required in different circumstances. Licensing agencies nearly always insist on a given level of certainty before they will grant approval for new treatments.

The greatest care is taken with drugs that are given to children or otherwise healthy people – such as vaccinations and oral contraceptives. The same principles apply to food additives and vitamin and mineral supplements. Much lower levels of proof can be acceptable in special circumstances – an experimental treatment that stands a chance of curing an otherwise terminal illness is the most obvious example.

Null hypothesis testing has many variants and thousands of different applications. We used drug testing as an example, but most quality-control procedures in manufacturing rely on null hypothesis testing.

We have described what is called a one-sided or one-tailed test. We were only concerned with how much better the new drug might be than the old one. We did not look at the left-hand tail of the normal distribution curve. Many quality-control systems use two-tailed tests. An engineering component, for example, may have an acceptable size range and we would need to reject badly made components that were too big or too small.

7 The chi squared test

In the previous topic we introduced the general idea of statistical testing and looked at the null hypothesis in detail. Tests like the null hypothesis cannot be used reliably unless the population is known to vary according to the normal distribution and unless sample sizes are relatively large.

In some situations we do not have enough information to assume that a population is normally distributed, or we know for sure that it is not. A lot of real-life problems also concern small samples or information that is collected together into a small number of groups. For these, a different type of statistical test is needed.

Chi (pronounced to rhyme with sky) is a Greek letter. Its symbol, χ, is very similar to the English letter X – be careful not to get the two confused. The χ^2 statistical test has many practical uses and it only involves short straightforward calculations.

Categorised information

Many trials or experiments give results which are grouped together in categories, classes or cells.

- Simple blood tests can place any sample of people into one of four blood groups – A, B, AB or O.

- Exam results are usually published not as detailed percentages but as grades, for example, from A to U.

- You could roll a dice a hundred times and count the number of times you scored 1, 2, 3, 4, 5 or 6 – giving six information categories.

The chi squared test compares the difference between theoretical or expected frequencies and frequencies observed in an experiment or trial. A statistic called chi squared is calculated from these differences and it can then be used to tell if there is a significant or meaningful difference between the expected and observed figures.

Honest and loaded dice

A perfectly made dice has an equal chance of showing each of the numbers from one to six every time it is rolled. Gamblers and casino operators call this an honest dice.

Loaded dice are sometimes used by gamblers to cheat casino owners and by casino owners to cheat gamblers. A good craftsman can load a dice in favour of any particular number and completely disguise the tampering. You cannot tell by looking, so how could you distinguish between an honest dice and a loaded one? χ^2 has the answer.

The dice are rolled a number of times and you keep records of the results. To make the sums easy, assume you have two suspect dice and you roll each one 60 times.

Number thrown	Dice A	Dice B	Theoretical or expected
1	8	22	10
2	11	3	10
3	12	10	10
4	7	11	10
5	9	7	10
6	13	7	10
Total	60	60	60

You would not be surprised if an honest dice did not show identical frequencies for the six numbers unless you were keeping track of a very long experiment, say 10,000 rolls. Nevertheless an identical frequency for all six numbers can be described as the expected or theoretical frequency.

The calculations

The tables show how to work out χ^2 for each dice:

$$O_n \quad = \quad \text{observed frequency}$$
$$E_n \quad = \quad \text{theoretical or expected frequency}$$
$$n \quad = \quad \text{number of groups or classes}$$

Dice A – 60 throws

Number	O_n	E_n	$O_n - E_n$	$(O_n - E_n)^2$	$\dfrac{(O_n - E_n)^2}{E_n}$
1	8	10	−2	4	0.4
2	11	10	+1	1	0.1
3	12	10	+2	4	0.4
4	7	10	−3	9	0.9
5	9	10	−1	1	0.1
6	13	10	+3	9	0.9
Total	60	60	zero		2.8

This number 2.8 is χ^2 for dice A.

Using summation notation:

$$\chi^2 = \sum_{1}^{6} \frac{(O_n - E_n)^2}{E_n} = 2.8$$

Dice B – 60 throws

Number	O_n	E_n	$O_n - E_n$	$(O_n - E_n)^2$	$\dfrac{(O_n - E_n)^2}{E_n}$
1	22	10	12	144	14.4
2	3	10	−7	49	4.9
3	10	10	0	0	0
4	11	10	+1	1	0.1
5	7	10	−3	9	0.9
6	7	10	−3	9	0.9
Total	60	60	zero		21.2

$$\chi^2 = \sum_{1}^{6} \frac{(O_n - E_n)^2}{E_n} = 21.2$$

If a third dice showed exactly equal frequencies of the six possible numbers in 60 throws, then a calculation would show χ^2 = zero, because all the numbers in the $(O_n - E_n)$ column would be zero. Clearly, χ^2 gets bigger as the observed frequencies depart more and more from the expected or theoretical ones. Our results show:

	χ^2
Dice A	2.8
Dice B	21.2

Assessing the chances

We can see that dice B is more likely to be loaded than dice A. Statistics textbooks contain tables of χ^2 and these are used to show how likely it is that a particular difference between observed and expected frequencies is due just to chance. As always we have to talk about probabilities, not certainties or absolute proof.

The relevant extract from the χ^2 table looks like this:

		Probability of a deviation greater than χ^2					
		1%	2%	5%	10%	30%	50%
Degrees of freedom	5	15.09	13.39	11.07	9.24	6.06	4.35

The degree of freedom is one less than the number of categories in the trial. In our example, therefore, this number is 5. The adjustment is made to correct for the possible distortions caused by small samples.

The table shows that for a six-category trial, a value of χ^2 greater than 15.09 indicates a less-than-1% probability that the difference between observed and expected frequencies happened purely by chance.

For dice B, $\chi^2 = 21.2$. This means that the probability that dice B is loaded is more than 99% and, of course, the chances of it being honest are less than 1%.

For dice A, $\chi^2 = 2.8$. This number is lower than even the χ^2 50% value of 4.35. It is unlikely that dice A is loaded.

8 The Spearman rank correlation coefficient

Here we describe a third kind of test which uses a statistic called the Spearman rank correlation coefficient. The name needs explanation.

Spearman first developed the test in 1904. He was a psychologist and therefore interested in human characteristics that cannot be directly measured, like extroversion and aggression.

Some things cannot be measured, but they can be ranked. You could arrange five different flavour ice-creams into an order or rank of preference, but you could not say that strawberry tasted 2.64 times better than vanilla for example. Ranking involves judgement – your ice-cream rankings might be different from somebody else's.

Correlation coefficients

A correlation coefficient is a number that shows how two variables are associated. It varies between +1 and –1.

A correlation coefficient bigger than zero, up to and including +1, shows that two variables are positively correlated – one increases in line with the other.

A negative correlation coefficient shows that two variables are negatively correlated – as one gets bigger, the other gets smaller.

The bigger the correlation coefficient, the closer the association between the two variables. Values close to zero show a weak or non-existent association.

The graphs give examples.

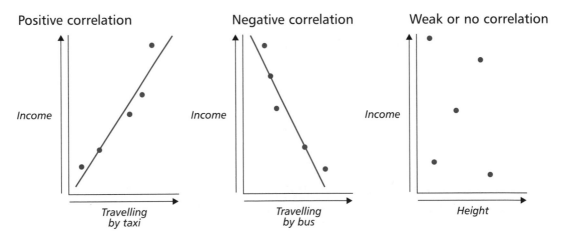

Correlation coefficients only show association. They cannot in any way prove that a change in one variable causes a change in the other.

A matter of judgement

Spearman's test is most often used to compare the results of two sets of 'judges' or investigators. Take the following example.

Promotion and recruitment often depend on the results of an interview board. In an ideal world, two different panels would give the same ranking to the same group of, say, six candidates. If the two interview boards were in total agreement, Spearman's coefficient would be +1. If they disagreed slightly, then the coefficient might be +0.7. Major disagreement or differences of opinion give very low or negative coefficients.

The calculations

Spearman's rank correlation test is easy to use and does not involve lengthy or complex calculations. The following example explains the method.

A large supermarket group uses two different panels to compare its products with those of seven competing retailers. The two panels taste or test products and are then asked to agree a ranking – the one they like best is ranked first and so on. Both panels test the same products under identical conditions.

The two panels are first asked to test eight pork pies. The table shows the rankings for each panel and the calculation for Spearman's rank correlation coefficient.

Pork pies

Pork pie	(X_n) Ranking panel X	(Y_n) Ranking panel Y	$(X_n - Y_n)$ Ranking difference	$(X_n - Y_n)^2$ Ranking difference squared
A	4th	2nd	2	4
B	2nd	4th	2	4
C	5th	3rd	2	4
D	1st	1st	0	0
E	7th	6th	1	1
F	3rd	5th	2	4
G	6th	7th	1	1
H	8th	8th	0	0
				18

It does not matter if the ranking difference is positive or negative because squaring the difference always gives a positive number.

Using summation notation:

$$\Sigma(X_n - Y_n)^2 = 18$$

Statistical theory shows that the rank correlation coefficient, symbol r_s, is given by the formula. You do not have to remember this.

$$r_s = 1 - \left(\frac{6\Sigma(X_n - Y_n)^2}{(n^3 - n)} \right)$$

n = number of items that are ranked.

Put more precisely, n = number of pairs of ranking results.

In this example, n = 8, because we are ranking eight different makes of pork pie, therefore:

$$\left(\frac{6\Sigma(X_n - Y_n)^2}{(n^3 - n)} \right) = \frac{6 \times 18}{(512 - 8)} = \frac{108}{504} = 0.214$$

$r_s = 1 - 0.214$

$r_s = +0.786$

The panels are then asked to test eight different competing white wines and finally eight different types of perfume.

White wine

White wine	(X_n) Ranking panel X	(Y_n) Ranking panel Y	$(X_n - Y_n)$ Ranking difference	$(X_n - Y_n)^2$ Ranking difference squared
A	8	8	0	0
B	7	6	1	1
C	2	7	5	25
D	5	1	4	16
E	6	5	1	1
F	1	4	3	9
G	4	3	1	1
H	3	2	1	1
				54

$n = 8$

$r_s = 1 - \dfrac{6 \times 54}{(512 - 8)}$

$r_s = 1 - 0.643$

$r_s = +0.357$

Perfume

White wine	(X_n) Ranking panel X	(Y_n) Ranking panel Y	$(X_n - Y_n)$ Ranking difference	$(X_n - Y_n)^2$ Ranking difference squared
A	8	4	4	16
B	3	7	4	16
C	2	1	1	1
D	6	2	4	16
E	4	8	4	16
F	7	3	4	16
G	5	5	0	0
H	1	6	5	25
				106

$$n = 8$$

$$r_s = 1 - \frac{6 \times 106}{(512 - 8)}$$

$$r_s = 1 - 1.262$$

$$r_s = -0.262$$

Comparing products and panels

On these three different kinds of products, how closely did the views of the two panels agree?

	Spearman's rank correlation coefficient, r_s
Pork pies	+0.786
White wines	+0.357
Perfumes	−0.262

If the panels had agreed exactly the same rankings for each product, then the correlation coefficients would have been +1.000 for pies, wines and perfumes.

The correlation coefficients show that the two panels broadly agree on their rankings for pies, they disagree more about wine and cannot agree at all when it comes to perfume.

Luck or judgement?

If both taste panels wanted to finish work early, they might just draw numbers out of a hat to decide rankings rather than go to all the time and trouble of actually tasting or testing the products. This random process would produce some level of agreement between the two panels, purely by chance.

As with the normal distribution and the chi squared test, there are statistical tables that show the probabilities of any particular rank correlation coefficient being reached just by chance. The appropriate section of the Spearman rank correlation coefficient table shows the following:

n	Coefficient	
8	5%	1%
	0.643	0.833

For a comparison of eight rankings, a correlation coefficient bigger than 0.643 has only a 5% probability of happening by chance. The correlation coefficient has to be 0.833 or more to reduce this probability to 1%.

Our pork pie rank coefficient is +0.786. This means there is better than 95% probability that the agreement between the two taste panels is genuine.

The wine coefficient of +0.357 and the perfume coefficient of –0.262 means that there is no reliable evidence of agreement or disagreement between the views of the panels.

A correlation coefficient of between –0.833 and –1.000, for instance, would strongly suggest that the views of the two panels were genuinely different or independent of each other.

To use Spearman's test in this form, you cannot include tied rankings.

The test only compares opinions. It obviously cannot show which is actually the best pork pie, wine or perfume.

9 Statistics – concept and detail

Many Access students, in particular those with little mathematical background, find the statistics unit one of the most demanding parts of the course. If this is your situation, these summary notes might help.

Background reading and private study

Theoretical statistics is a vast subject and much of the maths involved is intimidating. If you are struggling, talk first to your lecturers. Most higher-level specialist books will add to your confusion rather than increase your understanding.

Calculation

Do not be tempted into lengthy practice calculations. You can prove to yourself that you understand a basic idea by working with small sets of numbers. There is no need to wade through lists or tables of dozens or hundreds of figures.

You must be able to:

- Calculate an average or arithmetic mean.

- Understand negative numbers.

- Work out squares, cubes and square roots using a calculator.

- Know how brackets operate as a sequence instruction in mathematical formulae.

- Make sense of the Σ or summation notation.

In statistics, you should always work with neatly laid-out tables, where one calculation step follows another as you progress from left to right across the columns. Always double check additions and subtotals, column by column. If you ignore this advice, muddle, uncertainty and anxiety is inevitable.

Pictorial descriptive statistics

You should be completely comfortable with the interpretation of pie charts, bar charts, histograms, frequency polygons and graphs.

Numerical descriptive statistics

As well as calculating the arithmetic mean or average, you need to know how to find the median, mode and range of a set of figures. Definitions will not be provided as a guide in exams and assessments.

Concepts in inferential statistics

These points are vital:

- Inferential statistics works with samples taken from a population. These samples must be random and representative; otherwise statistical theory gives the wrong answers.

- Inference and proof are very different ideas. Taken in isolation, statistical theory cannot prove anything.

- Inference involves probability, not certainty. You can infer that a conclusion has, say, a 95% chance of being correct or false, but not that this probability is 100% or zero – that is, certainly true or certainly false.

Association, correlation, cause and effect

Again, this is a vital concept. Mathematics can show that two or more sets of numbers are associated or correlated. It can also produce a figure that shows the strength of this correlation or association. However, mathematics on its own can never prove cause and effect – that a change in one thing causes an alteration in another. To research cause and effect, maths has to be combined with some kind of science that suggests a mechanism to link two or more variables.

Formulae

The point of this unit is to give an understanding of concept, not detail. If you merely remember a list of formulae and then go on to apply these without a grasp of the main ideas, then your learning will be slow and difficult.

For inferential statistics, there are two things that you ought to commit to memory:

- The formula for calculating the sample standard deviation and how to use it.

- For the normal distribution, the approximate percentages of a sample that fall between the mean and the first three standard deviations.

Limits	% of a normal distribution
Mean ± one standard deviation	68
Mean ± two standard deviations	95
Mean ± three standard deviations	99.75

You do not need to remember the formulae for the null hypothesis test, the chi squared test or for Spearman's rank correlation coefficient calculations. However, if you are given these formulae and a set of numbers you should know what they are and what to do with them.

Statistical tables

You ought to know what statistical tables of the normal distribution, the chi squared distribution and Spearman's rank correlation coefficients look like and how to use them. Your lecturers will help.

Chapter 8

Applying psychology to health

National unit specification
These are the topics you will be studying for this unit.

1   Recap and revision

2   The biopsychosocial model

3   Addiction

4   Alcohol

5   Diet

6   Smoking

7   Behavioural change and compliance

8   Chronic illness

This final chapter includes a number of cross-references to material included in the earlier parts of the book. We suggest you read chapters one to seven at least once before you begin this last social science unit.

265

1 Recap and revision

The specification for this unit is very broadly written. Quoting from the current guidelines: '**students should be introduced to some key health issues in which psychology has made a major contribution**'.

However, it is difficult to think of any branch of modern healthcare that has not been significantly influenced by the work of psychologists. It follows that there are many different but equally valid interpretations of the specification.

In another way, this unit differs from most of the rest of the course because it introduces relatively little new material apart from a consideration of addiction and addictive behaviour.

Applying psychology to health is best studied as a summary or a collecting together of the social science units that make up the earlier parts of the health-related pathways.

You should already be familiar with some important concepts:

- The changing patterns of health and illness that have characterised the UK since the formation of the NHS in 1948.

- The biopsychosocial model of health.

- The influences of lifestyle, diet, environment, class, gender and culture on health and well-being.

- The relationships between stress and illness.

- The challenges and difficulties of health promotion.

- The Yale model of communication and its application to health promotion campaigns.

- The principle of informed consent, meaning that health-promoting behaviour cannot be enforced.

- The complexities of interpersonal and mass media communication.

2 The biopsychosocial model

It is unfortunate that the central concept in modern healthcare has been given such a clumsy label. What sounds like a complicated abstract theory is in fact a set of straightforward ideas that, taken together, underpin the health and social services in the UK.

The emergence of the model and its implications are more easily understood by looking back 60 years or so to the beginnings of the health service.

Beveridge's five giants

The blueprint for the NHS and the welfare state was the Beveridge report, published in 1942. Its author, William Beveridge, concluded that the country had a duty of care for its citizens **'from the cradle to the grave'** and that it could best fulfil this **'by slaying the five giants of want, disease, ignorance, squalor and idleness'**.

Beveridge was born in 1879 and was therefore close to retirement age in 1942. Unsurprisingly, some of his words now seem odd and old-fashioned, but with a little translation we can outline what were seen as the five major causes of ill health and misery 60 years ago.

Want

Want translates as poverty, but in the 1930s and 1940s, it described extremes that have been more or less eradicated from modern Britain. Direct and very significant connections between wealth, income, health and well-being persist. However, very few people now die or are made unwell because they lack the basic necessities of food, clothing and shelter. In the same way, the NHS provides treatment regardless of the ability to pay. The health service is frequently criticised, but it is probably at its best in response to accidents, life-threatening or acute conditions.

Disease

By disease, Beveridge almost certainly meant infectious disease, in particular those which killed or damaged the most vulnerable groups – infants, children, the elderly and the poorly nourished. It is easy to forget that, within living memory, tuberculosis, diphtheria, measles, whooping cough, gastrointestinal infections and pneumonia were constant daily threats to life and well-being.

Ignorance

To call an individual or group ignorant is much more of an insult than it used to be. Ignorance has come to mean the rejection of education or of social norms. By ignorance, Beveridge was describing what we would now call poorly developed basic literacy and numeracy. As he used the words, an individual could be highly intelligent, courteous and receptive to education – but still ignorant.

Squalor

There is still much sub-standard housing in the UK, but norms and expectations have risen very significantly since the 1940s. Squalor meant structurally poor housing but also overcrowded living conditions and the lack of heating, hot water, indoor lavatories, bathrooms, gardens and play areas.

Modern consumer durables like fridges, freezers, washing machines, driers and vacuum cleaners make major contributions to health and well-being. These were unavailable in Beveridge's time, or they were only within the reach of the wealthiest few per cent of the population.

Idleness

On 29 October 1929, there was a sudden and catastrophic collapse in share prices on the New York Stock Exchange. This single event, often called the Wall Street Crash, triggered a series of bank failures and business bankruptcies that eventually led to the Great Depression of the 1930s. American investment was withdrawn from Europe and governments around the word imposed trade barriers in futile attempts to protect their economies.

The net result of these actions was to produce massive unemployment across North America and industrialised Europe that lasted for most of the 1930s.

By idleness, Beveridge meant unemployment or casual insecure employment. The unemployment benefit and welfare systems of the time did not prevent millions of families from falling into health-threatening or health-limiting poverty.

The five giants are dead

Nobody can pretend that the UK of the 21st century is a perfect society, but the biopsychosocial model makes no sense without an understanding of how far we have travelled since the Beveridge report.

The implication of Beveridge was that once five major obstacles were removed, then the health and happiness of the nation would automatically, inevitably and rapidly improve.

The five giants arc dead, or at least laid low, but the outcome has not been one that Beveridge would perhaps have predicted.

Positive versus negative

The biopsychosocial model sees health as a positive idea, not merely the absence of illness. Extending the principle, health and well-being are not necessarily promoted and increased just as by-products of policies designed to provide full employment, education, curative medicine and material wealth. Public policies and strategies cannot be health promoting unless a concern for health is 'built in' from the outset and unless all aspects of public policy are integrated to achieve this end.

New giants

William Beveridge died in 1963. He lived to see the containment of the most serious infectious diseases, major reforms in education, the establishment of the welfare state and significant increases in the material wealth of the UK.

However, during the 1960s there was growing evidence that new patterns of disease and disorder were beginning to replace the old ones.

Essentially, the new giants have prosperity at their root rather than poverty. Cardiovascular disease and cancer, in all its forms, have replaced infections as the major causes of illness and premature death.

Acute versus chronic conditions

There are no sharp dividing lines between acute and chronic conditions, and some diseases pass through or alternate between chronic and acute or 'flare up' phases. This said, the distinction between the two types of illness or disorder often flows directly from the biopsychosocial model.

An acute condition usually has a sudden onset, a definable or single cause, a firm diagnosis and an established procedure for treatment. Immediate attention is essential and the condition does not usually persist. Obvious examples of acute conditions are things like appendicitis, injuries as a result of road traffic accidents, and the more serious infectious diseases.

In contrast, chronic disorders develop or worsen slowly over a period of years. They have many causes, each interacting and contributing to the illness, and treatment extends over long periods, usually without the prospect of complete recovery.

Healthcare in the UK is increasingly concerned with chronic rather than acute conditions. The biopsychosocial model explains the causes of much chronic illness and it is the foundation for health education, health promotion and preventative medicine. A heart attack could be described as the acute phase of gradually worsening chronic heart disease – which was itself brought about by poor diet, lack of exercise, stress, smoking and alcohol abuse. A similar chain of events is the underlying causes, or causes of much 'modern' illness.

Complex interactions

It is difficult to summarise the biopsychosocial model of health in a few words or with a simple diagram. By definition, it is complex and its main purpose is to demonstrate that health and well-being, or the lack of it, results from the interactions between very many different influences.

Health and illness are not simple or mutually opposing conditions. At any chosen time, our state of health and well-being could be placed on a scale or spectrum ranging between perfect health and, in the extreme, imminent death. As yet another consequence of the model, there must be many different definitions of health.

Any individual's position on the health–illness spectrum cannot possibly be determined just by the results of laboratory tests and measurements. Self-assessment may be just as important an influence as the views of health professionals.

Biology, psychology and sociology

The biopsychosocial model makes no distinction between mind and body. Put another way, health and well-being can only be understood by combining knowledge drawn from the natural sciences of biology – and also biochemistry, chemistry and physics – with the social sciences of psychology and sociology.

From previous units, you will remember that sciences are hierarchical. Cause, effect and process can be studied at any level from the individual human or object through to vast collections of people and objects. It can be argued that chemistry, biochemistry, biology, biomedical science and sociology form one continuous hierarchy, with psychology as a major influence at all but the simplest levels of organisation.

The diagram is an attempt to turn these ideas into a picture. You will almost certainly be able to add more detail and make many more interconnections.

An extended biopsychosocial model of health

3 Addiction

Most of us could easily list what we believe to be the characteristics of drug addicts and drug addiction. We might say:

- Addicts are younger rather than older, but no further generalisations in terms of gender, class, education, income or wealth can be made.

- Addiction leads to self-neglect. The typical user is thin, shabbily dressed and has no regard for personal hygiene.

- The most significant addictive drugs are heroin and crack cocaine; injecting is common.

- Drug addiction is a relatively new phenomenon and its incidence is increasing steadily.

- The manufacture, importation, supply and use of drugs is illegal.

- There is an inescapable connection between drugs and crime – in particular violent crime, theft and prostitution.

- Addicts are helpless and dependent in almost every sense of the words.

- Curing or treating addiction is very difficult, perhaps even impossible. Relapse is exceedingly common after short periods of abstinence.

These preconceptions are often wrong, if addiction is defined in a much broader and more meaningful sense to include dependency on, or habitual excessive use of, all potentially dangerous substances. In one way or another, self-destructive or illogical behaviour is the cause of most modern illness.

We have first to distinguish between addictive substances and addictive processes.

Addictive substances

There is no simple or single method for classifying addictive substances. Some have been known for thousands of years, others are recent products of the illegal or legal pharmaceutical industries. Drugs need not be complicated compounds that are difficult and expensive to produce, although some are. Many drugs are what would commonly be described as natural products or substances obtained very easily from cheap, widely available raw materials.

The drugs that cause the greatest harm to the greatest number – alcohol and tobacco – are not illegal in the UK and never have been.

Most addictive substances are eaten, drunk or inhaled. Intravenous administration is reserved for very few addictive materials.

The body has no physiological need for alcohol or tobacco but the wider definition of addiction includes the excess consumption of fats, in particular saturated fats and perhaps also caffeine and salt. We cannot live without carbohydrates, but all of these can be taken as starches rather than sugars. Sucrose, or added sugars, can be included in the list of the most common potentially addictive materials.

Confused legislation

The legislative approach to addictive substances could hardly be more complicated or confusing.

The Misuse of Drugs Act 1971 defines and categorises a number of controlled substances and criminalises their possession, production, cultivation, supply, giving, sharing, bartering, import and export. It is also illegal to allow premises to be used for supplying controlled drugs. Penalties vary according to the nature of the offence and the class of drug involved. A conviction for supplying a class A drug can result in life imprisonment.

Many potentially addictive drugs like Valium, amphetamines and barbiturates are also controlled by the 'prescription only' medicine system in the UK.

Anybody over the age of 16 can buy and use tobacco without restriction. Health warnings on retail packs are mandatory. Advertising is illegal but promotion and sponsorship – advertising in a different form – is not. The production and trade of tobacco is closely controlled, but more to prevent the loss of tax revenues than to preserve health. About 80% of the retail price of a packet of cigarettes ends up in the government's pockets through VAT and excise duties.

Alcohol is a controlled substance in the UK. Individuals are allowed to produce alcohol by fermentation for private use, but distillation without authority is illegal. Premises used for sale and distribution have to be licensed. There are regulations to limit opening hours, and under-age consumption is prohibited. There are many alcohol-related offences, in particular those connected with driving, operating machinery, caring for children while drunk and drunkenness in public places.

Drink advertising must not be targeted at children or designed to encourage alcohol abuse, but, with these provisos, this particular addictive drug can be advertised freely.

Like tobacco, alcohol is very highly taxed. Systematic evasion of excise duties and VAT are usually punished by imprisonment.

Solvents and solvent-containing products may not be sold to children.

Food legislation

In very general terms, any food or drink may be produced, imported, sold and advertised in the UK, provided it is wholesome and accurately described in terms of its country of origin, weight or volume, ingredients, energy value and nutrient content. Loose or unpackaged food and alcohol or food sold in catering outlets do not even have to meet some of these minimum requirements.

Food labelling, advertising and promotion may make positive health claims. However, the potential dangers of extended or excessive consumption of some types of food can be legally ignored by manufacturers and retailers. At the moment in the UK, the food industry is free to advertise any kind of food or non-alcoholic drink to any segment of the market. Many campaigns are aimed specifically at children and/or young people.

Addictive processes

Addiction usually combines an addictive substance and an addictive process. Nicotine is an addictive substance – the addictive process is smoking or, in some societies, chewing of tobacco or inhalation of tobacco powder or snuff. Many solvents are addictive – the process is commonly called glue sniffing.

An addictive process can exist in isolation without a corresponding or easily defined addictive substance – gambling is the best example.

Anorexia and bulimia are further examples of addictive processes.

Promiscuous unsafe sexual behaviour might be an addictive process for some people, as may dangerous sports and pastimes like mountain climbing, skydiving and motor racing.

Degree and potency

The traditional definition of addiction confines itself to hard drugs or to the unauthorised use of controlled or illegal substances which have significant effects and consequences in the short term when administered in relatively small quantities.

In 1993, the World Health Organization's expert committee on drug dependence defined addiction as:

'A cluster of physiological, behavioural and cognitive phenomena of variable intensity in which the use of psychoactive drug(s) takes on a high priority. The necessary descriptive characteristics are preoccupation with and a desire to obtain and take the drug and persistent drug taking behaviour. Determinants and the problematic consequences of drug dependence may be biological, psychological or social and usually interact.'

Rosenham and Seligman (1989) reached very similar conclusions but expressed them in rather easier language. They defined addiction as:

'dependence on a drug, resulting in tolerance and withdrawal symptoms when the addict is deprived of the drug.'

Those who choose to define addiction in a much wider sense to include everything, from heroin injection through to scratch-card gambling via health-threatening sexual promiscuity, must then answer the next and obvious question:

Why does the degree of addiction and the potency of the addictive substance or process vary so much between individuals and amongst different groups and societies?

Again, the biopsychosocial model of health is directly relevant – which also means there are no simple answers to this question.

- Vulnerability or resistance to addiction may be, in part, biologically or biochemically determined. In turn, this means there is almost certainly a genetic or inherited component in addiction. For example, we know that the children of alcoholics are more likely to become alcohol abusers than children whose parents are not alcoholics.

- The term 'addictive personality' is an inaccurate generalisation, but there is some truth in the idea. There are correlations between addiction and factors like introversion, extroversion, conformity and rebellion.

- Addiction cannot be understood without reference to sociology. Some groups tolerate or even encourage addiction. Others, according to the substance or process involved, criminalise addictive behaviour. Availability, advertising, promotion and price are key issues. Addiction is often judged in terms of the harm it does to the families, groups or societies to which the addict belongs.

The biomedical approach to addiction

Alcohol is produced naturally or by accident without human intervention when stores of fruit or vegetables are attacked by wild yeast. Mankind has used alcohol and had to come to terms with its effects for thousands of years. In a similar way, gambling is probably the addictive process with the longest history. All of the world's major religions disapprove of alcohol and gambling abuse. Islam and many Christian denominations prohibit them altogether. Generally, addiction has been seen as a sin, a crime, or a failure to resist temptation resulting from personal weakness.

If addiction is not a sin, then it can only be a disease or disorder – this is the biomedical approach. At its most extreme, this view has some disturbing consequences – it may mean that some people will inevitably become addicts, with only chance or availability deciding the substance or process.

Medical research into addiction is focusing on a series of biochemical reactions which maintain the body and the brain's level of arousal and alertness. The detail is complex and not yet fully understood. In outline, it involves an optimum level of a compound called dopamine which is an intermediate in the production of noradrenaline and adrenaline – which themselves result in or transmit feelings of pleasure and alertness.

Some individuals produce less dopamine than others or they are less able to make noradrenaline and adrenaline even if their biochemistry produces sufficient levels of dopamine. Dopamine deficiency may trigger addiction when the potential addict discovers that some external substances and processes produce pleasure and arousal that cannot be provided 'normally' or internally.

Biochemistry plays some part in addiction, but it is certainly not the complete explanation. We now have to look at the contributions of psychologists and sociologists.

The psychology of addiction

Some psychologists have not concentrated on a particular addictive substance or process. Instead, they have tried to understand addictive behaviour – characteristics and symptoms that are common to addiction in all of its forms.

One of the most useful summaries of addictive behaviour was suggested by Griffiths (1995). This research says that addiction has six elements or phases:

- Salience or preoccupation.
- Euphoria.
- Increasing tolerance.
- Withdrawal.
- Conflict.
- Relapse.

Salience

The first phase may develop over weeks, months or years. The substance or process becomes increasingly important and other aspects of life become less so. Priorities are more and more distorted until addiction is the major or sole concern. Dependency increases.

Euphoria

Feelings of pleasure, relaxation, self-confidence, arousal, elation or euphoria result. They may or may not be short-lived.

Tolerance

To reach the same state of euphoria, the addict has to increase the intensity or frequency of his or her addictive behaviour. Greater risks are taken and regard for consequences diminishes. At some stage, the pleasurable effects of the substance or process may be difficult or impossible to achieve – but addictive behaviour continues.

Withdrawal

Sudden withdrawal of the substance or process causes unpleasant symptoms. These may be biological, psychological, sociological or, as often, a combination of all three. A smoker trying to kick the habit will become irritable, ill mannered, clumsy, unable to concentrate and suffer from physical effects like a dry mouth and excessive tiredness. 'Cold turkey' is the classic description of heroin withdrawal symptoms – the condition mimics gastric flu, with stomach cramps, profuse sweating, often elevated body temperature and feelings of panic and despair.

It used to be thought that a substance could not be called truly addictive unless its withdrawal led to measurable, real or genuine changes in body function. This view, which is based entirely on the biomedical model, is now largely discredited. Withdrawal from an addictive process can produce physical symptoms. Gamblers in withdrawal sometimes develop tremor (Orford, 1985).

Conflict

The fifth phase of addictive behaviour has been given the general description of conflict. Many societies believe that mentally competent adults have the right to damage themselves, but very few think that sane, mature people should be allowed to cause harm to others.

Addiction has consequences that nearly always extend way beyond the individuals concerned. The temperance movement in the UK grew in response to the damage done to families and society by alcohol addiction amongst poor working-class men, and to a lesser extent their wives and female relatives.

Conflict may be internal, leading to shame, guilt and regret on the part of the addict, or external, causing family breakdown, financial problems and domestic neglect. The modern day link between drugs, violence and criminality is the best current example of external conflict.

Relapse

To call relapse the sixth characteristic of addictive behaviour is, at first reading, no more illuminating than simply saying addictive substances or processes are addictive – of course it is difficult, or very difficult, to change addictive behaviour patterns. This analysis is, however, meaningful because it helps in understanding how addictive behaviour might be treated or altered.

An addict's first attempts to alter his or her behaviour are unlikely to succeed, but often some progress may eventually be made.

Few addicts can break their addiction acting alone. Help and support from others is probably essential.

Addiction may not be curable, and therefore eternal abstinence is the price to be paid for the release from addictive behaviour. A speaker at an Alcoholics Anonymous group starts by saying, 'My name is John/Jane. I am an alcoholic' – not 'I used to be an alcoholic'.

The sociology of addiction

In theory, any society could legislate against the production and import of all addictive or potentially addictive substances and processes. At a stroke, the ill health and misery associated with addiction would be removed. In practice, in a free democracy, this 'perfect solution' is impossible. Most sociologists, politicians and health professionals also believe that this kind of law would make the problems of addiction worse, not better.

Prohibition

The largest and most extended experiment in history designed to eradicate addiction by legislation ended in complete failure. In January 1920, the 18th amendment to the American Constitution made the manufacture, sale, transport, import and export of intoxicating liquor illegal throughout the US. The prohibition of alcohol was repealed by the 21st amendment in December 1933. This 13-year ban produced many unintended consequences. Organised crime rapidly established a new production, transport, import and marketing system to supply illegal alcoholic drink on a huge scale. The profits involved were so large that extreme violence and corruption of public officials became commonplace and routine – to protect the business. Alcohol profits were used to establish and fund business diversifications into gambling, prostitution, hard drugs, property and stock market speculation.

Today, the regulations controlling alcohol use still vary significantly from one society to another. Islam forbids alcohol and this prohibition is effective in many Middle Eastern countries, largely with the consent of the majority of the population. Alcohol is still heavily regulated in Scandinavia and some US states.

Social control of addiction

In the UK, those outside the health professions have controlled, or tried to control, addiction in four ways:

- By legislation.
- By social disapproval.

- By restricting availability.
- By increasing price.

For most substances and processes, a combination of all four methods is used.

An absence of any of these controls combined with the operation of a free market amounts to the approval or encouragement of addictive behaviour.

Very few would argue against the heaviest penalties for a convicted large-scale heroin supplier. At the other end of the scale, the state encourages and promotes gambling for all through the national lottery and does virtually nothing to prevent the excess consumption of high fat, high sugar and high salt foods by children and young people.

It is important to remember that social disapproval or tolerance drives legislation. The best recent example is the change in the enforcement of the law and controlled status of cannabis.

The price mechanism in a mass market is subtle and easily misunderstood. All else being equal, the retail price of most addictive substances will remain stable or reduce in real terms. The long-term point of advertising is to increase market size and hence reduce production and distribution costs through economies of scale. In all but exceptional circumstances, only taxation can increase real prices and hence discourage consumption. If taxation is not constantly reviewed, its impact is gradually eroded by inflation and increased prosperity. In real money terms, the price of alcohol in the UK is tending to decrease year on year and the least healthy foods are probably cheaper than they have ever been.

UK tobacco tax has not been consistent. The present government is committed to annual increases in the retail price, over and above inflation, but demands for major price escalation or the ring-fencing of tobacco taxes to fund the NHS directly have been resisted.

Social norms and social values

For some, alcohol is an addictive and eventually life-threatening drug. However, the majority either do not use alcohol at all, or drink in moderation. The social value and benefits of alcohol have been recognised for thousands of years in many societies. The undoubted dangers of alcohol must be balanced against the positives of relaxation, creativity and sociability that responsible use brings to many millions. Supporters of the decriminalisation of cannabis use similar arguments.

Opium is the dried juice of the unripe seed capsule of the white Indian poppy. If grown under suitable conditions, opium contains around 15% by weight of morphine together with a number of related compounds including codeine. These natural products and their chemical derivatives – chiefly diacetylmorphine, the proper name for heroin – are called opiates.

Opiates have an invaluable role in medicine as the most effective of all painkillers. Their use was widespread, uncontrolled and socially acceptable until the end of the 19th century – laudanum was a mixture of opium and alcohol. Similarly, cocaine is a highly addictive illegal drug, but also a valuable local anaesthetic.

4 Alcohol

The Misuse of Drugs Act 1971 categorises heroin, crack cocaine, cocaine, methadone, ecstasy, LSD and amphetamines prepared for injection as Class A controlled substances.

A precise accounting for the human misery and unhappiness caused by addictive behaviour is impossible, but we can estimate the number of premature deaths, rates of illness and the costs to society of the most widely used and available addictive substances.

By any measure, the harm caused by tobacco, alcohol abuse and sustained unbalanced diets dwarfs the damage done by traditionally or legally defined hard drugs.

In this topic and the next two we try briefly to outline the size of the challenge posed to health by the three most commonly used addictive or potentially dangerous substances.

Probability, variability, risk and time frame

Very few adults would deliberately drink a solution that was clearly labelled 'sodium cyanide'. There are five reasons why this kind of illogical or self-destructive behaviour is exceedingly rare:

- The great majority of people know that cyanides are deadly poisons. We are well informed and educated in this respect.

- Human susceptibility to cyanide does not vary from one individual to another. Nobody is immune or resistant to its effects.

- The outcome of the action is totally predictable. Put mathematically, the probability of death is 100%.

- The gap or time frame between the action and its inevitable consequences can be measured in seconds or a few minutes at most. There can be no disputing cause and effect.

- There is no conceivable benefit or pleasure that can be balanced against the risks of drinking cyanide.

This illustration is bizarre but it makes some critical points that are directly relevant to health promotion relating to alcohol, tobacco and diet.

The direct link between smoking and lung cancer was first established beyond doubt in the 1960s. In the 40 or more years since, smoking has been found to be a major risk factor in many other diseases and disorders, in particular heart disease and strokes. There cannot be many UK adults who do not know that smoking is the primary cause of lung cancer but thereafter, knowledge tails off very rapidly. The risks and benefits of alcohol are poorly understood. Many people have little understanding of the connections between diet and health.

Health advice can never be delivered as personal certainties. Not all heavy smokers die young; not all who live blameless lives live to a ripe old age. The mathematics of probability make little sense to some people. '**My grandfather smoked 40 cigarettes a day and lived to 92**' might be a statement of fact, but it also describes an outcome that is statistically unlikely. The exception does not invalidate the rule.

Time frame is the central problem in health promotion. A tabloid newspaper would never print a headline that said '**If you carry on doing this for 30 years you will probably die**'. Humans are remarkably variable, but also incredibly resilient. Constant abuse over many decades causes illness and premature death. However, time breaks the link between cause and effect in many people's thinking.

The pleasures and rewards of alcohol, tobacco and eating are immediate, but the potential harm caused by abuse and excess consumption takes many years to develop. Again, time frame confuses the issue.

Measuring alcohol

Alcohol is a simple organic compound produced by the fermentation of fruits and vegetable materials. It is properly called ethanol or sometimes ethyl alcohol. Beers, cider and wine are made directly by fermentation. Spirit production is a two-stage process – fermentation followed by distillation.

Water and alcohol mix together in all proportions. Alcoholic drinks are relatively dilute solutions of alcohol in water. Pure alcohol is highly toxic and extremely unpalatable.

UK legislation obliges manufacturers and retailers to show the percentage of alcohol by volume in their products, but no other ingredient has to be declared. Alcohol sold in bars, clubs, pubs and restaurants is subject to measure control – for example a pint has to be a pint – but alcohol strength does not have to be specified.

Alcohol is less dense than water; 10 ml of pure alcohol weighs 8 grams, whereas 10 ml of water weighs 10 grams.

One gram of pure alcohol delivers 7 kcals. This compares with 4 kcals per gram for protein and carbohydrates and 9 kcals for a gram of pure fat.

Commercially produced alcoholic drinks vary in strength from about 3% by volume up to about 45% by volume for the strongest spirits. The table gives typical figures.

	% by volume	% by weight
Beers and cider	5	4
Wines	12	10
Spirits	40	34

Units, glasses, cans and bottles

The table shows the most common measures in which alcoholic drinks are sold or served.

Measure/package	ml
Spirits – single measure	25
Spirits – double measure	50
Wine – small glass	110
Wine – large glass	150
Beer – half pint	285
Beer/lager – can	440
Beer – pint	570
Wine – bottle	750
Spirits – bottle	750

Health advice is given in terms of units. One unit is 10ml or 8g of pure alcohol. With some simple arithmetic, a unit can be translated into something more meaningful. It should be remembered that these conversions are approximate. Drinks vary significantly in alcohol content and measures poured at home are usually larger than those bought away from home.

One alcohol unit is contained in:

- A half pint (285 ml) of ordinary-strength beer.

- A small glass (110 ml) of wine.

- A single measure (25 ml) of spirits.

There is growing concern that the unit definition for alcohol has been over-taken by market and social changes. The strength of drinks has risen and competition in the drinks trade has made measures more generous. This is especially so for wine.

	Volume ml	% alcohol by volume	Total alcohol ml
Original unit	110	9.0	9.9
Now more likely to be	150	12.5	18.8

Sensible drinking

Guidelines published in 1992 recommended that men should drink no more than 21 units a week, and women no more than 14 units a week. This advice was revised in 1995:

- Men should drink no more than 3 to 4 units per day; women 2 to 3 units a day at most.

- A heavy drinking episode should be followed by two non-drinking days.

- Consistent consumption at the upper limit is not advised.

Defining risk

Government-sponsored research has defined drinking patterns and the levels of risk associated with each.

Drinking pattern	Units consumed per week	
	Women	Men
Low to moderate	0–14	0–21
Moderate to heavy	14–35	21–50
Very heavy	35+	50+
Binge drinking*	6+	8+
		*in one session

Source: Strategy Unit Alcohol Harm Reduction Project

Increasing consumption

Drinking trends are measured in litres of pure alcohol consumed per person per year. The head count usually excludes those under the age of 16 or sometimes 14. UK consumption in 2002 was about 11.5 litres of pure alcohol per person aged 14 or over. This is equivalent to 385 pints of beer, or 115 bottles of wine, or roughly 35 bottles of spirits – or any combination of these. Remember these are average figures.

UK alcohol consumption fell considerably and consistently from 1900 to about 1950, but there has been a significant upward trend ever since. The table gives figures for selected years.

UK estimated alcohol consumption, selected years

Litres of pure alcohol consumed per person aged over 14					
Year	Beer	Spirits	Wine	Cider	Total
1956	3.86	0.82	0.29	0.10	5.07
1966	4.48	1.08	0.59	0.11	6.25
1976	5.68	2.14	1.19	0.23	9.23
1986	4.93	2.10	1.66	0.30	8.99
1996	5.16	1.72	2.14	0.59	9.61
1997	5.26	1.77	2.23	0.57	9.83
1998	5.10	1.66	2.31	0.57	9.64
1999	5.05	1.91	2.48	0.64	10.08
2000	4.95	1.93	2.69	0.61	10.18
2001	5.09	2.03	2.94	0.63	10.69
2002	5.18	2.34	2.98	0.63	11.13

Source: Institute of Alcohol Studies

The totals since 1991 are underestimates because they do not include personal cross-Channel imports. The Institute for Alcohol Studies believes that true consumption in 2002 was about 11.6 litres per head.

The heaviest drinkers in the world are the people of Luxembourg, followed closely by the Irish and the wine-producing countries of Europe. The UK is presently about number 12 in the world drinking league, but if present trends continue, we will soon overtake Greece, Spain, France and Portugal. We already drink more than the Italians.

Who drinks what?

	Number of UK adults, 2001 (million)		
	Men	Women	Total
Non-drinkers	1.6	3.1	4.7
Low to moderate	12.1	14.2	26.3
Moderate to heavy	3.9	2.5	6.4
Very heavy	1.4	0.4	1.8
Above daily guidelines	3.2	2.6	5.8
Binge drinkers	4.0	1.9	5.9

Source: ONS General Household Survey 2001

Nearly six million people in the UK drink more than the recommended daily maximums. Another 1.8 million are drinking at levels which are very likely to cause longer-term health problems

5 Diet

Students on the health-related pathways study diet as a specialist unit. Here we take a slightly different approach, looking at the psychological and social pressures that determine or encourage departures from sustained healthy eating. This subject is likely to become more and more important in the coming years. There are indications that diet-related diseases and disorders may replace smoking and/or alcohol abuse as the most important concerns for UK health.

Omnivorous apes

One of the secrets of our success as a species is that we are able to survive and prosper on a very varied diet. Unlike many animals, humans are omnivores. This fact has been key in our history of expansion into every corner of the world. Flexibility has evolved over a period of at least 150,000 years – perhaps much longer. Evolution never ends, but its pace is incredibly slow compared with the changes in lifestyle and diet that have occurred since the industrial revolution and even more so since about 1950 in the Western or developed world. There is a growing difference between what many of us eat and what our bodies were designed to eat. This nutrition gap is the root cause of diet-related illness – our dietary flexibility is not infinite.

The energy balance

Gaining weight is an essential survival mechanism – without it, our species would have become extinct. We store energy as body fat which is insurance against food shortage. Equally importantly, we can also store most of the vitamins and minerals that are vital for health. It is likely that the humans who were best able to store energy – those who put on weight most easily – survived and multiplied in greater numbers than those who were less efficient. What was once a huge advantage has become a potential health risk in modern society. The numbers are interesting.

	kcals for an adult woman
Maintenance need – sedentary lifestyle	2,000
Maintenance need – highly active lifestyle	2,450
Excess consumption needed to produce 1 lb of fat	3,200

These are average figures – individuals vary. Energy balance is simple arithmetic. A woman who is 14 lbs overweight is storing 3,200 kcals × 14 (or 44,800 kcals). She could survive without food for at least 22 days (44,800 ÷ 2,000) without ill effect. In practice, the body slows the metabolic rate in response to starvation, hence extending survival times.

A woman who was eating enough to support a very active lifestyle, but was in fact sedentary, would gain about one pound a week as body fat or stored energy:

$$2{,}450 - 2{,}000 = 450 \text{ kcals/day excess}$$
$$450 \times 7 \text{ days} = 3{,}150 \text{ kcals} = \text{about } 1 \text{ lb weight gain}$$

Balance and sustainability

Our precise diet can include very many different food combinations, but its balance in terms of the three macronutrients – carbohydrates, fats and proteins – cannot vary beyond certain limits without long-term damage to health. For many, alcohol is a fourth significant macronutrient. Current UK government guidelines are written as the percentage of total calories derived from each macronutrient. The guidelines also recognise the subdivision of carbohydrates into sugars and starches, and fats into saturated, mono-unsaturated and polyunsaturated. The sensible drinking limit can also be converted into the percentage of total daily calories obtained from alcohol.

The current guidelines

Macronutrient	% of total calories
Added sugars	10 maximum
Natural sugars and starch	37
Total carbohydrates	47
Saturated fats	11 maximum
Mono-unsaturated fats and oils	13
Polyunsaturated fats and oils	7
Trans fats and oils	2 maximum
Total fats and oils	33 maximum
Total proteins	variable
Alcohol	7 maximum
Total calories	100%

Source: *Dietary Reference Values for Food, Energy and Nutrients for the UK*
Department of Health, HMSO, 1991. © Crown copyright

Natural sugars are those found in milk, fruit and many vegetables. Added sugars are almost entirely common white sugar or sucrose.

Saturated fats are mostly of animal origin. Mono-unsaturated and polyunsaturated fats and oils come largely from plants and fish. Trans fats are man made and found most often in butter substitutes and processed foods like biscuits, pies and pastries.

A balanced diet must also include all of the essential vitamins and minerals and a minimum of fibre – which is essentially indigestible carbohydrate.

Energy density

The four macronutrients have different energy contents. Proteins and carbohydrates deliver 4 kcals per gram, alcohol 7 kcals per gram and fats are the highest with 9 kcals per gram. Nearly all foods are a mixture of carbo-

	kcals per 100 g
Chocolate	590
Crisps	510
Apples	35

hydrate, protein and fats, together with water and fibre (both of which have no calories). The most energy dense or energy rich foods have very high fat contents and/or high percentages of sugar, but very little water or fibre. Manufactured and processed foods are generally much more energy dense than the unprocessed alternatives. The table gives some examples:

Malnutrition

Malnutrition describes any major and sustained departure from a balanced diet. By this definition, many people in the UK are malnourished. Even the most unbalanced Western diets nearly always provide beyond the minimum needs of all the essential vitamins and minerals, although mild iron deficiency is not unusual in the UK.

The biggest problems are:

- Too many calories in total.
- Excess consumption of added sugars.
- Excess saturated fat consumption.
- Excess alcohol use.
- Not enough fibre.
- Not enough fruit and vegetables.

The health impacts of an unbalanced diet fall into two different categories. Excess calories from whatever source lead eventually to obesity and then a whole range of diseases and disorders like hypertension, diabetes, respiratory problems, limited mobility and circulatory diseases.

Over-consumption or the avoidance of particular macronutrients can be dangerous even if calorie intake and energy needs are balanced. There is a very well-established link between saturated fats in the diet, cardiovascular disease and some cancers. Alcohol abuse is associated with liver disease, some cancers and poor metal health. A low-fibre diet increases the risk of diverticular disease and bowel cancer. The health benefits of fruit and vegetables are wide-ranging and the subject of much current research. As a generalisation, they are needed to maintain the immune system, to give protection against many types of cancer and as major sources of vitamins, minerals and fibre.

Physical activity

In the last 100 years, the average maintenance energy requirement for UK men has fallen by about 500 kcals/day and roughly 400 kcals/day for women. This is a calorie reduction of around 18%. It is likely that the calorie needs of the average child have fallen even more in percentage terms. Few jobs now involve heavy manual labour, whilst the car and domestic machinery have replaced walking and strenuous activities like cleaning and washing by hand. For most, exercise has become an optional or leisure activity, not a daily unavoidable necessity.

Diet, class and culture

Compared with much of Europe, the UK is odd in that there is a class gradient in dietary habits. Poorer people eat differently from the richer middle classes. The more disadvantaged a family is, the more likely it is that their diet will be unbalanced and a threat to health in the long run. Income is clearly a factor, but not a complete explanation of these differences.

Targets for diet and health

The problems of alcohol abuse and unbalanced diets have three characteristics in common:

- Average figures for the UK suggest consumption or consumption patterns are posing risks to health.

- There is very significant variation within the averages, meaning that some groups are at considerable risk.

- In general, the problems are getting worse, not better, and there is increasing polarisation between healthy and health-damaging lifestyles.

Health educators and promoters are aiming at a moving target, so the figures that follow should be seen as no more than an outline or broad guide:

- The UK gets about 40% of its total calories from fats – it may approach 50% for some groups. This calorie contribution should be reduced to 33%.

- On average, saturated fats provide roughly 20% of UK calories. This is nearly twice the recommended maximum of 11%.

- Added sugar consumption is also nearly double the recommended maximum – about 18% of calorie intake compared with the guideline of 10% at most. Children and young people consume more than the UK average.

- The 'five portions a day' guideline for fruit and vegetables is a sensible minimum not an unrealistic ambition. This recommendation also provides more than enough fibre and guarantees sufficient levels of many vitamins and minerals.

In essence, the dietary health targets boil down to switching away from high-fat, high-sugar foods and increasing consumption of starches, fruit and vegetables.

Who decides what we eat?

Dietary choice is a good candidate for the most basic human freedom – personal preference decides what we eat. On closer examination, however, it becomes clear that preferences are heavily influenced by external factors and that choices need not be based at all on objective nutritional principles. For the UK today, we can summarise the most relevant and powerful external influences:

- Availability.

- Affordability.

- Knowledge and information.

- Cultural and social pressures, in particular advertising and time pressure.

We all have to eat – this is biology. How much we eat and what we eat is determined in large part by psychology and sociology.

Availability

The UK food industry is one of the most sophisticated and profitable in the world. Amongst developed nations, the UK is also unusual in that our food retailers are generally bigger and more powerful than UK food manufacturers. The reverse is true in the US.

The larger food retailers argue that their success has resulted directly from understanding then supplying what their customers want. This logic is difficult to deny – if we wanted very many small food shops, then they would still be in business. There might be a difference between what customers want and what they need for a balanced diet, but the wants are easily defined. UK food retailers have succeeded by providing the largest range at the most competitive prices. The product range now includes many more processed, part processed and ready-to-eat foods than it used to. Seasonality and country of origin no longer restrict choice.

School dinners, prison food and hospital food are often used as terms to describe food that is bad or unappetising. Availability has another dimension – depending on circumstances, many people have to eat what others give them, or go hungry.

Machinery and equipment are a third aspect of availability. A car, access to a car and efficient public transport all increase dietary choice, as does the ownership of fridges, freezers and microwave ovens.

Affordability

Availability and affordability are closely linked. The richer you are, the greater the range of affordable choice in goods and services. For the majority in the UK, a balanced diet has never been more affordable or more available – but steep price gradients amongst products still exist because there is an inescapable connection between price and volume. For a food manufacturer or retailer, the perfect product in profit terms sells in very high volume, is instantly recognisable by consumers, can be standardised in pack and content and has a very long shelf life. Some of the unhealthiest foods fit this definition – most of the healthiest do not.

The fast food catering and restaurant industry has mushroomed because it combines availability, affordability, standardisation and very high public awareness. None of this has anything necessarily to do with good nutrition.

The price/volume relationships can set up a virtuous or vicious circle. The greater the demand, the lower the price, and vice versa. The food industry would supply healthier food at lower prices if more people decided to buy it.

Knowledge and information

Infant and primary schools are defined as the first and second stages of the education system. In fact, they are the second and third. Our first teachers are our parents, grandparents and other close relatives. Nutrition and good diet, like any other subject, can be taught and learned formally or informally. If you cannot cook or prepare food and you have not been taught the basics of food hygiene and nutrition – then you become dependent on the efforts and motives of others. We all have to eat and we all have to feed our families.

There is no lack of food information in the UK, but there is almost certainly not enough unbiased, soundly based basic information.

Money rich, time poor

By developing new products, new packaging and new presentations, the food industry tries to create new demand and therefore greater profits. However, it cannot force anybody to buy anything. The industry reacts to social trends – it very rarely creates them. The typical supermarket sells more processed, ready-to-eat, higher energy density foods because people have less time, less ability and less inclination to cook. The second major influence is the shift away from formal meals at home and towards snacking or 'grazing' away from home.

Advertising and promotion

The great majority of food and drink advertising spending does not try to sell nutrition or food-related health and well-being. Campaigns focus on food as enjoyment or as an entry ticket to a desirable group or lifestyle. The most heavily promoted products are soft drinks, crisps, confectionery, alcohol and fast-food outlets.

6 Smoking

In our approach to this unit we have chosen to give considerable attention to poor diet and alcohol abuse as two of the three factors that potentially cause the greatest harm to the greatest number in the UK. Some lecturers may take a different view and devote most of your time to a study of smoking and its consequences. This is because:

- No genuine cost/benefit analysis can be applied to smoking. In health terms, there are no identifiable advantages to set against a huge array of harms and dangers. Tobacco tax and excise revenues may not even cover the direct costs of treating smoking-related diseases – it depends how the accounting is done, and who does it.

- There is no safe level of tobacco consumption because the product contains carcinogens as well as toxic materials. In theory, even the tiniest quantities of some compounds can trigger cancer.

- Nicotine has been proven to be highly addictive.

- Alcohol abuse and poor diet have wider consequences for families and society at large. However, the damage transmission methods are psychological and sociological. Passive smoking is directly harmful and the mechanism is biological.

- Smoking is a global issue, not a national one. Production and distribution is mostly controlled by multinational companies who have chosen to concentrate their marketing efforts in the countries and regions with the fewest restrictions. The legal status of tobacco manufacture and supply is insecure. At some stage, probably in the US, the tobacco companies may be forced to compensate their customers for the damage done by smoking. The sums of money involved, when and if this happens, are potentially enormous.

Nicotine, tar and carbon monoxide

Nicotine is one of a large family of compounds called alkaloids, which are produced naturally by a few species of plants. Other examples of alkaloids are atropine, caffeine and quinine. Nicotine is a psychoactive addictive drug. It also induces changes in body function – in particular raised blood pressure, increased heart rate, fluid retention and a greater release of free fatty acids into the blood. In combination with the carbon monoxide in tobacco smoke, nicotine also increases the rate of blood clotting.

Burning tobacco generates a mixture of at least 200 different identifiable solids, liquids and gases. The solid and liquid components, called tar, include around 20 proven carcinogens and many more irritants and toxic materials.

The third major ingredient in tobacco smoke is the gas carbon monoxide. This molecule is very similar in shape and size to oxygen and its harmful effects all follow from its ability to bond with haemoglobin and hence reduce the oxygen-carrying capacity of the blood. Narrowing of the arteries and tissue damage are direct results.

There is no safe brand or type of cigarette. Carbon monoxide inhalation is inevitable. Switching to 'low tar' brands makes little difference to the health risks.

The list of the likely or potential consequences of smoking could fill many pages. Research continually identifies new dangers. It is the primary cause of lung cancer and a major factor in cardiovascular disease in all of its forms. Most chronic respiratory diseases are caused or made very much worse by smoking. Nicotine crosses the placenta and smoking reduces the oxygen supply to the foetus. Increased infant mortality has been directly associated with smoking in pregnancy.

The long-term trends

Except as shown otherwise, the information that follows is sourced from the campaign group Action on Smoking and Health (ASH).

In 1948, the first year for which reliable UK surveys exist, 82% of adult men were smokers. Historically, women have smoked considerably less, with numbers varying between about 40% and 45% of all adult women between 1948 and the mid-1960s.

Looking at the period between 1975 and today, three trends are evident:

- There was a significant reduction in smoking between 1975 and about 1995.

- Since 1995, the number of smokers has stabilised or perhaps decreased slightly year on year.

- The gender gap has narrowed. Nearly as many women as men are continuing smokers.

Year	% of UK adults who smoke		
	Men	Women	Total
1974	51	41	45
1978	45	37	40
1982	38	33	35
1986	35	31	33
1990	31	29	30
1994	28	26	27
1996	29	28	28
1998	28	26	27
2000	29	25	27

Bringing these numbers up to date is difficult because different surveys reach different conclusions – under reporting of smoking is usual. In 2004, smoking prevalence may have been 1% or 2% below the year 2000 figures.

There are about 12 million adult cigarette smokers in the UK and roughly 11 million ex-smokers.

Smoking and age

The heaviest smokers are aged between 20 and 24; thereafter, smoking declines. This age relationship is a new factor in the UK and follows directly from the number of older people who have given up.

Years	Smokers – % by age group					
	16–19	20–24	25–34	35–49	50–59	60+
1978	34	44	45	45	45	43
2001	28	37	34	29	26	22

The figures for smoking amongst children aged between 11 and 15 may not be reliable because some young people will be reluctant to admit to the habit and others may exaggerate out of bravado. Few in this age bracket have enough money to support heavy or even daily smoking so definitions become confused.

Two conclusions can be drawn from the available surveys – neither are reassuring:

- Nearly 25% of 15-year-olds are regular smokers, although this may involve only a few cigarettes a week.

- Since the mid 1980s, girls have become heavier smokers than boys – the traditional gender gap has reversed.

Smoking and class

There has probably always been a relationship between smoking and class, but this has become steadily more significant ever since the link between smoking and lung cancer was first established in the early 1960s. King George VI was a very heavy smoker and this led to his premature death in 1952. Before the 1960s, many GPs were regular smokers; today very few are.

The table shows the relationship between class, gender and smoking for the year 2000.

Class, defined by occupation	% of adult smokers 2000	
	Male	Female
I Professional	17	14
II Managerial and technical	23	20
IIIN Intermediate/junior non-manual	27	26
IIIM Skilled manual	33	26
IV Semi-skilled manual	36	32
V Unskilled manual	39	35
All non-manual	23	22
All manual	34	29
All adults	29	25

Source: Social trends 2003. Crown copyright

The message is clear – the more wealthy, more fortunate and better educated have taken more notice of smoking cessation campaigns.

Polarising lifestyles?

Health promotion and health education in the UK is likely to become increasingly concerned with class. Alcohol abuse, poor diet, smoking and lack of exercise are each health-threatening in isolation, but yet more so in combination. The most alarming predictions suggest a growing polarisation of lifestyles and the concentration of all the most serious self-destructive behaviours in the poorest and least fortunate families.

7 Behavioural change and compliance

Medical advance and increasing prosperity in the UK has brought about a paradox. Health and well-being for all is becoming more difficult to achieve, not less so. Addictive, self-destructive or illogical behaviour is difficult to cure, reverse or treat.

Previously, we have discussed health education, health promotion and the Yale model of communication in detail. You should read or re-read Chapter 2, *Health in a changing society*.

In this topic we look at a model of behavioural change and discuss the problems of compliance.

The spiral model of behavioural change

Prochaska, Di Clemente and Norcross (1992) proposed a five stage model that helps understand the mechanisms that lie behind changes in behaviour. This is thought to apply generally to hard drugs, alcohol, diet, tobacco, exercise and addictive processes like gambling. Prochaska called the five stages:

- Precontemplation.
- Contemplation.
- Preparation.
- Action.
- Maintenance.

Precontemplation and contemplation

In the beginning, the individual does not recognise the need for change, although partners, relatives, friends and colleagues may do so. Behaviour is self-justified as eccentricity or a feature of personality.

Contemplation means 'thinking about it'. A problem is recognised, but no firm plans are made. The contemplation phase may be very brief or it can extend indefinitely.

Preparation and action

Preparation involves the firm intention to act in the near future. Lifestyle and habits may alter to avoid environments and situations that encourage addictive behaviour.

Action without preparation is not usually successful – it most often involves complete cessation, for example of drinking alcohol, smoking, taking hard drugs or gambling.

Maintenance

The individual tries to avoid relapse and makes the most of his or her release from addictive behaviour.

The model is described as a spiral because relapses are the rule not the exception. It may take three or four repeats of the process before the final termination stage is reached.

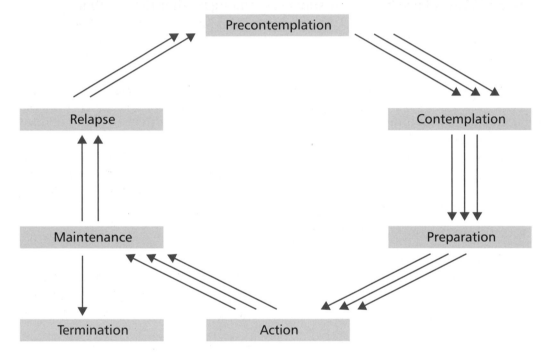

Compliance

In everyday English, a compliant person is one who does as he or she is told by others, without argument or protest. The word has negative associations of timidity, weakness and deference. In health psychology, compliance is a different issue – we need to understand why many people do not comply with or take action based on sound health advice.

It has to be remembered that, in the UK, no mentally competent adult can be forced into compliance or treatment with the exception of those diagnosed with a few rare notifiable infectious diseases.

Health compliance requests may be long term, short term, positive or negative. For example, to keep an appointment to have a child vaccinated, to eat five portions of fruit and vegetables every day for the rest of your life, or never to drink more than two glasses of wine a day.

Ethical considerations and the multi-factional nature of many conditions makes judging or assessing compliance difficult and often impossible. Progress checks and laboratory tests may indicate non-compliance, but other influences might be at work – thus confusing measurements like blood pressure, blood sugar levels and urine analysis.

Rationality and non-compliance

It is tempting to see any degree of non-compliance as illogical or irrational. This assumption is false because it supposes, amongst other things, that the giver and receiver of a health request have identical knowledge, culture, background beliefs, values and priorities – in short, that they have the same psychology and sociology.

Rationality cannot be judged objectively or externally. We all justify our actions or lack of actions differently. The most common reasons for non-compliance can be listed:

- Many people believe compliance is impossible although they recognise the risks of non-compliant behaviour. This is thought to be the main reason why a majority of smokers carry on smoking. Moderation does not solve the problems and cessation is not a realistic alternative.

- Often, compliance involves such a major change in lifestyle that it is not judged to be worthwhile. The playwright John Mortimer once said, '**I cannot think of any pleasure that is worth forgoing for the sake of another three years of life in a nursing home**'. Personal judgements of risks, consequences and time frame need not be accurate or well informed.

- Denial is a highly effective self-defence mechanism because most self-destructive behaviour does not have inevitable or certain consequences. The mathematics of probability provide a 'get-out clause'. The justification for health-damaging behaviour is identical to that which compels many people to buy lottery tickets.

- Personal values can be very different from those accepted by the mainstream and by health professionals. An anorexic teenager and an obese 50-year-old may both see themselves as attractive to individuals they want to attract.

- There can be conflict between compliance and role expectations: 'I cannot afford to be ill and I do not have time to be ill because I have to go to work and look after my children.' Broken appointments with GPs and out-patient clinics are routinely justified by this kind of thinking. Denial and avoidance are contributing factors.

- Short-term pain, discomfort or anxiety are common reasons for non-compliance. Nobody looks forward to routine dentistry, X-rays or blood pressure tests.

- Therapies and drug regimes may be complicated, poorly explained and difficult to comply with. This is a major issue for the elderly.

- Side effects, even if trivial, can trigger non-compliance with medical treatment. Only the individual involved can decide if the disadvantages of something like drowsiness, constipation or loss of libido is a price worth paying for the containment of a more serious condition.

8 Chronic illness

In topic 2 we outlined the differences between chronic and acute conditions and made the point that the balance between the two patterns of illness is shifting. Increasingly, healthcare is concerned with the treatment, containment and understanding of chronic conditions. We are able to extend life expectancy but not necessarily maintain the quality of life for some patients and clients.

Some definitions

A chronic illness is one that develops relatively slowly and usually worsens over a period of time. There may be an obvious single cause, a variety of factors at work, or sometimes no obvious or straightforward diagnosis.

The population of the UK is ageing. The table gives some selected figures from the 2001 census.

Age bracket	Number (millions), 2001		
	Men	Women	Total
60–69	2.651	2.825	5.476
70–79	1.877	2.429	4.306
80–89	0.710	1.357	2.067
90 and older	0.083	0.288	0.371
Total	5.321	6.899	12.220
Total population	28.611	30.225	58.836
% aged 60 and older	18.6%	22.8%	20.8%

Source: Census 2001. © Crown copyright

More than one person in five is over 60. Although many people no longer want to 'grow old gracefully', chronic illness usually accompanies ageing. The commonest examples are deterioration in hearing and sight, arthritis and loss of mobility, reduced respiratory efficiency and conditions like angina.

The diseases and disorders resulting from smoking, alcohol abuse, poor diet and lack of exercise usually have a slow onset, but these are obviously not confined to the older age groups. Heart disease, some cancers and diabetes – if untreated or undetected – cause a gradual worsening of health and well-being.

The relatively recent significant increases in reported cases of asthma may be due to improved detection. However, pollution is implicated in this and other chronic respiratory disease and disorders.

Kidney or liver failure used always to result in rapid death. Drug treatment, dialysis, and in some cases the wait for transplant surgery mean that these disorders may have extended chronic phases.

There is probably a genetic component in most illness. However, single gene mutation conditions like cystic fibrosis and Huntington's disease typically have chronic phases that continue for many years.

AIDS is a chronic disease, more so if the sufferer has access to appropriate care and drug therapy.

Back pain

Chronic illness need not be life threatening, simply defined or readily explained. Back pain is one of the most common reasons for visiting a GP and for taking time off work. Acute conditions give permission for the sufferer to adopt the 'sick role'. However, some chronic disorders are not always recognised as genuine illness by employers, friends, family and society generally. From time to time, the courts have been asked to give opinions concerning the reality and the causes of chronic illnesses like repetitive strain injury (RSI) and myalgic encephalomyelitis (ME), also called post-viral syndrome or 'yuppie flu'.

Uncertainty

The biology of chronic illness is hugely variable, but its psychology and sociology have many features in common. Illness generates uncertainty which, in turn, can lead to psychological and behavioural changes – most commonly anxiety, depression or denial.

Chronic illness changes not only how people see themselves, but also how others see them. Major changes in lifestyle, social role, family life and employment are often or eventually unavoidable. The table illustrates these points by contrasting acute and chronic conditions. Clearly not all of the comparisons apply in all instances.

This is a long list, but it is not complete or exhaustive. More importantly, the usual consequences of chronic illness interact. Dramatic reductions in income and/or mobility, for example, influence every aspect of life.

Control

Psychologists use an idea called locus of control. Locus just means location or place. The concept recognises that individuals vary in the amount of control they believe they have over their own lives. Loss of control or independence is a central theme of chronic illness. People's ability to cope – and to resist depression and anxiety – is thought to be largely determined by differences in this belief or perception.

Factor	Acute illness	Chronic illness
Duration	Short and predictable	Extended, perhaps never-ending and always uncertain
Cause(s)	Usually definable and simple	Often multi-factorial and difficult to pin down
'Blame'	Sufferers see themselves, and others see them, as blameless	Sufferers may blame themselves for their illness – so might others
Recovery and outcome	Complete recovery probable or outcome and time frame is predictable	Recovery improbable or impossible, time frame is unpredictable
Medication	Short term and often administered by others	Perhaps life-long and self-administered. Side effects a major issue in many cases
Diet	Normal or usual diet rapidly resumed	Major changes or restrictions essential or advisable
Alcohol	Habitual pattern rapidly resumed	Abstinence or severe restriction often needed
Self-assessed physical attractiveness	Reduced only in the short term	Sufferers may see themselves as no longer attractive to others
Sex life and libido	Unaffected in the long term	Libido and sexual function may be impaired
Leisure, family and social life	Unaffected	Physical and intellectual leisure activities might no longer be possible. Narrower circle of friends. Changing family relationships.
Working life	No enforced change	May no longer be able to work – at all, or full time, or in previous occupation. Inevitable implications for income, lifestyle and social contacts

Individuals whose locus of control is internalised think that their fate is mostly in their own hands. They are able to take steps and make changes that result in a better outcome – for themselves and those around them.

As a generality, these groups suffer less from the psychosocial consequences of chronic illness than individuals with an externalised model. However, there can be an unbridgeable gap between the perceived and actual control that is possible for some conditions. An overly developed or unrealistic internalised model causes frustration and eventually exhaustion.

There are two types of externalised model. Events like ill health may be seen as just a matter of chance or luck – nobody has control, least of all the individual concerned. Alternatively, the controller can be identified – this may be a particular health professional or a healthcare group, or it might be a matter of faith or religion.

Control versus compliance

There is no reason for a patient or client who has a fatalistic externalised model of control to comply with health requests. They would argue that compliance or non-compliance makes no difference.

Externalised models focused on health professionals often result in complete compliance but they may also limit practitioner–patient communication. Side effects and the unexpected consequences of treatments can be ignored or under reported.

There is no simple relationship between internalised models and compliance. The patient or client will decide what is good for them and may choose to ignore or take notice of sound advice. The usual pattern involves picking and choosing – and therefore disruption to integrated therapies and treatments. Some diabetics take dietary advice but do not limit their alcohol consumption. Many chronic conditions can be controlled using a cocktail of three or four self-administered drugs. Without reference to or advice from a doctor, one or more of the prescribed medicines may be discontinued.

For similar reasons, many people do not complete a prescribed course of antibiotics once they judge themselves 'better' or 'cured'.

Treatment and containment

Chronic disorders can, by definition, only be cured or reversed with major advances in medical science. 'Breakthrough' is one of the mass media's favourite words, but quantum leaps in healthcare and science generally are much rarer than is usually imagined. Drug therapies are widely prescribed to treat anxiety, depression, pain and the physical symptoms of chronic illness. With varying success, psychosocial techniques are used in conjunction with drugs.

There are local, national and international self-help groups for virtually all chronic disorders. These give mutual support as well as information and advice.

The tax and benefit system in the UK recognises the financial and material consequences of chronic disorder, although the level of help provided is widely criticised.

Counselling is sometimes advised, as are relaxation techniques, hypnotherapy, yoga and other branches of complementary medicine.

References

Fordham, M. (1992) Ethics. In Brooking J.I. et al. *A Textbook of Psychiatric and Mental Health Nursing.* Churchill Livingstone, Edinburgh.

Griffiths, M. (1995) *Adolescent Gambling.* Routledge, London.

Lalonde, M. (1974) *A New Perspective on the Health of Canadians.* Government of Canada, Ottawa.

Maccoby, E.E. (1980) *Social Development, Psychological Growth and the Parent Child Relationship.* Harcourt, Brace, Jovanovich, New York.

Mayor and Sharpe (1997) Treating unexplained physical symptoms. *British Medical Journal* 315: 561– 62.

Orford, J. (1985) *A Psychological View of Addiction.* John Wiley and Sons Ltd, Chichester

Piaget, J. (1948) *The Moral Judgement of the Child.* Free Press, New York.

Prochaska, J.O. et al. (1992) Applications to Addictive Behaviours. *American Psychologist* 47: 1102 – 1114.

Rosenham, D. and Seligman, M. (1989) *Abnormal Psychology.* 2nd ed. Norton, New York.

Thiroux, J.P. (1980) *Ethics Theory and Practice.* 2nd ed. Glencoe Publishing Co. Inc, Maidenhead.

Watzlawick, P. et al. (1967) *Pragmatics of Human Communication.* Norton, New York.

Wilson, M. (1975) *Health is for People.* Darton Longman & Todd, London.

Bibliography

Banyard, P. (1999) *Applying Psychology to Health*. Hodder & Stoughton, London.

Butter, D. and Kavanagh, D. (1997) *The British General Election of 1997*. Macmillan Press, London.

Department of Health. (1991) *Dietary Reference Values for Food, Energy & Nutrients for the UK*. HMSO, London.

Ellis, R.B. et al. (1995) *Interpersonal Communication in Nursing*. Churchill Livingstone, Edinburgh.

Faulkner, A. (1997) *Effective Interaction with Patients*. Churchill Livingstone, Edinburgh.

Field, D. and Taylor, S. (1998) *Sociological Perspectives on Health, Illness and Health Care*. Blackwell, Oxford.

Gross, R.D. (1997) *Psychology The Science of Mind and Behaviour*. (3rd ed.) Hodder and Stoughton, London.

Ham, C. (1999) *Health Policy in Britain*. Macmillan Press, London.

Helman, C.G. (2000) *Culture, Health and Illness*. Butterworth Heinemann, Oxford.

Haralambolos, M. et al. (2000) *Sociology: Themes and Perspectives*. Harper Collins, Oxford.

Leatherard, A. (2000) *Healthcare Provision: Past, Present and into the 21st Century*. Stanley Thornes, Cheltenham.

Luft, J. (1969) *Of Human Interaction*. National Press. Palo Alto, Ca.

Nadoo, J. and Wills, J. (2000) *Health Promotion: Foundations for Practice*. Bailliere Tindall, London.

Purtillo, R. (1999) *Ethical Dimensions in the Health Professions*. W.B Saunders, London.

Sinnet, I. et al. (1999) *Evidence Based Health Promotion: Principles and Practice*. John Wiley and Sons Ltd, Chichester.

Woodward, K. ed. (2000) *Questioning Identity, Gender, Class and Nation*. Routledge, London.

Wright, M. and Gidding, M. (1997) *Mental Health Nursing*. Stanley Thornes, Cheltenham.

Index